PERGAMON INTERNATIONAL LIBRARY
of Science, Technology, Engineering and Social Studies

The 1000-volume original paperback library in aid of education industrial training and the enjoyment of leisure

Publisher: Robert Maxwell

Industrial Movement and Regional Development:

The British Case

THE URBAN AND REGIONAL PLANNING SERIES

For a complete list of titles and other titles of interest see the end of this book

Industrial Movement and Regional Development:

The British Case

by
MORGAN SANT

PERGAMON PRESS
OXFORD · NEW YORK · TORONTO
SYDNEY · PARIS · BRAUNSCHWEIG

Pergamon Press Offices:

U.K.	Pergamon Press Ltd., Headington Hill Hall, Oxford, OX3 0BW, England
U.S.A.	Pergamon Press Inc., Maxwell House, Fairview Park, Elmsford, New York 10523, U.S.A.
CANADA	Pergamon of Canada Ltd., 207 Queen's Quay West, Toronto 1, Canada
AUSTRALIA	Pergamon Press (Aust.) Pty. Ltd., 19a Boundary Street, Rushcutters Bay, N.S.W. 2011, Australia
FRANCE	Pergamon Press SARL, 24 rue des Ecoles, 75240 Paris, Cedex 05, France
WEST GERMANY	Pergamon Press GmbH, D–3300 Braunschweig, Postfach 2923, Burgplatz 1, West Germany

First edition 1975

Library of Congress Catalog Card No. 75-7830

ISBN 0 08 017965 7

Urban and Regional Planning Series
Volume 11

(C

Printed in Great Britain by A. Wheaton & Co., Exeter

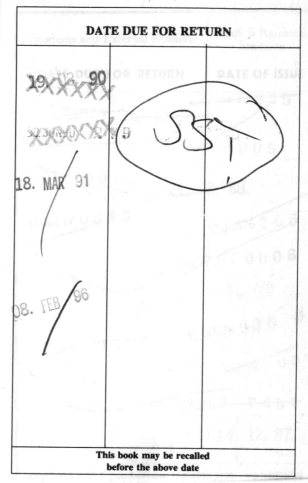

Contents

LIST OF FIGURES   vi

LIST OF TABLES   viii

PREFACE   xi

CHAPTER 1   Regional Equilibrium, Political Intervention,
             and Industrial Movement   1

CHAPTER 2   Perspectives on Industrial Movement   36

CHAPTER 3   Time Series   67

CHAPTER 4   Geographical Distributions   110

CHAPTER 5   The Prospects for Industrial Mobility   160

CHAPTER 6   The Impact of Industrial Movement   185

CHAPTER 7   The Future of Regional Policy in Britain   211

APPENDIX A   Areas Used in Recording the Movement of
             Firms   225

APPENDIX B   Explanations and Definitions   229

APPENDIX C   Employment in Industrial Movement   233

REFERENCES   239

INDEX   249

List of Figures

Fig. 1.1. Hypothetical relationships between the propensity to move, rates of growth and levels of inducement   25

Fig. 1.2. The assisted areas in 1972   32

Fig. 2.1. The distribution of origins and destinations of moves by sub-regions, 1966–71   39

Fig. 2.2. Greater London: employment in (a) small factories, (b) large factories   42–43

Fig. 2.3. Moves to the Outer Metropolitan Area and the Outer South East from the outer divisions of Greater London   47

Fig. 2.4. The spread of the factories of Clarks Ltd., from Street in Somerset, 1939–67   49

Fig. 2.5. Movement generation 1945–65 (employment) as a percentage of manufacturing employment in 1951   61

Fig. 2.6. Movement attraction 1945–65 (employment) as a percentage of manufacturing employment in 1951   62

Fig. 2.7. Net employment from industrial movement 1945–65 as a percentage of manufacturing employment in 1951   64

Fig. 2.8. The contribution of industrial movement to employment change   65

Fig. 3.1. The operation of economic and structural variables in an hypothetical time series of industrial movement   69

Fig. 3.2. The effect of temporal variations in revenue on locational attraction in a "spatial margins" model   70

Fig. 3.3. Time series of industrial movement and post-move closures in Great Britain, 1946–66   72

Fig. 3.4. Time series of selected economic and structural variables, 1946–65   73

Fig. 3.5. Time series of industrial movement in Great Britain, 1966–71   74

Fig. 3.6. Time series of industrial movement by macro-region, 1946–65   75

Fig. 3.7. Time series of industrial movement by standard region, 1946–65   77–78

Fig. 3.8. Interregional time series correlations, 1946–65; (a) dendrogram of regional links, (b) main correlation bonds   79

Fig. 3.9. Annual closure rates of mobile establishments, 1945–66   103

Fig. 3.10. Cohort closure rates, 1945–66   104
Fig. 3.11. Age specific closure rates, 1945–66   105
Fig. 4.1. Generation of industrial movement, by area and period,
           1945–71   112
Fig. 4.2. Attraction of industrial movement, by area and period,
           1945–71   113
Fig. 4.3. Flow of industrial movement from Greater London, 1945–
           65   116
Fig. 4.4. Major flows of industrial movement from provincial
           sources, 1945–65   117
Fig. 4.5. Main source areas, 1945–65   119
Fig. 4.6. Inter-area dominance, 1945–65   120
Fig. 4.7. Industrial movement originating abroad, 1945–65   122
Fig. 4.8. Employment in manufacturing, 1951   126
Fig. 4.9. Average gross weekly earnings, 1968; (a) male manual
           workers, (b) female workers   127–128
Fig. 4.10. Female activity rates, 1951   129
Fig. 4.11. Rates of unemployment, average 1961   130
Fig. 4.12. Urban employment density, 1961   132
Fig. 4.13. Levels of urbanization, 1961   133
Fig. 4.14. Assisted area weights, by period   135
Fig. 4.15. New towns and town expansion schemes, 1946–71   136
Fig. 4.16. Numbers unemployed, average 1951   139
Fig. 4.17. Residual distributions of movement generation, by period   155
Fig. 4.18. Residual distributions of movement attraction   156
Fig. 5.1. A systematic view of changes in the volume and distribution
           of interregional movement   164
Fig. 5.2. Hypothetical model of long-term trends in industrial
           movement   173
Fig. 6.1. Actual and expected employment in manufacturing indus-
           tries (excluding shipbuilding and metals), composite
           development areas, 1951–70   187
Fig. 6.2. Unemployment rates, differences and ratios in the develop-
           ment areas and the United Kingdom, 1951–70   191
Fig. A1.   Areas used in recording the movement of firms, 1945–65   224
Fig. A2.   Areas used in recording the movement of firms, 1966–71   228

List of Tables

1.1.   Interregional migration in Great Britain, by age groups, 1965–6   6
1.2.   Selected regional indicators in Great Britain; indices and ranks of standard regions   16
1.3.   Major items of expenditure on regional policy, 1945–70 (£m at current prices)   29
2.1.   Generalized distribution of origins and destinations of industrial establishments in Great Britain, 1966–71   38
2.2.   Selected characteristics of establishments moving to peripheral areas and the rest of Great Britain, 1945–65   41
2.3.   Distribution of sales and purchases of establishments moving to locations within South-east England   47
2.4.   Generalized directions of industrial movement between standard regions, 1952–9 and 1966–71   51
2.5.   Factors in the decision to move   54–55
2.6.   Factors in the location decisions of interregional movers   57
2.7.   Post-move progress towards profitability in North-east England   59
3.1.   Correlation matrices of regional time series, 1945–65   80
3.2.   Independent variables used in time series analysis of industrial movement, 1945–65   85
3.3.   Correlation coefficients (r) between regional series and independent variables (lagged models), 1945–65   90
3.4.   Intercorrelation matrix r of independent variables in the national series, 1945–65   91
3.5.   Coefficients of multiple correlation (r^2) obtained in the best lagged regression models, by region, 1945–65   93
3.6.   Best lagged regression equations (standardized) for time series of movement, macro-regions, 1945–65   97
3.7.   Best lagged regression equations (standardized) for time series of movement, standard regions, 1945–65   99
3.8.   Coefficients of multiple correlation (r^2) obtained in the best regression models of time series of regional shares of total movement, 1945–65   102
3.9.   Adjusted closure indices in the peripheral areas and the rest of the United Kingdom, 1945–71   106
3.10. Closure ratios by categories of origins and destinations, 1966–71   108
3.11. Closure indices for branch plants and transferred establishments, 1966–71   109

4.1.   Independent variables used in the analysis of movement gener-
       ation and attraction   138
4.2.   Correlation coefficients (*r*) between numbers of surviving moves
       generated by areas, and independent variables   141
4.3.   Matrix of intercorrelations between independent variables used in
       generation and attraction analyses, 1960–5   144
4.4.   Movement generation models, 1945–71   146–147
4.5.   Correlation coefficients (*r*) between numbers of surviving moves
       attracted by areas, and independent variables   149
4.6.   Movement attraction models, 1945–71   152–153
5.1.   Summary of 1960–5 cross-sectional forecasts based on 1952–9
       models   169
5.2.   Classification of selected sources of change in long-term inter-
       regional industrial mobility   172
5.3.   Industrial characteristics, employment change and industrial
       movement   175
5.4.   Assistance approved under the Local Employment Act and
       employment estimated to arise from assisted projects, 1963–73 182
6.1.   Net internal migration and natural increase in population, by
       standard region, 1951–70   193
6.2.   Net migration to the South East and West Midlands, 1965–6   194
6.3.   Employment changes in the United Kingdom and selected stan-
       dard regions, 1950–72   195
6.4.   Employment changes by sector in development areas and non-
       development areas, 1951–63 and 1963–70   196
6.5.   Net output per employee, 1958–68   202
6.6.   Industrial productivity by region, 1963   202
6.7.   Productivity in the United Kingdom and the South East, 1963,
       by SIC group   204
C.1   Number of firms and employment in movement: regression
       analysis, 1945–65   234
C.2.   Correlation coefficients between employment in moves generated
       and attracted by areas and independent variables, 1945–65   235
C.3.   Attraction and generation models based on employment in moves 237

Preface

THIS study concentrates upon the movement of manufacturing establishments between British regions. Little attention is given to local movement, to the migration of non-manufacturing activities, or to the differential birth and growth rates of industries found among and within regions. It is, therefore, a review of only one part of the total complex of spatial readjustment in the national economy. The scale of this readjustment, however, should not be underrated; in 1965 about one in ten of the total manufacturing labour force in Britain worked in establishments which had carried out an inter-regional move since 1945 (Howard, 1968). Between 1966 and 1970, moreover, the rate of interregional movement increased, despite generally unfavourable economic conditions. These changes add up to a considerable transfer of resources between regions in a relatively short time. To a large degree, the postwar volume and pattern of movement have been influenced by political intervention for the purpose of securing more desirable distributions of employment opportunities and real wealth. However, there is not a simple relationship between intervention and industrial movement. On the one hand, different measures can yield different responses; on the other hand, regional policies are only a small part of the total array of factors relevant to regional development. Direct intervention in industrial location is, in turn, only one of those policies, albeit an important one. Thus, the context for setting the three objectives of this study is a broad one.

First, an important aim of this study is to provide information about the nature and correlates of the temporal and regional patterns of movement which occurred in Britain between 1945 and 1971; the data consists of unpublished tabulations supplied by the Department of Trade and Industry. The time series relate to annual movements in the country as a whole (including moves from abroad) and movements to each of the ten standard regions comprising Great Britain (Northern Ireland has been excluded) during 1945–65. In addition, series have been constructed for three macro-regions, the development (or "peripheral") areas, South-east England and East Anglia, and the rest of Great Britain. The distribution of moves (cross-sections) into and out of areas can be analysed at a finer geographical level, using the forty-nine regions into which Great Britain was divided for the collection of data for the three subperiods into which the main time series has been divided (1945–51, 1952–9, and 1960–5) and the sixty-one regions used in 1966–71. No account has been taken of movement into Northern Ireland. These sets of data provide a good basis for description and allow the testing of hypotheses about interregional movement which forms our second objective.

In choosing hypotheses it is valuable to distinguish the level of resolution appropriate to the study. The emphasis here is upon macro-economic movements—upon patterns rather than individual actions—and it follows that classical location theory, though not irrelevant, occupies a less important role. In the present context, industrial movement has much greater affinity with the concepts of international trade theory than with either the price theory, upon which the classical systems of Weber (1929), Losch (1954), and subsequent writers (Hoover, 1948; Isard, 1956; Smith, 1971) developed their hypotheses, or the behavioural concepts (Pred, 1967; Townroe, 1971) which have gained currency in more recent years. Rather, the aim has been to show industrial mobility as an open, dynamic system, in which the role of movement is to transform *inputs* (especially regional policy and regional variations in factor returns) into *outputs* (i.e. regional development). In a perfectly competitive, completely open international or interregional system, an equilibrium is obtained where the marginal returns to each resource in every region are equalized; any shift from equilibrium leads to countervailing movements of factors of production, particularly labour and capital, between regions until equilibrium is restored. However, as is well known, systems are neither fully competitive nor completely open, but are subject to constraints, both absolute and relative, on migration of labour and movement of capital, and disequilibrium can persist indefinitely. At the regional level, in contrast with the international, such restrictions tend to be the result of impediments inherent in the system rather than of barriers imposed politically. Nevertheless, it is hypothesized that movement does take place in response to regional variations in factor returns, even though it may be necessary for intervention on the part of government to assist and encourage movement.

However, this does not account for the variations in movement found to have occurred from year to year for which a supplementary hypothesis is necessary. Lack of movement has occasionally been attributed to "inertia" without any further consideration of the meaning of this term. (Of course, inertia is lack of movement, and neither term explains the other.) Now inertia may be due to a number of factors, but they can all be reduced to a lack of incentive or opportunity to move as perceived by the decision-makers of a firm. This may be due to their own myopia or to an absolute lack of advantage in moving (which is probably true of the vast majority of firms) or to a temporary or marginal lack of advantage. In the present context, we hypothesize that it is the third category which controls the annual volume of movement. That is, when conditions are favourable firms will be more likely to move to (or, in effect, invest in) other regions. Favourability of conditions, in turn, depends upon the state of the national economy (a buoyant economy is associated with greater investment and, hence, probably more movement) and the level of regional incentives (investment grants or allowances, labour subsidies, the construction of new towns, and so on).

The third objective is to relate industrial movement and its impact to the possible future evolution of regional policy. This requires, on the one hand, an understanding of how the mobility system operates and the prospects for further mobility in the future, and, on the other hand, an assessment of regional requirements. It also requires, as we argue in conclusion, a clear identification of the time-scale of regional objectives and policies. Industrial movement was selected, implicitly, to meet short-term objectives—the amelioration of disparities in unemployment arising from an imperfect labour market. As such, it will continue to play a fundamental role in influencing the *rate of change* (stimulating growth or moderating decline) in particular regions. But what is also required is a long-term perspective for regional development which takes account of other variables as well as industrial movement.

In conception, therefore, this study is an attempt to bring together the normative and the positive in economic geography. An important part of the policy-making process is the monitoring of past achievements and present trends. In turn, these help in identifying future problems and in informing the debates which might lead to new objectives and policies. Here the emphasis is on monitoring, but there are also some tentative conclusions for the future of policy drawn from the implications of our results.

Acknowledgements

The opportunity to conduct the research on which this study is based was made possible by the Leverhulme Trust, which provided financial support, and the Department of Industry, which supplied vital unpublished data. The research was carried out as part of a programme of studies in the Centre of East Anglian Studies at the University of East Anglia, and a special debt is owed to my colleagues in the Leverhulme Project, Malcolm Moseley, Peter Townroe, and Margaret Camina, for advice and criticism. The several drafts of the manuscript were patiently typed by Anita Schweinberger.

CHAPTER 1

Regional Equilibrium, Political Intervention, and Industrial Movement

1.1. Regional Equilibrium and Industrial Movement

Industrial movement takes place in response to changes in economic and geographic equilibrium. However, "equilibrium" has many different connotations. Without extending the classification very far, it is possible to distinguish three basic dichotomies: micro- and macro-economic, static and dynamic, partial and general. From these it is possible to derive combinations of locational models ranging in complexity from the static, partial, micro-economic approach of Weber (1929), for example, to the attempted dynamic, general, macro-economic theory of Isard (1969). In addition, it is possible to introduce non-economic theories of allocation mainly based on behavioural concepts (Pred, 1967). Finally, it is also possible to construct theories based on a notion of disequilibrium in which new conditions are met, not with countervailing responses, but with cumulative changes which cause divergence from equilibrium (Myrdal, 1957).

In this study no attempt is made to work within a truly "general" context; such an approach would be unwieldy and too abstract to be useful. On the other hand, the subject demands a less partial framework than that normally found in industrial location analysis if only because the introduction of time series makes it necessary to look at wider economic processes. For the same reason, any theory of inter-regional movement must be biased towards dynamic factors; the act of movement and the ensuing effects bring about a new interregional equilibrium. Further, while it is possible to conduct a study of movement strictly within the limits of micro-economics, concerned only with the behaviour of individual units, at the scale which applies in this study (namely, aggregate behaviour over large areas), the relevant approach here is a macro-economic one which treats industrial movement as a form of resource reallocation.

The last point can be illustrated in the following way. Assume that firms occupying single factories are ideally located with respect to their ability to maximize profits. At a point in time a change occurs which makes some other locations potentially more profitable. Now the micro-economic approach concentrates attention on the cost/revenue differentials for individual firms at the alternative locations. In a macro-economic analysis, however, the questions of interest are considerably wider. In the first place, changes in locational values must be seen in the wider context of regional factor supplies and costs. For example, if labour supply becomes inadequate in one region compared with another, the reason may be not only that the firm's requirements have increased (which may be the primary, micro-economic cause), but also that within the region as a whole labour might have become a more scarce factor relative to other inputs. Secondly, in the macro-economic approach the distribution of firms and industries is seen as a function of regional variations in comparative or absolute advantage. That is, not only do locations suit the firms which occupy them, but also the firms and industries found within a region are the ones most suitable to the region's own characteristics. Thus, industrial movement is not only a response to changing locational values (again, the micro-economic approach), but also it can be seen as a selection process by each region to adapt its industrial composition to its own requirements. Of course, this is an oversimplification because "regions" do not take decisions, and the effect of the behaviour of individuals within the region (and outside it) may give imperfect or unintended results. Thirdly, the micro-economic approach concentrates upon readjustment within the firm with locational change as one outcome among several alternative responses to a given change (Krumme, 1969b; Townroe, 1969). The macro-economic approach, while also viewing movement as a form of readjustment chosen from several alternatives, has a different context. For a firm, the alternative to moving is remaining in the same place, possibly making non-spatial readjustments in order to substitute high economic efficiency for low "geonomic" efficiency (Renner, 1947). For the region, however, the alternatives to industrial movement include labour mobility, capital transfers, or even an acceptance of unequal factor returns. In the macro-economic approach, therefore, it must be asked why industrial movement should occur in preference to other forms of interregional change.

The conditions for static equilibrium in an open interregional system have been stated as follows (Richardson, 1969). Assuming perfect competition, without any shifts in technology or demand functions or in other underlying parameters, and with constant returns to scale, equilibrium occurs when there are:

(a) equal factor prices between regions;
(b) equal marginal physical products of each factor in the production of each good in every region;
(c) with zero transport costs, equal prices of identical goods in all regions.

Given such conditions, the regional system will be characterized by a stable distribution of households and industries with specialization based upon the resource endowments (labour, capital, and natural resources) of regions. Such changes as do occur among regions will be the result of growth or decline in their basic (export) sectors transmitted to their non-basic sectors, and will be immediately met by countervailing forces operating through perfect factor mobility (implicit in the assumption of perfect competition) to restore the equilibrium. In other words, as long as equilibrium exists there will be no tendency for interregional movements of any form except for trade in commodities and services.

However, static equilibrium models are, at best, no more than a rigorous discussion of logical relationships; they make no pretence of describing realistic conditions. In the present case it is possible to level two sets of criticisms against the notion of factor price equalization, namely that it is based on unreal assumptions and that it ignores the dynamic elements of regional systems. Thus, in the first category, it is unrealistic to assume (i) perfect competition (factors are not perfectly mobile or freely substitutable), (ii) constant returns to scale (agglomeration economies and scale economies might both be obtainable in certain situations and may result in higher payments to a particular factor of production), and (iii) zero transport costs (as Lefeber, 1958, has demonstrated, transport costs can afford an element of regional protection, and factor and commodity prices are likely to be equalized only after the deduction of transport costs, if at all).

Secondly, the dynamic element referred to may take the form of disequilibrating movements, particularly when responses to changes are sectorally selective, where there are increasing returns to scale and agglomeration and where there are major discontinuities in the availability or use of resources. Thus, in a dualistic system such as that described by Myrdal (1957), disequilibrium is not met by countervailing forces but by a set of cumulative changes which reinforce regional differentials. The difference, at least in short-run changes, between this and the static equilibrium model can be seen from two examples. In the equilibrium model, labour migration in response to regional income differences leads directly to equalization; in a cumulative causation model, in contrast, it leads to a widening income differential as the receiving region is able, via increasing returns to scale, to employ additional increments of labour. Similarly with capital; in the equilibrium model returns on investment become equalized, whereas in the cumulative causation model the region which starts with higher profitability continues to hold its advantage. Myrdal's "backwash" effect, which embodies this pressure for concentration, might in the very long run be succeeded by a "spread" effect when returns to scale at the original centre begin to diminish or when the terms of trade between the centre and periphery begin to favour the latter, but the authors of cumulative causation models have stressed a need for political intervention in order to hasten the development of backward regions.

Now, in the British context particularly, it is clear that neither the static equilibrium model nor the cumulative causation model provides an accurate description of the regional system. Instant, or even short-run, equilibrium has never applied; and too many regions developed large agglomerations associated with rich resource bases (coal, iron, coastal situations, etc.) for the dualistic cumulative causation model to have more than localized importance. Thus, as is often the case, reality takes the form of a compromise between conflicting theories. The system may be described as containing the elements for achieving equilibrium in the long run, but that these tend to operate sluggishly, so that there is a continual gap between what ought to happen in theory and what actually happens. Moreover, being a dynamic system, the desired equilibrium is never constant for more than a brief moment.

The nature of responses of different factors of production to long-term disequilibrium have been discussed in some detail elsewhere (Richardson, 1969; Stilwell, 1972), but it is useful to summarize their roles. First, in a completely open regional system the movement of either of the two main factors, labour and capital, can be used to provide an equilibrium state. Moreover, in reality, we find that both main factors are mobile and have moved freely between regions in the expectation of gaining higher returns. However, (i) there are differences in the effects of mobility among the various factors, and (ii) in addition to regional equality governments have other economic and social goals, some of them as (or more) important, which militate against certain types of movement.

Thus, concerning the movement of labour, it has been postulated by Richardson (1969) that mobility is a function of (a) the costs of moving, (b) the expected gains (in money wages), and (c) the social costs of dislocation. As a result it might be expected that movement is found to be greatest (proportionately) among the young and the skilled, leaving residual populations with lower average productivity in areas with net outflow and doing little to restore regional equilibrium (Table 1.1). Moreover, Needleman and Scott (1964) have argued that the same selectiveness adds to growth pressures in the reception areas; by their calculations every five employed migrants to South-east England created a demand for about one additional job.

Capital redistribution, in the form of industrial movement, is no less complex. There is not an automatic spatial readjustment by firms when their optimum location changes. Although Hoover (1954) has argued that in modern corporations managements tend to act more in the mould of traditional "economic man", it has also been contended by Eversley (1965), and shown emphatically by Townroe

TABLE 1.1. INTERREGIONAL MIGRATION IN GREAT BRITAIN
BY AGE GROUPS, 1965–6

(a) Total interregional migration per 10,000 resident population in Great Britain.

aged	1–14	13·5
	15–44	19·4
	45–59 (F) 45–64 (M)	5·7
over	65 (F) 65 (M)	6·1
	Total	13·2

(b) Net migration per 10,000 resident population by selected standard regions.

Age	South East	East Midlands	Scotland
1–14	−11·5	+33·7	−37·2
15–44	−0·8	+51·1	−52·9
45–59 (F) 45–64 (M)	−14·1	+13·3	−12·6
over 60 (F) 65 (M)	−23·4	+6·6	−0·1
Total	−11·8	+35·7	−30·2

Source: Sant (1974a).

(1971), that there is much imperfection in movement decisions and search procedures, stemming from a mixture of social and psychological values, incomplete knowledge, and lack of resources to conduct complete locational surveys. In addition, as is shown later, in the short run the volume of movement is controlled less by interregional differentials than by national cyclical and structural (policy) parameters, while in the long run it is doubtful whether the amount of movement capable of taking place over a given period would ever be sufficient to achieve regional equality in incomes or unemployment. Moreover, it can be asked whether the "indirect" and "induced" effects (as distinct from the "direct" effects of employment created) remain within the area receiving the movement or whether large leakages occur which transfer many of the benefits to other regions. This problem has underlain much research on the nature of growth centres; Yeates and Lloyd (1970) and Moseley (1973) have shown that in the relatively short run there may be considerable leakage before the reception areas are able to readjust their basic/non-basic ratios.

Recognition that other goals might be as important as, and possibly conflict with, regional equality is, of course, crucial in discussions about the policies which interventionist governments might apply. This is part of the theme of the next section, but it might be noted here that they contribute to a wider concept of regional equilibrium in which social values put a constraint on economic adjustments. Thus, for example, the equilibrating conditions for short-run full employment in all regions might differ from those relevant to long-run full employment; or, avoidance of metropolitan congestion might require actions different from achieving maximum efficiency of resource utilization and economic growth, and so on. The implications, therefore, are that equilibrium exists only within closely defined terms, and with the political conditions existing at any given time it might be neither desirable nor feasible to use certain equilibrating factors to their maximum, or even at all.

1.2. The Politics of Industrial Movement

In the United Kingdom the politically chosen instrument for attempting to achieve an interregional "balance" (rather than an indefinable equilibrium) of jobs, social welfare, and earnings is industrial movement. This is not to say that other processes do not also operate but these (such as voluntary migration and national wage bargaining) do not have the status that is found in the measures dealing with industrial location which are contained in the Industry Act 1972 (Cmnd 4942), the Local Employment Act 1972, and their predecessors. Why this emphasis should exist is not altogether a simple matter. Certainly, it is not because only industrial movement can have an equilibrating effect: other measures could have the same impact and there may be some—as yet untried—which might be effective. Above all, the reasons for choosing industrial movement as the keystone of regional policy are that (i) it is politically and socially the most attractive and least disruptive in the short term, (ii) also in the short term it is unlikely to conflict too strongly with other economic goals, and (iii) by dealing with impersonal units (company organizations, usually medium to large in size) it is easier to impose direct controls as well as fiscal incentives.

1.2.1. *The Case for Intervention*

In so far as it is possible to identify them, the major national economic goals are related to (i) growth, (ii) stability, and (iii) equity. However, stated baldly like this, goals take on the character of slogans, whereas, in reality, none of them is an easily defined or measured quantity. Moreover, other goals, not much less important, can be specified, such as (iv) the prevention of resource under-utilization, (v) achieving an optimal allocation of resources between sectors, (vi) the avoidance of excessive inflation, and (vii) the avoidance of balance of payments disequilibria (Stilwell, 1972). Expanding the list thus, it becomes obvious that, apart from their vague wording, there are potential conflicts between goals and that there are no *a priori* solutions as to where emphasis should lie. Thus, over the lives of successive democratic governments it is to be expected that different goals will take priority. For example, during the late 1960s the chief concern in the United Kingdom lay in establishing a strong balance of payments position at the expense of growth in domestic consumption and, to some degree, the redistribution of resources towards greater equality. In the early 1970s emphasis shifted towards greater growth and more freedom for resource allocation to find its own level before the world crisis in energy supplies and raw materials led to a new constraint on expansion.

Given such a set of national goals and a small unified territory, it is possible, as some have argued, to relegate regional policy to an insignificant role. Richardson (1969) has illustrated one basis for such a case by showing that "the sum of maximized income per head in each region does not equal maximized national income per head, *except in a world of perfect competition*" (p. 366). That is, by maximizing the income of one region it might be necessary to commit resources to uses which are inefficient from the national viewpoint.

This inefficiency might take the form of bad locational choice for potential growth industries or investment in declining sectors which are geographically concentrated. Extending the argument, it is likely that regional and sectoral mis-allocation will cause scarcities, probably in capital and possibly in labour, in areas with the greatest potential for growth, leading to demand-pull inflation emanating there but being transmitted later to other regions. One set of unbridled advocates of national growth and efficiency might argue, therefore, for a system which contained no checks and balances on regional development other than those inherent in the static equilibrium model (West, 1966).

However, this is by no means the only view to take, and two rejoinders can be made to this argument. The first is that national growth and efficiency can be enhanced by regional policies; the second is that, in any case, arguments based purely on growth and efficiency are superficial since they ignore other deep-seated social and economic goals. In the first case, the argument which might be put forward is that regional systems are so imperfect that national growth can be impaired by the persistent underutilization of resources (especially labour) in some regions; in effect, misallocation results from imperfect knowledge of opportunities in other regions and constraints upon factor mobility. Needleman (1968) has argued that if the high unemployment and low activity rates that characterize the regions that remain depressed were to be brought into line with those in the south of England, the national labour force might be increased by 2 or 3%, and that the cost of public intervention necessary to achieve this would be far outweighed by the resultant increase in output. Although his calculations are based on static comparisons and ignore the long-term constraint on growth which might result from expanding sectors being faced by labour shortages, the initial thesis, that regional systems are very imperfect, is a compelling one. Moore and Rhodes (1973) have extended the argument by estimating the contribution to the national economy during 1963–70. Their case is that the large Exchequer cost associated with regional policy (about £300m in 1970) has diverted attention from the real possibility that the resource costs are close to zero or even negative. Much of the expenditure is recoverable, and that which is not brings into operation productive capacity which might otherwise not be employed. They calculated that the addition to national output of the 250,000–300,000 jobs, attributable to regional policy during 1963–70, was between £400m and £500m per annum greater by the end of the period than it would otherwise have been. By itself, this does not prove the case for intervention, at least in the form that has been adopted (other approaches may, in the long term, yield at least as high a return), but it does help to put into perspective the resource cost arguments concerning regional policy.

Secondly, intervention gains support when equity goals are taken into account, even if the pursuit of these means some reduction in efficiency and growth. Acceptance or rejection of inequality of real incomes is, of course, a political issue; economic theory is unable to determine what the optimum sectoral or regional differentials should be. From the politician's viewpoint, however, inequality in a democratic society can be either a social evil or a sure way to lose votes. In consequence, he will intervene, to a greater or lesser extent, either to effect some real redistribution or to give the impression of showing concern. In Downs's (1957) economic model of the working of a two-party democracy, this is embodied in two forces which, simultaneously, ensure at least a moderate level of intervention and restraint upon the level of expenditure. The first is the tendency for both parties to try to capture the middle ground; the second is the need to weigh marginal costs of policies (which, if we accept the Moore and Rhodes thesis, should read perceived marginal Exchequer costs) against the marginal gain in votes. If, as happens in Britain, one party piles up very large majorities in assisted area constituencies, there is little to be gained by either party in massively bidding-up the level of assistance.

The goal of securing long-term national stability may also require intervention. Serious cyclical fluctuations may be due to exogenous factors such as worsening terms of trade caused by undersupply of important materials, or the substitution of commodities leaving an exporting region economically stranded, or they may be due to misallocation of resources within the system. Nordling (1967) has put forward, as an explanation of the 1929 great depression in the United States, the theory that in the construction industry in the years before the fall there was not only an excess of demand but also that it was regionally misplaced. Whether such an imbalance could occur in the United Kingdom is doubtful, but the implication is that a well-designed system of information and control could secure greater stability. In British examples, Needleman and Scott (1964) argue that migration to areas of full employment, like South-east England, is inflationary, and Moore and Rhodes (1973) have suggested that cyclical tendencies can be dampened by resource allocation such that the overheating which occurs in the South East and Midlands (while there is still spare capacity in other regions) and which results in a premature halt to expansion, can be delayed if not suppressed.

Thus a discussion of the case for regional intervention needs to decide, firstly, whether or not such action reduces growth and efficiency, and, secondly, whether in any case growth and efficiency provide the only—or even the principal—goal of the society. Moreover, in making the second decision it should be emphasized that growth is not indivisible; the choice lies not between growth and no growth but between different combinations of alternative growth rates and alternative rates of progress towards equity or whatever other goal is desired. Thirdly, given this choice (and no country has more than a general notion of what it wants), the next question concerns what combination of vehicles of regional intervention to adopt.

1.2.2. *Intervention and Industrial Movement*

There is no major conflict (in theory, if not in practice) between the two major ways of achieving interregional equity; movement of industry and the mobility of labour are not competitive solutions and there is no reason why both should not be encouraged. However, in the practice of regional intervention, political choice has lain firmly with the use of industrial controls and incentives. By far the greater part of labour mobility, in contrast, has been entirely voluntary. For example, the 1966 census reported that about 705,000 people, of whom perhaps half were in employment (i.e. excluding juveniles and inactive females), had moved between regions during the previous year (i.e. the ten standard regions). In contrast, during the period 1967–8 the Department of Employment and Productivity reported that about 5700 people had been assisted under the various schemes dealing with labour mobility, and many of these were aided under the Key Workers Scheme (i.e. they were moving into development areas as part of the labour force of mobile industry). Thus the schemes concerned with the transfer of people to more prosperous regions affected only minute numbers compared with unassisted voluntary migration. Moreover, the Hunt report on the Intermediate Areas (Cmnd 3998, 1969) advocated only that the Department of Employment and Productivity schemes be reviewed from time to time, and that no widespread subsidization of movement or attempts to "plan" mobility, except in specific cases such as movement from conurbations to new towns, should be undertaken.

A large number of reasons for concentrating on industrial location, rather than labour mobility, has been assembled by various authors and, while it is not intended to discuss them in depth here, it is useful to list the main ones along with some of the arguments against them. It might be emphasized, in passing, that none of them is absolutely proven; their status is that of propositions upon which action has been based rather than that of axioms.

The first group of arguments is economic:

(i)   Industrial location decisions in a free market tend to be imperfect. Evidence for this has been collected by Townroe (1971), and others have argued that social and psychological factors play a greater role than cost factors (Eversley, 1965). However, while there is much truth in this, it might be commented that (a) the degree of imperfection in location decisions is not known, i.e. they may be within tolerable limits, even if they are not perfect, as Smith, 1971, has argued in his concept of spatial margins to profitability, and that (b) exactly the same charge can be levelled at household location decisions.

(ii) In an imperfect system, national growth may be enhanced by industrial mobility for the purpose of absorbing unemployment and underemployment (Needleman, 1968; Moore and Rhodes, 1973).

(iii) Labour migration to fully employed areas tends to be inflationary (Needleman, 1968).

(iv) Social capital and industrial infrastructure already exist in areas with underemployment and will continue to be replaced. It is, therefore, an efficient use of resources to encourage industrial growth there in order to avoid wastage. However, Cameron (1974) has questioned the validity of this argument, pointing out that, allowing for obsolescence and changing consumer preference, about 2% of social and economic overhead capital falls due for replacement each year. Unless population is falling by more than 2%, or there is an age-specific group whose population is decreasing faster than the capital it uses, the problems of redundancy and duplication do not apply. In fact, no standard region in Britain has suffered a net loss of population since 1951, and even the subdivisions which have declined have not done so at this rate.

(v) Overconcentration of population and employment imposes social costs. This argument is illustrated (Klaassen, 1965) by the concept of optimum city size, which can be developed to show that the gap between *per capita* income and *per capita* costs of operating the urban complex increases with city size up to some point and then diminishes. Unfortunately, it has neither been shown that there is, in fact, a discrete optimum (figures put forward for optima in the United States range from 200,000 to 1 million population), nor that the two curves (*per capita* income and operating costs) must inevitably converge (Richardson, 1972). Moreover, analysis of the distribution of migration in recent decades shows that, on balance, the conurbations, especially London, have been losing population and the main net gains have been in areas of relatively low population density.

The second set consists of political arguments for industrial mobility:

(vi) In the Barlow report (Cmnd 6153, 1940) serious consideration was given to the strategic consequences of industrial concentration. At that time industrial dispersal to the west and north offered greater safety. It is doubtful whether this argument has carried any weight since 1945.

(vii) More important today is the strength of economic regionalism. As McCrone (1969) has stated: "whatever government is in power in the United Kingdom ignores the regional problem at its own peril" (p. 26). Indeed, one could go further and state that any overt attempt to solve the regional problem other than through industrial movement and public investment would be politically unacceptable at the present time since one of the attributes of regionalism seems to be the jealous guarding of the region's population. It may be facile to point out that no regional plans—other than for London—have actually proposed a reduction in population and employment (and even in London it has recently been feared that continued out-migration will undermine the economic base of the conurbation—Greater London Council, 1970), but the fact remains that regional leaders are unable, for political reasons, to advocate policies which are perceived to be "against" the interests of their constituents.

Thirdly, social reasons have been given for favouring industrial movement:

(viii) Labour mobility breaks up communities (Stilwell, 1972). Of this there can be little doubt; families can be split or whole settlements disrupted by the selective migration of workers. Moreover, at the larger community scale it is the young, the skilled, and the more adaptable who are most mobile, and little is done, in the short run, to alleviate the problems of local unemployment and unbalanced population and age structures by migration. The alternative—industrial movement—may cause a different kind of change to communities, but this is seen to be preferable. West (1973) has strongly criticized this as a regional economic objective.

(ix) Control over industrial location is a necessary adjunct to maintaining and improving environmental conditions. But, whether this requires interregional movement (as against careful intraregional planning) is questionable.

Finally, there is a strong administrative reason for working through industry rather than households:

(x)   Industrial units are fewer in number, more easily identified and classified, and, being "impersonal", are more amenable to legislation than households. This is important both because it allows the use of direct controls on location and eases the problem of applying fiscal incentives.

Throughout this discussion the intention has been to preserve the notion that there are no absolute arguments for preferring one regional policy to the exclusion of others. Although the above list appears to contain quite a formidable case for concentrating on industrial movement, many of the items have been challenged, and probably only the last remains unscathed. However, as we discuss in the next few paragraphs, there are two fundamental questions which still need to be considered. The first is that the regional system is considerably more complex than has been acknowledged in most statements on policy-making. There are no straightforward dichotomies between rich and poor, congested and open, or growing and depressed regions in Britain. Rather, there are many spectra upon which regions can be placed according to their characteristics (Table 1.2). Regions have a mixture of good and bad features, and although, as expected, the major assisted areas have a preponderance of the latter and the South East is placed first on nine of the thirteen indicators, there is, nonetheless, a different rank order on every one. Moreover, each region has attractive and repulsive features for industrial location, and each competes in some way with every other. Secondly, the supply of industrial mobility is limited; all areas cannot have their wishes gratified at the same time, and it may be that none can ever be satisfied with the amount of movement they attract. We need, therefore, to consider (i) what commitments, in terms of industrial movement, are undertaken by governments, (ii) what the likely effect is of the measures by which they intervene in locational decisions, and (iii) what success they can hope to achieve towards meeting their commitments.

TABLE 1.2. SELECTED REGIONAL INDICATORS IN GREAT BRITAIN: INDICES AND RANKS OF STANDARD REGIONS (GB = 100)

	North	Yorkshire and Humberside	East Midlands	East Anglia	South East	South West	West Midlands	North West	Wales	Scotland
Sickness benefit per man at risk: 1965–9	148	119	91	58	51	93	89	129	181	127
1970	9	6	4	2	1	5	3	8	10	7
Pupil teacher ratio: 1970	104	103	103	96	94	96	101	105	100	103
	9	6	8	2	1	2	5	10	4	6
Pupils aged 16 or over: 1966	84	97	87	81	121	99	87	82	123	101
	8	5	7	10	2	4	6	9	1	3
Per cent employment in declining industry 1970	144	178	191	102	46	78	93	104	167	118
	7	9	10	4	1	2	3	5	8	6
Activity rates (female)	90	98	100	89	108	81	106	105	76	104
	7	6	5	8	1	9	2	3	10	4
Unemployment: 1965–70	177	99	79	85	67	109	88	106	171	170
	10	5	2	3	1	7	4	6	9	8
Net output per employee: 1968	100	88	95	105	110	98	95	101	105	97
	5	10	9	3	1	6	8	4	2	7
Net change industrial floorspace: 1964–7	207	59	129	232	41	154	100	41	123	—
	2	7	4	1	8	3	6	9	5	NA
Net change, commercial floor-space: 1964–7	86	94	164	117	114	112	111	85	83	—
	7	6	1	2	3	4	5	8	9	NA
Retail turnover, *per capita*: 1966	89	94	96	104	118	97	96	102	87	102
	9	8	6	2	1	5	6	3	10	3
Population per car: 1969	128	121	94	83	89	81	96	121	100	128
	9	7	4	2	3	1	5	7	6	9
Net income *per capita* (total): 1968–9	92	97	99	99	107	97	102	95	93	93
	10	6	3	4	1	5	2	7	8	9
Per cent earning less than 50p per hour: 1970	114	124	116	145	78	125	76	104	101	120
	5	8	6	10	2	9	1	4	3	7
Employers, managers, professional workers as per cent of all employment: 1966	83	89	96	108	119	106	90	91	90	88
	10	8	4	2	1	3	6	5	7	9
Net migration: 1951–66 (%)	−3·7	−2·2	+2·9	+6·3	+3·6	+7·2	+1·9	−2·4	−1·5	−9·6
	9	7	4	2	3	1	5	8	6	10
Net change in employment: 1961–70 (%)	0	−3·4	0	+7·6	−2·6	0	−2·6	−3·7	−3·8	−1·6
	4	8	3	1	6	2	7	9	10	5

Source: Sant (1974a).

1.2.3. *Objectives of Locational Intervention*

During recent decades there has been a large volume of legislation designed to control aspects of regional economic behaviour. Modern governments in the United Kingdom and elsewhere are therefore in a position, unparalleled in history, to shape the regional development of their territories through selective expenditure and fiscal policies and the subordination of private actions for public motives.

It is, however, easier to identify commitments than to evaluate them, particularly when they involve industrial movement and when the entire regional system is dynamic. For example, one commitment undertaken in 1963 was to stimulate "viable growth" in Central Scotland, using public investment as well as the full range of locational controls and incentives then existing (Cmnd 2188, 1963). However, viable growth is as difficult to define as any other economic concept, since it requires a value judgement about what will be accepted as "viable". At its most strict, this could be taken to mean a self-sustained growth in *per capita* incomes without any form of protection at a level at which full employment could be maintained with a balanced distribution of factor movements. However, "viability" fundamentally revolves on "acceptability". Thus, if the South East and Midlands grow at 5% per annum, will a figure of 3% be acceptable in Central Scotland? Is it more acceptable if both groups of areas grow at 3% per annum? Also, it is no less difficult to define growth. It could be interpreted in many ways; for example, as the increase of employment or activity rates or the decrease of unemployment, or the increase of real incomes. Each presents a different target, although most are interrelated. But the most important omissions from regional policy statements are firm, quantitative targets. Partly, this is due to the normal political process of raising smoke-screens; vague targets have the advantage that they are less easy to subject to damaging criticism (Downs, 1957). Unfortunately, they also have the ability of obscuring the planner's own view of things.

Therefore, in the absence of firm statements of commitments, it is necessary to make our own interpretations. For this it is not unreasonable to assume that the implicit long-term commitments embody a "pareto-optimal" shift; that is, ultimately to remove regional differentials by improving the position of the deprived areas without harming the viability of the better off and to bring about less congested, but no less viable, conditions in the major conurbations. In Britain these aims have been approached through assisted area legislation and the programmes of new towns. The latter can be treated briefly since they are easier to deal with. In effect they represent, in most cases, little more than a redistribution of population and jobs within a standard region. They are important, however, because they require a considerable volume of industrial movement from the sources which would otherwise supply the assisted areas with most of their new industry. Thus the more new towns there are designated, the more difficult, other things being equal, is the task of the assisted areas.

The requirements of the assisted areas have changed from time to time. In the 1950s they were regarded as minimal, but in the 1960s, following the accelerated run-down to basic industries concentrated in peripheral regions, the requirement grew rapidly. It was possible to estimate in the early 1970s that 1 million jobs were needed in the five main problem regions (Scotland, Wales, Northern England, Yorkshire and Humberside, and the North West) in order to achieve parity in employment between the assisted areas and the rest of the country (Ridley, 1972). This consisted of:

(a) 120,000 in order to bring down the rate of unemployment to a national average of 1·5%, at which point the country is assumed to have full employment;
(b) 150,000 to increase female activity rates to the national average;
(c) 350,000 to meet the expected growth in labour supply assuming no change in the rate of out-migration;
(d) 300,000 to offset expected redundancies in the coal, steel, textiles, shipbuilding, and engineering industries.

All of these were regarded as necessary within a decade. Furthermore, it should be emphasized that they relate to employment parity. Income parity might require more selectivity in types of occupations and industries or a contrived excess demand for labour, neither of which is realistic within the short run. Thus the task of achieving parity by any measure is formidable. Moreover, in general the development areas lack the necessary basis of labour intensive growth industries to generate such an expansion of jobs. Although indigenous firms have, in places, produced a significant gross increase in employment, this has usually been offset by the contraction of other indigenous firms, leaving a net loss or small net gain. Inevitably, therefore, the increase in the demand for labour must come from the movement of industry, particularly from the manufacturing sector.

But these are static comparisons and assume that a once-and-for-all parity could be achieved by a single massive transfer of resources. In fact, while large numbers of jobs have been created through industrial movement, the progress of the development areas towards parity with the remainder of Britain has been insignificant although it must be remembered that, in the absence of regional policies, disparities might easily have grown. West (1973) has dissented from this view, but Brown (1972) has presented evidence that the industrial composition effect was responsible for the employment growth in the development areas during 1921–61 running behind the national average; in Wales, the discrepancy amounted to about 0·5% per annum. During 1961–6 the composition effect showed signs of becoming even larger. Up to the mid 1960s, unemployment and activity rate differentials had failed to close and, while production per employee appeared to have grown faster, this was as much due to the contraction of labour intensive industries as to the expansion of capital intensive ones. Above all, before 1960 personal incomes in the problem regions as a whole tended to fall further behind the national average; the only major exception in Britain was the South West. Despite the greater level of incentives for industrial development and movement in the second half of the 1960s, there is no evidence that the gap was significantly reduced, and the cyclical recession in this period may, indeed, have had an adverse effect.

Failure to remove disparities in the past has been due to a number of factors. First, job creation through movement and indigenous responses to incentives has partly been offset by closures in old industries such as shipbuilding and mining. Second, investment in development areas very often has multiplier effects outside these regions, providing, in fact, a further impetus to prosperous areas. Third, the prosperous regions themselves have continued to grow despite having much of their growth potential "hived off" to the development areas. As long as these three factors remain, it is doubtful whether the implicit commitment of regional policies will ever be met. At the same time, political factors demand that while disparities remain, regional policies are unlikely to be substantially reduced.

1.3. Locational Inertia and Industrial Movement

Although interregional industrial movement is important as a means of redistributing resources and has the highest significance for firms involved in relocation, the proportion of manufacturing industry engaged in the process at any one time is not large. In the United Kingdom the highest number moving (transferring their entire operation or setting up branches) in any one year between 1945 and 1965 was 300, whereas the 1958 census of production reported the existence of about 60,000 establishments employing more than ten workers in manufacturing. Allowing for the existence of multi-plant companies, this means that interregional movement affects not much more than 1% of firms in Britain even during peak years. From this it might be possible to draw two conflicting inferences:

(a) that a large reservoir of industry, hitherto uninvolved in movement, can be used to solve problems of regional development (Needleman, 1965); but,

(b) that the rate at which firms move is too slow to provide satisfactory solutions and that any major attempt to increase it will have serious disadvantages to the national economy (Richardson and West, 1964).

However, it seems that before any progress can be made towards resolving these two views, there should be a thorough-going review of the factors which control the volume and direction of movement and, conversely, the factors which determine that the overwhelming proportion of firms remains static.

The term "locational inertia" has never received more than cursory treatment (although Dziewonski, 1966, has attempted to classify locations in terms of the strength of forces for stability and relocation likely to be found in them), perhaps because it denotes a neutral state, lacking the positive functions associated with movement and choice of location. Moreover, when it has been discussed, emphasis often appears to have been placed on the role of inertia in giving rise to anomalies (steel production at Consett, the manufacture of ships chains at Cradley, for example), and there has been little attempt to incorporate the notion of inertia in a general framework of location theory except in recent studies of decision-making. The generaliz-ations found in the earlier descriptions of inertia tend to be con-cerned with the continued use of a location after the initial reasons for its choice have disappeared. The reasons, according to Estall and Buchanan (1961), are that expansion on site is often cheaper than movement and that other advantages of a location may grow to supplement the original one. Chisholm (1966) has suggested, with greater precision, that inertia might be caused by the marginal product of capital being higher at the time of an investment in the existing plant rather than at a new one. In addition, there tends to be a lag between bid rents and actual rents; in a period of inflation, actual rents are generally less than the true value of sites. Hence, the observation that "the power of a locality to hold an industry . . . greatly exceeds its power to attract" (Ross, 1896).

There is nothing inaccurate or misleading in these early statements, but they are, nevertheless, unsatisfactory for two reasons. The first is that they do not "universalize" the occurrence of inertia; the second, is that they fail to place inertia in a clear, temporal framework. That is, their appreciation of inertia is too narrow for the development of a useful concept because they concentrate, implicitly and explicitly, on particular cases over very long periods; in the Estall and Buchanan case the emphasis is on the survival of old-established industrial areas. With a wider understanding of locational inertia, however, the term takes on much greater value.

Thus it becomes necessary to consider all firms to be inert unless they are engaged in a move. The level of inertia is, broadly, dependent upon two sets of criteria relating to conditions both external and internal to firms. Different firms respond in different ways to the same external force, whether it be a change in transport costs, a regional incentive, or some other stimulus; likewise, the same firm and the same external force might yield different results at different times, depending on the nature of other conditions. Resulting from this, it is expected that the volume of movement will differ from year to year as the level of inertia rises and falls in response to changed internal and external conditions.

These generalizations apply to the behaviour of individuals, but there is a further feature of the definition which has interesting connotations. That is, inertia includes the notion of uniform motion. Thus we might also conceive of an "areal-interactive" inertia, in which a pattern of movements between areas is sustained without any alteration over an infinite period of time. However, this adds a new dimension to the concept of inertia and, while not undesirable, it should be kept strictly separate. In effect, this relates to inertia of geographical patterns as distinct from time series of movement.

Of course, this approach by itself does no more than open up an interesting avenue for discussion. It gives a picture of inertia without explaining why firms opt for a "state of rest" rather than locational innovation or vice versa. In general, it can be postulated that at any given moment each firm contains a combination of social and economic attributes against which it balances, usually implicitly but occasionally explicitly, the strength of the various external forces. An examination of this balancing act has been made by Townroe (1969), in which the locational decision is seen as an alternative choice among many different strategies. The choice between alternative investment projects might be made entirely on economic grounds or it may be dominated by other motives. In addition, since relocation—like other forms of investment—requires optimism about future economic conditions in the long term, the likelihood of a move will be reduced if the production time-horizon is limited and when there is uncertainty about adaptability to innovations (Cameron and Johnson, 1969). However, the balance is not static; social resistance to movement can change, the external forces can vary in strength, and the economic environment within which the firm operates can also alter. Thus it might be hypothesized that movement is most likely to occur when firms expect to gain the greatest advantage from this course of action rather than another. However, it is not always, or even often, possible for firms to withhold investment projects until the optimum moment, and it may be that short-term needs preclude relocation. Even so, there ought to be a positive relationship between the volume of movement and the strength of external forces and propitiousness of general economic conditions (e.g. growth in production and ease of credit). As noted above, inertia also has implications for the geographic distribution of movement. It might be expected, firstly, that moves which occur in the absence of constraints would involve the least possible effort in order to achieve a given objective, and, secondly, that movement patterns would tend to be stable, with the same areas continuously receiving or generating movement. Over a period this "uniform" motion might take the form of a steady flow of firms from a conurbation to its suburban fringe; or, less likely in practice, from an old resource region to a new one. In this context, disturbance of inertia means simply the diversion of flows from existing sources of movement to new destinations by the exertion of some external force.

Now the role of political intervention can be clarified. It is to encourage the creation or diversion of movement, or both, by pro- moting the conditions for reducing the level of inertia in the system. The range of actions by which these effects can be achieved is very broad, and most are likely to influence both creation and diversion, but in practice the aim is, or should be, to achieve the desired volume and pattern of mobility for the minimum outlay. In a federal system, where states within the nation have a significant economic autarchy, it is possible for each state to divert movement to itself by offering local monopolies and other benefits which have little direct impact on public expenditure. An example occurs in Australia where most states have successfully attracted industry (Linge, 1967). In such a case the main cost falls upon the consumers, who are restricted in their choice of commodities, and probably incur higher prices. Conversely, there are regions which have gained from the removal of barriers of movement. The formation of common markets with no internal tariffs provides the conditions for well-located regions to benefit. In western Europe, for example, tariffs prior to the 1956 Treaty of Rome placed a major constraint on development in the Netherlands (Clark *et al.*, 1969). The removal of tariffs and the emergence of a new set of market potential surfaces encouraged some additional movement into the European Economic Community, but also had a marked impact on the attraction of Dutch locations (Smidt, 1966).

In the United Kingdom, as in many other unitary states with large private sectors, creation and diversion of movement involve a complexity of intervention far in excess of tariff manipulation or the provision of local monopolies. Here the range of action extends from the use of information and promotional services by local and regional authorities (Camina, 1974), through controls on industrial development to the creation of growth centres (Boudeville, 1974), the provision of infrastructure, and the production of entirely new cost surfaces in the form of financial incentives (Wilson, 1973). All of these influence both the creation and the diversion of industrial movement to varying degrees, and each is liable to incur different costs and have different effects. Thus promotion by local authorities is designed as a diversionary strategy, usually costs little, but has only a minor impact on the total pattern of movement, although individual areas have been known to gain considerably. Controls on development (e.g. industrial development certificates in the United Kingdom) are mainly negative forces in the sense that their purpose is to prevent undesirable industrial growth in certain areas, but inevitably they also provide conditions for creating movement, as also does the use of compulsory purchase orders for urban redevelopment. The designation of new towns (which may be regarded implicitly as "growth centres") and the scheduling of assisted areas, on the other hand, place emphasis upon the diversion of industrial movement, although they, too, usually have a dual effect, since incentives are often great enough to induce movement among firms who would otherwise have remained static.

Apart from these deliberate interventions, or external forces, inertia is also affected by general economic conditions. Thus the pursuit of a growth policy, requiring a high level of capital formation, is of fundamental importance in the creation of industrial movement; firms are unlikely to invest in new plant and machinery unless they expect to operate at full capacity. Likewise, since much expansion is internally financed, company liquidity needs to be kept at a high level, which has implications for tax policy. In effect, therefore, regional policy needs, for maximum success, to be geared as closely as possible to national economic policy.

This notion of locational inertia is particularly useful in providing a "basing point" upon which the results of statistical analyses of movement patterns can be evaluated. In effect it allows each change in external forces (controls, incentives, new growth centres) or general economic conditions (e.g. the rate of growth in production, levels of company liquidity, etc.) to be viewed as a potential act working positively or negatively against the inertia existing in the immediate past. From this it is possible to make some estimate of the effectiveness of different factors influencing the volume and pattern of movement and, ultimately, to suggest how successful different regional policies might be in achieving objectives.

We can illustrate this in the following way. In the absence of external forces (e.g. regional controls and incentives) there will be, over the entire population of manufacturing firms, a range of levels of inertia or propensities to move in response to given economic conditions. For example, in Fig. 1.1(A) it is expected that as the level of manufacturing output (and, implicitly, investment) increases, so,

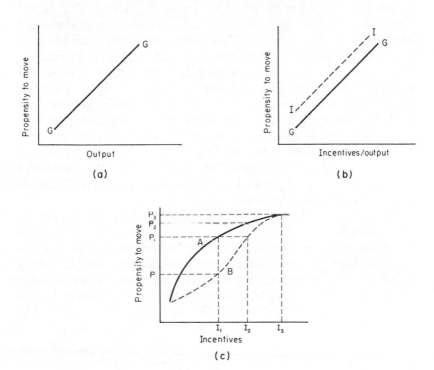

Fig. 1.1. Hypothetical relationships between the propensity to move, rates of growth and levels of inducement (see text).

too, does the propensity to move. In effect we have a supply curve *GG* of moves in which extra marginal returns offset the disutility of movement of an increasing number of firms. This disutility may take the form of costs attributable to the move or the social disruption of people involved in the move; but whatever its cause there is a level of inducement which is sufficient to outweigh it. In some cases the necessary inducement will be negligible or even zero (the extremely "footloose" firms), while in others it will be very high.

Next, we may consider the effect of regional incentives. Clearly the intention of these is twofold—to increase the propensity to move and to divert movement along desired paths. Assuming the two objectives to be completely complementary, we can postulate that a given financial incentive has the effect shown in Fig. 1.1(B). That is, the incentive raises the supply curve of industrial movement above that attributable to growth alone. Two points are worth considering at this stage, however. Firstly, we cannot be sure whether the incentives have an equal effect on all firms; that is, whether curve *II* is parallel with curve *GG* or whether it diverges. Ideally, it might be argued, the best incentives are those which cause divergence because they imply increasing marginal propensity to move in response to inducements and, with the effect of the incentive concentrated at the upper end of the scale, there is less wastage. Secondly, it is apparent that the addition of regional incentives, while raising the movement supply curve, may yet yield a low volume of movement if the rate of growth of manufacturing output is low.

Finally, we have in Fig. 1.1(c) a problem to resolve concerning the costs and effectiveness of alternative regional incentives. It is quite likely that policy instruments incurring the same costs to the government will have different effects on the propensity to move. This may be because the incentives fall in such a way that the firms incur different costs; for example, infrastructure improvements or investment allowances are less likely to affect the firm's balance-sheet than direct grants. Let us assume, however, that two different instruments are available. Both will ultimately, for the same outlay, yield the same amount of movement, but at lower outlays have markedly different effects. For example, the lower curve *B* may represent the effect on the propensity to move of incentives based on investment allowances and the upper curve A may reflect the influence of grants. These two are realistic examples: the latter has normally been thought to be the more effective incentive to date (McCrone, 1969).

Now at the highest level of incentives, I_3, both policy instruments have the same effect, yielding a propensity to move, P_3, which may be sufficient to meet the political objectives. In this case, other things being equal, the government will be indifferent between the two. However, the case is likely to occur that finance which can be devoted to regional policy, rather than to other social objectives, amounts only to I_1. Clearly the more effective measure in this instance will be A, which yields a propensity to move of P_2 compared with P_0 when policy B is followed. But the problem does not end there, for it may happen that further assistance, I_1 I_2, becomes available. The choice might still appear to lie with A, because at I_2 it still yields an overall propensity to move greater than B. However, the marginal increase in propensity to move when inducements are raised from I_1 to I_2 are relatively small in the case of policy A. So that it may now be time to introduce B to augment A. Unfortunately, it is impossible at this stage to say whether this is a valid approach because we have, in effect, introduced a third policy instrument (i.e. the combination of A and B), the response to which might not be simply the sum of the other two, and in these circumstances it might still be safer to opt for A alone unless it can be proved that the new policy will be more effective.

Above all, what the last statement implies is the need for identifying the complex relationships between industrial movement (or its converse, inertia), on the one hand, and external forces and general economic conditions, on the other hand. If progress can be made towards this end, two benefits might ensue: the ability to forecast the effect of alternative policy packages and to make assessments of the gap between the likely outcome of policies and the ultimate objectives for regional economies. Thus the most important questions to which the deepest consideration should be given are logistical: it may be that the answers to questions about what is *possible* will lead to new questions about what is *desirable* in regional policy.

1.4. The Commitment to Regional Development in Britain

To be fulfilled, regional policies require resources to be diverted between areas and, as a measure of commitment to the achievement of regional policy objectives, there is no better indicator than the expenditure incurred. However, care is needed when interpreting the figures involved because, over time, the value of money has fallen and in some items of expenditure the regional component has to be separated from a general sum. Also, some of the expenditures are recouped through taxation and loan repayments, while a further component is offset by savings in other expenditures such as unemployment benefits. Nevertheless, it is possible to derive a good estimate of the amounts devoted to raising standards in the assisted areas between 1945 and 1970; these are contained in Table 1.3.

Two major features dominate these figures. The first is the growth in total quinquennial expenditure since 1960. Before that, the sum was relatively small, although taking account of inflation, the level between 1945 and 1950 was not far below that in the early 1960s. Between 1965 and 1970 the total reached about £1400m (£270m per annum).

The second feature is the change in the dominant categories of regional expenditure. Until 1960 the main item was factory building by the Board of Trade, which accounted for over 75% of spending. The effect of this has been embodied in the expansion and proliferation of industrial estates in the assisted areas. By 1969 there were over 100 of those, administered by estates corporations, containing over 1000 establishments, not including those which had been purchased by their occupiers, with more than 250,000 employees working on them (European Free Trade Association, 1971). However, after 1960 the picture altered radically as other policy instruments were augmented or introduced. Between 1960 and 1965, Treasury loans and grants were raised tenfold to over £80m per year, and building grants were brought in mainly for firms moving to purpose-built sites not on estates and to extend existing premises. There is in this shift of emphasis a realization of the need to adjust inducements not only to increase the supply of mobile industry but also to foster employment growth in firms indigenous to the assisted

TABLE 1.3. MAJOR ITEMS OF EXPENDITURE ON REGIONAL POLICY, 1945–70
(£m AT CURRENT PRICES), QUINQUENNIAL TOTALS

Item	1945–50	1950–5	1955–60	1960–5	1965–70
Expenditure under Local Employment Act, etc.					
BoT (factories, industrial estates)	36	21	21	50	70
Treasury (loans and grants)	2	5	8	81	87
Building grants				22	101
Plant and machinery grants				9	14
Special operational grants					10
Other expenditures (differential element)					
Investment grants (estimated)					265
Regional employment premium (estimated)					369
Tax allowances, free depreciation (estimated)					400
Other (estimated)					90
Total (estimated)	38	26	29	162	1406

Financial years—April–March.

areas. Investment grants, first paid in 1967, were applied nationally, but with a regional differential worth about £60m per annum. This form of assistance is industrially selective in its impact, tending to favour the more capital intensive sector. Almost a quarter (23·4%) of the sum paid on machinery and plant during 1967–70 went to the chemical industry, which employed only about 5% of the workforce in mining, manufacturing, and construction in Britain. In addition, there were, throughout the 1960s, taxation allowances, including free depreciation, with regional differentials to the value of about £40m per annum, which also tended to favour profitable capital intensive firms. Although it is desirable to foster capital intensive industry, this fails to meet all the requirements of regions with an oversupply of labour. Hence the last major inducement, namely the regional employment premium, with its approximate annual cost of £100m. The regional employment premium was introduced in 1967 as a standard *ad hominem* labour subsidy equivalent, initially, to about 7·5% of average labour costs, though this later diminished under the effect of inflation (Brown, 1972).

Thus over the 26-year period covered by this study the list of policy instruments related to industry expanded to cover not only industrial movement (first through the provision of premises and later by loans and grants) but also through investment and job creation in indigenous industry. The policy was further strengthened and extended by the terms of the Industry Act and the Finance Act in 1972 (Cmnd 4942, 1972), which not only augmented conventional instruments but also introduced two others—selective financial assistance to projects to create or safeguard employment and assistance to the shipbuilding industry. Paralleling the increase in assistance to industry, the level of public investment in infrastructure was stepped up sharply, reaching a regional differential in favour of assisted areas of about £40m per annum. Likewise, inducements for the clearance of derelict land, helping to improve the environment in many parts of the assisted areas and old industrial districts, were also increased.

Commitment to regional development also requires the designation of areas to receive assistance although, of course, lines on a map mean nothing without the resources to carry out the objectives. Since 1945 the definition and extent of assisted areas have been changed from time to time, but the overall trend has been towards their enlargement and intensification. By 1973 there was a hierarchy of areas with no fewer than seven recognizable ranks according to the level of assistance or control (Fig. 1.2). At the top, with the highest rates of inducement, were special development areas (8·4% of the UK population); these were followed by development areas (14·1%), intermediate areas (21·7%), derelict land clearance areas (4·0%), "neutral" areas (our own term) divided into those containing new towns and town expansion schemes under the 1947 and 1952 Acts, respectively, and those with no planned growth areas, and, finally, at the lowest end, subject to strict constraints on factory and office development, Greater London and the West Midlands conurbation.

The route towards this situation passed a number of landmarks in the concept of what criteria should be used to justify designation for assistance. The first development areas, designated in 1945, were characterized by being compact and, for the most part, continuous regions, similar to the old prewar special areas, but now including the major cities (Glasgow, Newcastle, Cardiff, and Swansea) located within their boundaries or adjacent to them. In the years following, additional, less-compact, areas were also designated. The three in North-west England and that in Wales (at Wrexham) were justified on the grounds of actual or imminent high unemployment. Another, in Scotland (Dingwall/Inverness), was scheduled on the basis that it would act as a focal centre for the Highlands as a whole. In the designation of these areas there was considerable optimism that areas were being selected for growth potential; other areas had rates of unemployment at least as high and relatively marked out-migration, but were not designated. To have designated these would have been a negative act, treating regional policy as a short-term "rescue" operation rather than an instrument for long-term growth. However, this is what occurred in the late 1950s following high cyclical unemployment in many peripheral areas. The Distribution of Industry Act 1958 added to the existing development areas, smaller areas where the Treasury was empowered to make loans or grants on the criterion that these areas had high unemployment rates which were likely to persist. The legislation which was next enacted, the Local

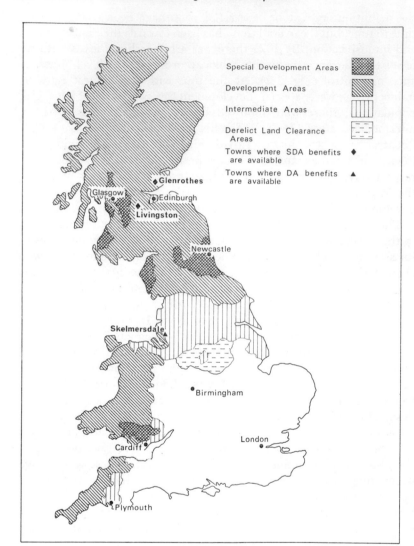

Fig. 1.2. The assisted areas in 1972.

Employment Act 1960, continued this preoccupation with unemployment rates although it did extend the criterion to include areas where high rates were imminent; unofficially, the figure of 4·5% was adopted as the critical threshold. In effect, the new development districts which ensued included the old ones, but also contained several which were new. But, most seriously, adherence to the criterion of a particular level of unemployment meant that areas were scheduled and descheduled with bewildering frequency (McCrone, 1969); the proportion of the country's population in development districts was 12·5% in 1961, 7·2% in 1962, and 16·8% in 1966.

The replacement of development districts by much larger development areas, following the Industrial Development Act 1966, marked the adoption of two new criteria—the need to have stable definitions of assisted areas and greater freedom of choice for firms to locate where it best suited them while, at the same time, enabling them to benefit from the incentives offered. However, the subsequent legislation introducing special development areas appears to run contrary to the notion of broadly defined assisted regions in which growth ought to concentrate in areas of greater potential. The special development areas contained areas with acute structural problems (all of the earlier ones were coalfield areas) and high unemployment. Intermediate areas, first set up in 1970, were recommended by the Hunt Committee (Cmnd 3998, 1969) on the grounds that they were growing slowly and suffered from poor environments; to a degree this was attributed to their being put at a disadvantage by the concentration of assistance in development areas. Hence an intermediate range of inducements was recommended and applied. These included assistance for infrastructure investment and land clearance and also incentives for industrial development. The aim of the last item was to modernize and stimulate existing industry rather than attract new firms at the expense of the development areas, but it would be unreasonable not to expect some diversion.

Thus, overall, the trend in the designation of areas for assistance has pointed generally towards the relief of localized distress. Apart from the early development areas in the 1940s and, to a lesser extent, the areas set up in 1966, the main criteria has been unemployment rates, with little positive attempt to identify and concentrate development in areas of high growth potential. More seriously, preoccupation with this criterion has two detrimental implications—it diverts attention from consideration of long-term objectives and it dilutes the assistance which can be given to particular areas.

There are three ways of measuring the significance of commitments. The first—and least important—is to make international comparisons. Per head of population, only two European countries—Belgium and Italy—spend more on regional policy, and both have regional imbalances which are greater than Britain's. Secondly, the purpose of most of this regional expenditure is to change the cost surface of the country. This is difficult to measure for a number of reasons (not only does the surface differ between industries, but also it varies from year to year, following inflation), but it has been estimated that the average inducement afforded in development areas in the late 1960s was approximately 5·5% of total operating costs (Thomas, 1969). However, the cost advantage to individual firms could be larger or smaller depending on the character of the firm (its capital intensity and amount of new employment created), rates of taxation, the rate at which investments were discounted, and the level of profit (unprofitable concerns gained less). Clearly this was not a large differential in favour of development areas, though it was an improvement over the early 1960s; Thomas also calculated that in 1963 their advantage averaged 3·6%. However, it can be compared with the proportion of operating costs incurred in transport. Over all census of production industries in 1963 this averaged about 5%; among the more mobile industries the proportion was considerably less. Broadly, therefore, regional policy went a long way towards levelling the transport cost surface of Britain.

The third, and most important measure of their significance, is the effectiveness of these expenditures in assisting the achievement of regional objectives. Unfortunately, it is in this area that the greatest problems arise. As we indicated earlier, there is a high degree of ambiguity in the specification of objectives; they lack quantitative bases and different objectives may conflict. Moreover, not all objectives are overtly publicized; some are taken for granted. An additional problem is that long- and short-term objectives for regional development must be differentiated. Implicitly, British policy has been short-term, aiming to avoid serious dislocation arising from secular changes. Recognizing that household migration is likely to be constrained (e.g. by low family incomes in disadvantaged areas and high house prices and the shortage of private rented accommodation in congested areas), the aim has been to prevent regional disparities from widening while, at the same time, allowing a steady flow of migration to areas with higher demand for labour. In this it can be regarded as having been relatively successful. However, the ultimate measure of achievement (given that there will always be substantial populations in the areas presently assisted) is the ability to withdraw assistance in the confidence that in these regions they can attain the same rates of growth in all welfare criteria as the other regions. This requires the servicing of long-term objectives geared to promoting conditions for growth. Such conditions include the improvement of industrial composition, replacing declining sectors, the creation of new infrastructure, and concentration of development in strategically located growth centres to exploit economies of scale. Progress towards this long-term objective has been less successful than the short-term holding operation. To some extent this can be attributed to slow rates of growth nationally; too few resources have been available to divert to assisted areas. But it can also be held that insufficient planning has been given to the use of resources which have been available.

CHAPTER 2

Perspectives on Industrial Movement

AT ANY given time a region is likely to be experiencing a variety of changes in its economic structure arising from the expansion and contraction of its indigenous industries and from industrial movement. Ultimately, the balance of these changes determines the region's rate of growth or decline and contributes in large measure to the internal redistribution of its economic system. Thus, although interregional industrial movement has been the main instrument of policy and an interesting subject for study in its own right, it is important to view it in the perspective of a wider framework which incorporates both intraregional movement and indigenous change. In the two sections of this chapter, therefore, we consider, firstly, industrial movement at its various levels, and, secondly, aspects of the contribution of industrial movement to regional development.

2.1. Distributional and Developmental Industrial Movement

The role of an industrial move can be regarded as either distributional or developmental, depending on the nature of its impact within a regional context. Each mobile establishment contributes to a new configuration of the space economy and may, at the same time, set up or augment a process of growth within its new locale. However, the definition of developmental and distributional moves depends upon a number of factors, and the division between the types is not necessarily clear-cut. The movement of a firm over a very short distance, say from a city centre to its periphery, as a result of an urban renewal scheme is unlikely to have significant multiplier effects or to involve a major change in its workforce and may, therefore, be regarded as a distributional move. On the other hand, longer distance moves which involve the creation of employment and add to regional output (e.g. from the non-assisted to the assisted areas) are likely to be developmental. In between there may be less clarity. For example, a move from London to a town expansion scheme in East Anglia might be regarded as both a redistribution within a non-assisted part of Britain and, more narrowly, as a developmental impetus within a rural region.

It should be emphasized that the distinction between distributional and developmental moves is related only to impact. There are (as discussed below) variations between mobile firms, and these are broadly related to the types of move which they undertake. But these variations tend to be continuous rather than discrete, and the relationships are only identifiable after movement: there is no way of accurately predicting what form of locational adjustment a specific individual firm might make in response to changing conditions. Partly, this is due to randomness within the decision process, but more significantly it also reflects instability of exogenous factors (especially planning and policy constraints) which influence decision-makers in the firm. What this amounts to is that the same decision-makers in the same situation could rationally take different locational decisions at different times.

2.1.1. *The National Pattern*

The closest approach to a full national breakdown of industrial movement according to its origins and destinations is found in the unpublished data collected by the Department of Trade and Industry for the period 1966–71. Although this does not allow a very close analysis, it does permit a classification of moves according to whether the origin and destination were in the same subdivision, different subdivisions within the same standard region, or in different standard regions. As Table 2.1 shows, of the 3392 moves with origins and destinations in Britain, just over half began and terminated in the same subdivision (see Appendix A), while only a quarter crossed the boundaries of standard regions. There was, however, a strong contrast between the assisted and non-assisted areas, with the former having 52% of their moves to destinations within the same subdivisions and 37% from other regions compared with the latter's

TABLE 2.1. GENERALIZED DISTRIBUTION OF ORIGINS AND DESTINATIONS OF INDUSTRIAL ESTABLISHMENTS IN GREAT BRITAIN, 1966–71

	Origin and destination			
	(1) Within same subdivision	(2) Within same region excluding (1)	(3) Within GB excluding (1) and (2)	(4) Total
BY DESTINATION				
Assisted area destinations	939 (52%)	205 (11%)	660 (37%)	1804 (100%)
Other destinations	926 (58%)	408 (26%)	254 (16%)	1588 (100%)
BY ORIGIN				
Assisted area origins	939 (71%)	205 (15%)	183 (14%)	1327 (100%)
Other origins	926 (45%)	408 (20%)	731 (35%)	2065 (100%)
Total moves	1865	613	914	3392

Source: unpublished DTI tabulations.

58% and 16% respectively for the same categories of move. Although the detailed, subdivisional breakdown (Fig. 2.1) emphasizes these figures by showing only a marginal overlap between the

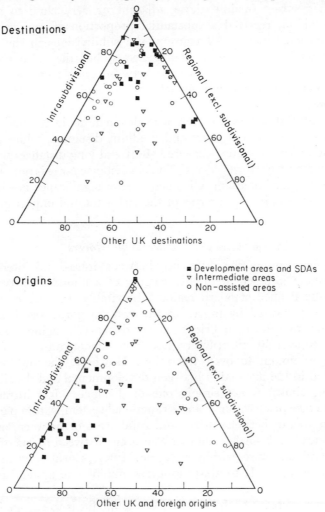

FIG. 2.1. The distribution of origins and destinations of moves by sub-regions, 1966–71.

assisted and non-assisted areas, there was, nevertheless, a wide within-group dispersion. Several in the non-assisted group were almost entirely dominated by intrasubdivisional moves, while another subset (mainly those adjacent or very close to a major conurbation) received a substantial proportion of regional, extra-subdivisional moves. As a group, the subdivisions in the assisted areas tended to be more homogeneous, but they also showed a significant range in their balance between types of move—in their case between intrasubdivisional moves and moves from other regions.

Broadly, therefore, the moves to destinations in the non-assisted areas mainly covered short and medium distances, while those to assisted area destinations covered short and long distances with very few in between. However, variations in distance *per se* is not especially interesting or important. Of much greater significance is what such variations can imply in terms of the character and impact of mobile firms.

2.1.2. *The Characteristics of Intraregional Movers*

By convention, the difference between intra- and interregional movement is based upon the crossing of a boundary between the officially defined standard regions. Inevitably, this means that the distances covered by moves in the two categories overlap. Intra-regional movement in Britain covers distances ranging from a few yards to over 50 miles; interregional movement can range from the same minimum to over 400 miles. However, the difference (as implied in the distinction between developmental and distributional moves, above) is not simply one of distance. Most intraregional moves take place within a single functional system, within parts of an urban area or between urban and rural areas or between large and small towns. A smaller number also occur between towns of similar size and structure within a region. Interregional movement, by comparison, tends to shift resources out of one system and into another.

The preference of the majority of mobile firms to engage in short rather than long moves can be attributed to several factors. But at the heart of the explanation lie two broad dichotomies between the types of establishment undertaking long and short moves and between the locations of large and small plants. In the first case, the evidence from the Department of Trade and Industry (Howard, 1968) permits a comparison of moves to peripheral area locations with those shorter moves to locations elsewhere in Britain during 1945–65. This ignores intrasubdivisional moves, which would have widened the differences. Nevertheless, Table 2.2 illustrates how the longer moves tend to be

TABLE 2.2. SELECTED CHARACTERISTICS OF ESTABLISHMENTS MOVING TO PERIPHERAL AREAS AND THE REST OF GREAT BRITAIN, 1945–65

Destination	Median distance moved (miles)	Branches as % of all moves	Mean employment 1966	
			Branches	Transfers
Peripheral areas [a]	Approx. 150	83	395	310
Rest of Britain	Approx. 50	52	285	175

Source: unpublished DTI tabulations.
[a] See Appendix A.

larger (both for transfers and branch establishments) and to be dominated by branch plants. The second dichotomy is illustrated by Martin's (1969) maps, showing the distribution of employment by size of plant in Greater London (Fig. 2.2), although the patterns are repeated in other major urban areas. Small plants tend to be more nucleated and more central than large ones.

Thus it is characteristic of short-movers that they tend to be smaller and comprise an above-average proportion of transferred plants and that the basic stock from which they come tends to be located more centrally within urban areas. However, this still does not explain why such firms, since having decided to move, elect only to migrate over relatively short distances. The answer to this appears to lie in their relationship with the local economy in the form of external and urban economies.

The advantages of centrality in urban locations are those accruing from accessibility to labour (of sufficient quantity and quality),

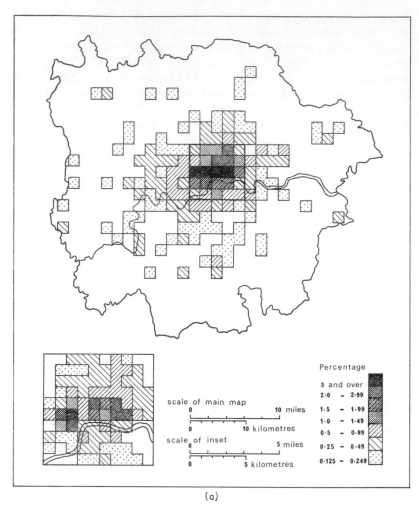

(a)

FIG. 2.2. Greater London: employment in small factories (with less than 20 operatives) (1954). Percentage of Greater London total (138,000) in each square.

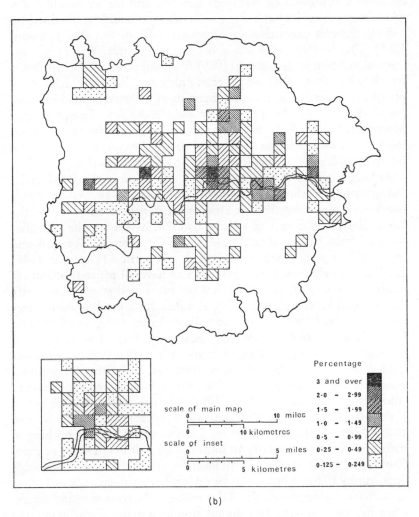

(b)

FIG. 2.2. Greater London: employment in large factories (with 100 operatives and over) (1959). Percentage of Greater London total (651,000) in each square.

customers, concentrated transport termini, and the availability of a wide range of services at lower unit costs than could be obtained by industrial firms producing for themselves (Cameron and Johnson, 1969). The findings of a study of American intrametropolitan industrial location by Goldberg (1969) lends supports to the last factor by showing that while scale economies are inversely related to proximity to the urban core, the benefits of external economies were positively related to both proximity and the density of employment. Moreover, many of the external services available in central areas tend, partly as a function of size and partly through necessity, to be internalized by the companies located on the urban periphery.

Although Wood (1969) has argued for a concept of industrial linkage which embraces the flow of information as well as goods between firms, most British studies have concentrated upon the latter. Early definitions of linkage concentrated upon the identification of links by the direction of sales; for example, forward and backward, diagonal, horizontal, lateral, and vertical (Florence, 1948; Estall and Buchanan, 1961). While these have all proved difficult, if not impossible, to measure, this has not prevented attempts to verify the concept. Keeble (1969), using as a definition local flows of intermediate goods between firms, investigated the strengths of linkages in north-west London. Broadly, these were related to the size of firms and their processes: small firms with unstandardized products tended to have the highest linkages. However, comparing his findings, which related to an outer part of the metropolitan area with those of studies in inner London (Hall, 1962; Martin, 1966), Keeble found it doubtful that linkage had been of equal importance in the two zones. Many of the firms in outer London owed little or nothing of their growth and prosperity to local linkage, although some of them found that their metropolitan location afforded them a valuable opportunity to forge linkages on a regional or national scale.

With its concentration of metal working and engineering industries, often in small firms, and its domination by a major conurbation, the West Midlands has also provided fruitful ground for linkage studies. Lomas and Wood (1969), basing their analysis on the circumstantial evidence afforded by employment data rather than an interview survey, first classified firms in the metal and engineering trades on the basis of their processes, arranging them on *a priori* expectations of their linkages, and then classified towns on the basis of their specialization in these categories. The result showed a distinct gradation, with the conurbation and inner towns exhibiting specialisms in the most linked categories (e.g. supplying particular processes as a service to other manufacturers, subcontracting, and components manufacture), while the outer towns were dominated by assembly and firms making final products.

The opportunities to form interfirm linkages and the consequent effect upon industrial structure are not the only advantages of centrality. Passenger transit systems in urban areas generally favour movement between centre and periphery, allowing producers operating near central termini to draw on a larger pool of labour than firms in the suburban periphery. Also, while land values in central areas tend to be very high, this is offset, for small firms at least, by the advantages of having an available supply of relatively cheap premises to rent which, to a firm with limited capital, provide an adequate base. Moreover, for firms which have bought such premises, Cameron and Johnson (1969) point out, there is no realistic alternative. Many fail to budget sufficiently for depreciation, and a move to a new factory, possibly with new machines, would require considerable liquidity. Such firms are therefore given a kind of protection by the existence of older industrial districts, so that even when forced to move, by urban renewal for example, they often show a preference for relocation in similar central premises.

Thus we may begin to understand why there is a preference for short moves, especially among smaller firms. Indeed, the constraints on movement in many cases have been even narrower than initially supposed. Smith (1970), investigating mobility of metal-working in the West Midlands conurbation, found that although many were potentially mobile, the majority were unable to move substantial distances (above 30 miles) because of the linkages with the rest of the West Midlands economy. Experience, however, tended to show that even this view of intraregional movement was overoptimistic, at least as far as the metal trades were concerned. Of the 705 establishments moving from sites in Birmingham during 1956–68, 65% stayed in Birmingham, 16% went to other parts of the conurbation, and only 13% went to overspill schemes within the West Midland region. Put another way, almost a third moved less than a mile and a further third between 1 and 5 miles. Tulpule (1969), examining the dispersion of industrial employment in Greater London, found that the more concentrated industries (i.e. enjoying external and urban economies) moved least. Similarly, Keeble (1969) found a correlation between size of firm (and, by implication, linkage) and mobility, with small firms (employing between 11 and 75 workers) providing less than half the number of migrant factories that might have been expected, had all size-groups behaved identically. Even the larger engineering firms tended to move no further than was necessary in order to preserve continued links with the specialist subcontractors and finishers who had remained behind. These findings can be compared with those by Hall (1959) in New York, which showed that firms moving out of the city were characterized by standard, specialized processes, and a demand for cheap, unskilled labour, while firms moving inwards or newly established in the center had a lack of standardization, unpredictable markets, and a need for the urban and external economies provided there. Movement also involves labour turnover and recruitment. This imposes a cost which most firms would attempt to reduce, something which is most readily achieved by short rather than long movement. An analysis in the South East indicated a sharp rise in the proportion of new staff recruited with distance: firms moving less than 5 miles recruited, on average, little more than a tenth of their workforce, while those moving over 60 miles recruited 86% (South East Joint Planning Team, 1971).

A further implication of the advantages of accessibility is that when movement does occur it tends to be radial: there is little point in a firm putting a large congested urban centre between its new location and its former one, where its linkages are concentrated. Evidence of radial intraregional movement has been cited by a number of authors (Keeble, 1968; Sant, 1970; Brown, 1966) and is well illustrated in Fig. 2.3.

Many of the findings relating to intraurban location and movement also apply to intraregional movement in general. The local linkages of firms moving from London are reduced by distance from the metropolis, as Table 2.3 indicates, but for mobile firms there remain

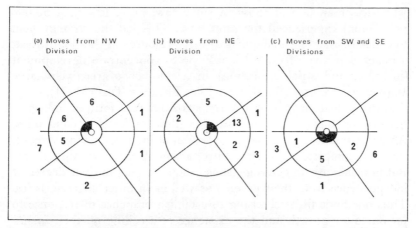

FIG. 2.3. Moves to the Outer Metropolitan Area and the Outer South East from the outer divisions of Greater London. (From South East Joint Planning Team, 1971.)

advantages of location in the larger non-metropolitan centres of the region. Among these, the same study found, was the ease of labour recruitment: two-thirds of firms in large towns found little difficulty,

TABLE 2.3. DISTRIBUTION OF SALES AND PURCHASES OF ESTABLISHMENTS MOVING TO LOCATIONS WITHIN SOUTH-EAST ENGLAND: BY SUBREGION

	Sales		Purchases	
Location in	% within 30 miles	Rest of South-east	% within 30 miles	Rest of South-east
Inner London	45	15	27	14
Outer London	31	16	26	16
Outer Metropolitan Area	26	22	20	19
Outer South-east (North)	17	31	8	25
Outer South-east (South)	13	30	11	28
All areas	28	21	21	19

Source: South East Joint Planning Team (1971), vol. 5.

while less than half of those in small towns (i.e. less than 50,000 population) experienced the same ease. This led the strategy plan to conclude that since labour is a scarce resource in the South East, a major objective of policy should be to concentrate development (including industrial relocation) in a number of relatively large employment centres (South East Joint Planning Team, 1971).

Intraregional movement also reflects a different form of linkage— that of organization and control within multiplant companies. Although branch moves are more typical of interregional movement, they also comprise a substantial proportion of moves within regions. But branches are an heterogeneous group, varying in their degree of independence from their parents as well as in other characteristics. Thus one finds firms choosing to establish branches in response to pressures for growth and the existence of a ceiling on their *in situ* expansion (due to lack of space or insufficient labour, for example), but, at the same time, wishing to retain close control over management or requiring a frequent interchange of products. The result in such cases is a preference for intraregional movement and, possibly, a "colonization effect" when the parent or the early branches spawn subsequent branches. An example is illustrated in Fig. 2.4, which describes the sequence of branch formulation in South West England by a shoe-manufacturing firm in search of pockets of labour (Spooner, 1972).

Finally, the preference for intraregional movement must be related to the nature of the search process for new locations. There is now little doubt that decision-makers operate in a less than perfect manner (Townroe, 1971). Nevertheless, it seems necessary to stress that, within the limits of their knowledge and the resources available to meet the non-recurrent costs of the search, they do tend to behave rationally and purposefully (Logan, 1966; Stewart, 1974), even though the end result may be described as a "satisfactory" rather than a "maximizing" solution. With certain objectives to be met, such as the need to avoid undue risks from higher costs and isolation from the previous location or the need to conduct the search quickly and cheaply, it is reasonable to look first at alternative or additional (in the case of a branch plant) locations in the immediate neighbour- hood, only looking further afield when these prove unsatisfactory or

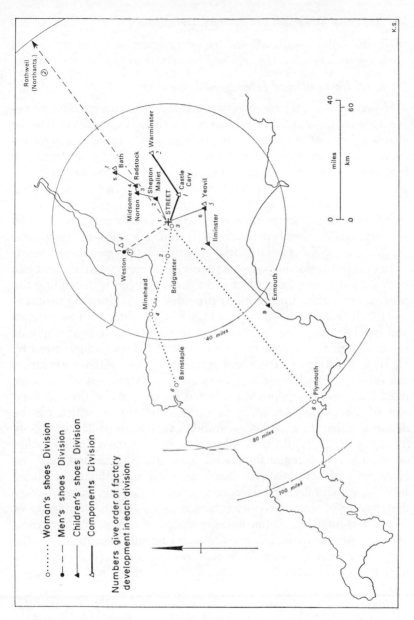

Fig. 2.4. The spread of the factories of Clarks Ltd., from Street in Somerset, 1939–67.

when the inducements offered by government to move to assisted areas are seen to offset the real and perceived costs of a longer move.

2.1.3. *Characteristics of Interregional Movement*

However, the differences between intra- and interregional movement are not absolute. As has been noted, there is some overlap in the characteristics of the two groups and, given a change in exogenous conditions, many firms might respond differently to pressures for locational adjustment. Decision processes are also broadly similar for all mobile firms, with each having to decide whether to move, what sort of move to make, and where to move to. However, while there exist these general similarities, there are also sufficient differences in motivation, locational requirements, and response to exogenous factors to bring about a substantial volume of interregional movement.

In classical regional economic theory, interregional movement can be regarded as one form of capital flow which (notwithstanding the presence of public intervention) provides an equilibrating mechanism for the adjustment of macro-economic variables such as incomes and employment. The direction and volume of movement responds to the marginal efficiency of capital which, in turn, is influenced by regional variations in costs and revenues. Now, without exploring the validity of such a model, it can be asked what sort of firms are most likely to be significantly affected by such variations and what sort of moves they are likely to make. The answer which can be deduced is that the most likely candidates are firms which can supply (or aspire to supply) the national market, either from a single location or from a set of regionally based locations. In the first case the emergence of new low-cost locations, with or without a regional subsidy, which offset the dislocation costs of moving, will encourage the transfer of single-product establishments and the setting up of specialized branches within multiproduct companies. In the second instance, new low-cost locations may not be sufficient to induce the complete relocation of single product establishments (due perhaps to high transport costs), but may result in regionally oriented branch plants.

These are general statements and not easy to verify in detail. But one trend which can be identified is the movement from regions having high demand for resources (especially labour) to regions of lower demand (Table 2.4). Comparing flows between three categories of standard regions during 1952–9 and 1966–71, it can be seen that the patterns were broadly similar even if the magnitudes were not. The first period was one of low regional policy inducements and a

TABLE 2.4. GENERALIZED DIRECTIONS OF INDUSTRIAL MOVEMENT BETWEEN STANDARD REGIONS, 1952–9 AND 1966–71

(a) 1952–9 (*percentages*)

Destinations[a]		Origins				
		Assisted areas		Non-assisted areas	Abroad	Total
		A	B			
Assisted areas	A	1	9	16	9	35
	B	2	5	21	4	32
Non-assisted areas		1	6	19	7	33
Total (*n* = 374)		4	20	56	20	100

(b) 1966–71 (*percentages*)

Destinations[a]		Origins				
		Assisted areas		Non-assisted areas	Abroad	Total
		A	B			
Assisted areas	A	2	7	42	8	59
	B	1	1	10	2	14
Non-assisted areas		1	2	22	2	27
Total (*n* = 800)		4	10	64	12	100

[a] Assisted areas: A, Scotland, Wales, Northern England; B, North West, Yorkshire and Humberside, South West. Non-assisted areas: South East, East Anglia, East Midlands, West Midlands.
Source: unpublished DTI tabulations.

I M.R.D.—C

major concentration of effort on building up the metropolitan new towns. Even so, there was a movement towards less pressured regions; almost three-fifths of the moves within Britain were in this direction, while only 12% went the opposite way—from less- to more-pressured regions. The latter period coincided with the major expansion of expenditure on regional policy following the 1963 Local Employment Act and a greater polarization of movement towards the less-pressured regions, now given impetus by the larger subsidies and stronger controls. Only 5% went to regions of higher demand for labour, while 68% went in the other direction.

The motivations of interregional movement have been documented in a number of studies (McGovern, 1965; Cameron and Clark, 1966; Keeble, 1969), but two recent ones are especially interesting. The first, an analysis by Forsyth (1972) of American companies locating in Scotland (hitherto the main reception area in the United Kingdom for foreign industrial investment), though strictly a study of inter-national movement, gains extra value because the origin and the destination of the firms are so far removed. This means that the motivations are clear-cut and easily identifiable. As a group, these expressed their motives for movement (usually setting up branches) out of the United States as being the need to meet market expansion in the United Kingdom and Europe (82 out of 171 firms responding to the survey) or to maintain their share of the market (28) or to overcome barriers to trade (28). Market orientation was thus an over-riding consideration in their decision to move. The second stage in the process was where in the United Kingdom to locate. Their choice of Scotland was motivated chiefly by labour supply (53 firms out of 228), inducements made under regional policy (52), low wage rates (18), good transport and communications (18), market growth in Scotland (14), and Industrial Development Certificate policy (13). Primarily, therefore, they were influenced by labour factors and by the instruments of regional policy. Linkages, the factor attributed such importance for the short-distance movers, received scant attention. Indeed, the level of integration between these firms and the rest of the Scottish economy was minimal, a condition also found by Lever (forthcoming) in firms moving to Scotland from other parts of Britain.

The second is a major investigation (the Industrial Location Attitudes Group survey) carried out by the Department of Trade and Industry (House of Commons, 1973). Questionnaires were presented to all firms who had opened a new manufacturing plant at some time during 1964–7 in an area (see Appendix A) where they had not manufactured previously. The population therefore included both transfers and branch plants, but not firms which were entirely new to manufacturing. The inquiry dealt with four broad topics: factors causing firms to investigate opening a plant in a new location, factors determining their choice of location, their decision processes, and their post-move experience. Questions were also asked about the impact of the regional employment premium (the standard *per capita* labour subsidy for firms in the development areas) which came into operation in 1967. Altogether, 835 moves were identified, though some were separate branches of a single company, and 787 firms were approached; of these, 632 returned usable questionnaires and 543 were interviewed.

The decision to consider opening a new plant in a new location is not always a simple one, but may arise from a gradual accumulation of pressures from a number of sources. Thus, when firms classified these motivations (Table 2.5) according to their importance (minor, major, outstanding), there was, inevitably, an element of double counting. Nevertheless, the overwhelming motive was to undertake expansion. By itself, this was a major reason for 83% of respondents and the outstanding reason for 20%. In addition, the next two factors (inadequate premises or site and unsatisfactory labour supply) were also related to expansion as, indirectly, were several of the others. Significantly, the impact of policy on this stage of the decision process was quite small. The positive influence of the activities of official bodies on firms' initial thinking, through the provision of inducements and facilities, was a major reason for only 27% of interregional movers (atmost, only half of those going to assisted areas were affected) and an outstanding reason for only 2%. The percentages are higher in the second stage of the decision process, dealing with where to locate, reflecting the result of information gained after the initial decision to move.

Further analysis of responses, classified by industrial group, type,

TABLE 2.5. FACTORS IN THE DECISION TO MOVE

Question numbers (b)		Percentage of all respondent firms[a]		
		Major[c] reason	Minor[d] reason	Outstanding[e] single reason
B1–2	To permit an expansion of output	83	8	20
B12–15	Inadequate existing premises or site	50	11	8
B26–29	Unsatisfactory labour supply at existing location	40	11	15
B30–31	Inducements and facilities made available by official bodies	27	14	2
B22–25	Opportunity to purchase or rent premises or site at new location	20	8	3
B4–6	Too far from established or potential markets	19	1	9
B20–21	Refusal or expected refusal of IDC	12	4	5
B18–19	Town planning difficulties	11	3	4
B16–17	Lease of former premises fell in, or good offer received	5	2	3
B33	Desire to be in more attractive surroundings	4	8	1
B7–11	Too far from supplies, actual or prospective, of materials or services	3	2	1
B34	More profitable to operate elsewhere, no other postulated reason being major	1	—	1
B35	No one outstanding reason	—	—	28
				100

(a) Questions B1–34 were asked of 531 firms—the 543 firms interviewed less 12 cases classed as enterprises new to manufacturing, for whom the questions were not appropriately worded. Question B35 was asked of 492 firms, having been added after some interviews had taken place.

(b) B3 and B32 did not postulate individual reasons.

(c) Percentage replying "major" to at least one of the questions in the group named.

(d) Percentage replying "minor" to at least one of the questions in the group named, provided "major" had not been answered to any question in the group.

(e) Percentage replying as indicated to B35: Was any one of the above reasons (B1–34) outstandingly more important than the rest in causing you to open a new plant in a new location? If so, which?

Source: House of Commons (1973).

and size of company, type of move and origin of move, indicates a considerable variation on each of these factors. Branch plants have a greater association with expansion than do transfers; inadequate sites are more commonly found in the conurbations; labour intensive industries are motivated by inadequate labour supplies to a much greater extent than capital intensive ones; the food-processing industry is sensitive to both markets and supplies, in contrast to clothing and footwear, which is sensitive to neither. These are just a few of the findings of the first part of the Industrial Location Attitudes Group survey, but they indicate that, whatever the shortcomings of the process of locational change, the pressures to move tend to be identified in a consistent and rational manner.

The same can be said of the specification of the attributes that determined which location was selected. Comparing Table 2.6, which ranks these attributes, with Table 2.5, which describes the initial motivation, one can see a strong consistency. Expansion requires resources (especially labour) and accessibility to markets and supplies, all of which score highly in the choice of location. Likewise, at this stage there comes a greater appreciation of the positive influence of official agencies and regional policy. Moreover, as before, there are substantial differences between the categories of move. For example, comparing moves to locations in Wales (an assisted area) and the South East, the former are seen to be related more strongly to labour supply and government inducements, while in the latter the main objectives are labour retention (most of the moves to the South East originated in London), availability of managerial skills, and access to markets, with "amenities" as a significant bonus. Differences also occur between capital- and labour-intensive sectors, between different industries, and between type of move. In the latter case it is evident that decisions involving branches take greater heed of inducements and labour supply than do transfers. Of interest also are the reasons for rejecting particular regions given by firms which considered alternative locations. Thus of the firms which rejected the South East, only 15% did so because of transport or communications problems or remoteness from markets or suppliers, whereas the same reasons were given by 57% of those rejecting Wales (and 71% of those rejecting Scotland). In contrast, a lack of suitable sites was

TABLE 2.6. FACTORS IN THE LOCATION DECISIONS OF INTERREGIONAL MOVERS
(PERCENTAGE OF REPLIES NAMING FACTORS SPECIFIED)

Principal question		Major factor	Minor factor	Outstanding single factor
C4	Availability of labour at new location	72	20	20
C10	Knowledge or expectation that IDC obtainable immediately or in future	48	18	2
C2	Accessibility to markets or supplies	39	21	9
C7	Availability of government inducements	39	7	7
C9	Assistance or encouragement from LAs or promotional bodies	36	30	3
C1	Accessibility to one of firm's plants or to location from which moving	32	18	7
C3	Access to specified transport facilities	31	20	2
C6	Good amenities and environment	29	41	1
C8	Availability of suitable non-government factory	28	5	6
C5	Special characteristics of site	20	17	3
C11	Other factors	12	2	3
	No outstanding single factor	—	—	38
				100

Source: House of Commons (1973).

quoted by 31% of firms rejecting London, but by only 18% of those rejecting Wales and 8% of those rejecting Scotland.

For the individual firm (if not for the national economy) the rationale of industrial movement is tested by its post-move experience. Here the evidence of most studies, including the ILAG survey, proves inconclusive due to the number of variables internal and external to the firm which have to be taken into account. In addition, the assessment ought strictly to take notice of what might have happened in the absence of a move. For obvious reasons, this is difficult to do for a large number of firms. As a result, it is not possible to state confidently whether the terms of the regional economic equilibrium model are fulfilled and whether the firms gain a real, rather than a perceived, benefit. Luttrell's (1962) findings show a tendency for unit costs to be high initially, but to fall rapidly towards equality with those at the original location, but the period covered was insufficient to see whether the trend continued to bring about lower costs. A slightly different approach was adopted in a study of firms moving within and into Northern England (North East Development Council, 1973). The two groups were asked how long, following the move, it had taken to break even and to achieve profitability (Table 2.7). The evidence implies that the extra disturbance of a longer move impedes the rate of achievement, but that the majority quickly approach a break-even position, if not profitability. The latter might have been held back by the national recession, which coincided with the early life (1967–72) of this cohort. The ILAG survey was, in this sense, less rigorous since it sought only broad comparisons. It reported overall satisfaction in 79% of cases, but this clearly reflects different standards. For example, while 72% found semi-skilled and unskilled labour easy to recruit, only 35% said the same of skilled labour. Only 27% found pay rates lower, and 36% had higher output per unit labour cost, although, where the regional employment premium was taken into account in the development areas, the proportion rose to 56%. However, 81% found rents to be lower, while 75% of those buying their factories found purchase prices to be lower than at their previous locations. The gains, therefore tend to be related more closely to experiences with premises and the ability to achieve plans for expansion—both at the time of

TABLE 2.7. POST-MOVE PROGRESS TOWARDS PROFITABILITY IN NORTH-EAST
ENGLAND

(How many years elapsed from the commencement of production until the
plant was (a) breaking even, and (b) profitable, using the standard of profit
appropriate to your company?)

	Break even		Profitable	
	Within region moves (%)	Moves into the North-east (%)	Within region moves (%)	Moves into the North-east (%)
Less than 1 year	55	38	43	26
1–3 years	27	25	19	13
More than 3 years	14	25	24	26
Not achieved by time of survey	4	12	14	35
Number of respondents	22	24	21	23

Note: the survey was carried out in the second quarter of 1972 and
covered establishments known to have moved within or into the North-east
during 1966–8.
Source: The Move to the North, North East Development Council, 1973.

the move and subsequently. The major cost elements—labour and
materials—appear to be affected to a lesser degree.

2.2. The Relative Incidence of Interregional Movement

Regions differ in their absolute and relative abilities to generate and
attract industrial movement. Absolute disparities are the subject of
the analysis in later chapters. Relative disparities, however, are an
important guide to the dynamism inherent in regional economies or
induced in them by the operation of policies. Four diagnostic variables
can be identified which indicate, firstly, the relative incidence of
interregional movement and, secondly, the importance of this source
of employment in each region's development.

By expressing gross employment in movement generated and

attracted over a period as a proportion of base-year employment in manufacturing, a set of patterns emerges describing the relative status of each region in the national system. Discontinuities in the methods of data collection (Appendix A) make it impossible to analyse distributions through to 1971, but those for 1945–66 (see Figs. 2.5– 2.8) cover the greater part of the period and show patterns similar to those for 1966–71.

The ability of a region to generate high relative levels of industrial mobility could, in theory, be related to a variety of factors. High levels, for example, might signify the loss of comparative locational advantage, with a region's industries subsequently migrating to other locations. In the British context, however, this can be almost completely ruled out. Rather, high rates tend to indicate rapid industrial growth with firms actively seeking conditions for further expansion, augmented by the spatially discriminant effects of policy. Thus, as might be expected, the main concentrations of relative out-movement lay in the South East (Fig. 2.5). But this is not a homogeneous region either in industrial composition and development or in the factors giving rise to the high rates of generation. Greater London's position was a relatively simple one, with an outward flow engendered by congestion and planned or policy-induced movement. In the belt north of London, stretching from Oxford to Essex, the picture was not so straightforward. In general, congestion can have played a much smaller part here than in London, although factor shortages, especially of unskilled labour, were acute in many parts of the region; it appears that pressure to move originated chiefly in this constraint. But reference to Fig. 2.6 shows this region also to be one of the main destinations of movement from London. There is some evidence of a radial, step-wise flow of firms through the outer South East to other parts of Britain, but it is unlikely that this is as significant as movement generated by firms indigenous to the region, especially in the vehicles and engineering industries. The areas of high relative out-movement extended into the Midlands, with the Coventry belt, like Oxford, Luton, and Dagenham, providing a source for the movement of the motor-car industry and the West Midland conurbation and south Staffordshire providing a major flow of engineering establishments.

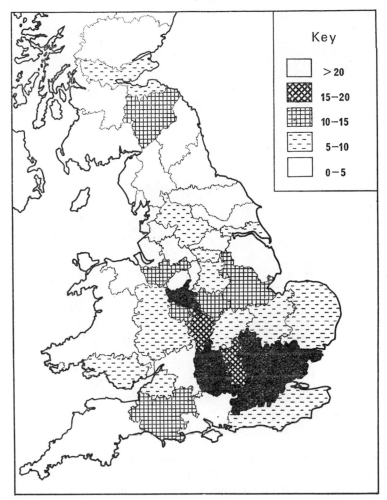

FIG. 2.5. Movement generation 1945–65 (employment) as a percentage of manufacturing employment in 1951.

Attraction of movement is not the direct converse of generation, as Fig. 2.6 shows. The peripheral areas, as expected from their combination of labour supply and government assistance, gained

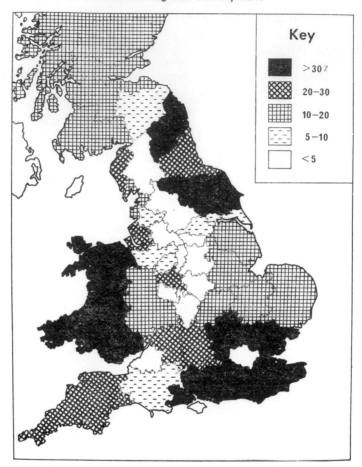

Fig. 2.6. Movement attraction 1945–65 (employment) as percentage of manufacturing employment in 1951.

significant rates of inward movement, but so also did the South East outside Greater London. From an analysis of the characteristics of the moves to these two sets of regions Keeble (1971) has suggested a dual population hypothesis, in which movement is comprised of two groups, long- and short-distance (analogous with intra- and interregional movement, discussed above). The existence of the two groups allows this bi-modal locational distribution in both the relative and the absolute incidence of movement. However, the dual population hypothesis, as is shown later, is augmented by a gravity relationship, so that both the assisted and the non-assisted regions closest to the main sources of growth, other things being equal, attract the greatest amount of movement. Thus, in relative terms, Wales—the closest of the assisted regions to the main sources of movement—gained more than Scotland.

Summarizing these distributions in terms of the net changes in relation to manufacturing employment in 1951 (Fig. 2.7), it is possible to describe regions in terms of both the magnitude of gains or losses and the manner in which these arose. Although one-third of the regions had a deficit, for most it was a case of a small loss out-weighing an even smaller gain. These included, most notably, two northern conurbations (South-east Lancashire and the West Riding) which at the time lay outside the assisted areas, and other urban regions such as Sheffield, Nottingham/Derby, and Bristol. In contrast, the deficits in London, the West Midlands, and Leicester were large, and all arose because of relatively high proportions of outward movement. Similarly, the areas registering net gains can be subdivided. The South East, as implied, witnessed what may be described in aggregate terms as a massive "turnover", but still exhibited major gains, while the peripheral areas generally benefited from a large one-way movement. In between, there came regions (such as East Anglia, the Potteries, North-east Lancashire, and East Central Scotland) where both gains and losses were small or moderate.

The above discussion compares employment in movement with manufacturing employment near the start of the period. Figure 2.8 carries the analysis a step further by comparing employment in movement with total employment change during 1951–66. That is, it investigates the contribution of industrial mobility to regional development. In defining this it has been necessary to assign regions where net employment in mobile industry has been more than offset by indigenous decline. In such cases it has been assumed that the contribution is equivalent to that where net employment in mobile industry is equal to all the growth in total employment.

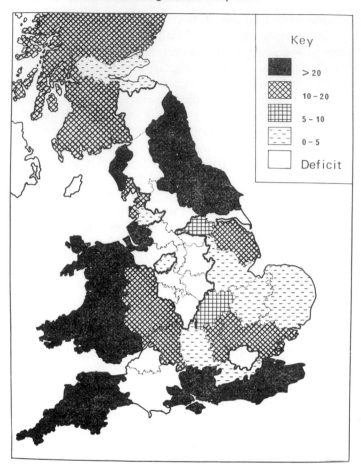

FIG. 2.7. Net employment from industrial movement 1945–65 as
a percentage of manufacturing employment in 1951.

Comparison of this map with Fig. 2.7 shows that there has been
little correlation between a relative gain in manufacturing employment through industrial movement and total employment change.
This occurs for several reasons. In the South East the large net gain
from movement was, in fact, relatively small compared with indi-

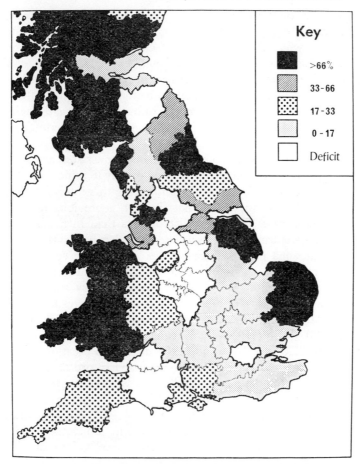

Key

■	>66%
▨	33-66
⦂	17-33
▢	0-17
□	Deficit

Fig. 2.8. The contribution of industrial movement to employment change.

$$\left(\text{KEY}: \quad \frac{\text{Net employment in moves (1945–65)}}{\text{Change in employment 1951–66)}} \times 100. \right)$$

genous growth in manufacturing (Keeble and Hauscr, 1971). On top of this, moreover, there was a rapid growth in the service sector. In contrast, the eastern part of East Anglia presents another set of circumstances. Prior to 1966, the service sector did little more than offset the rapid, regionally very important, contraction in agricultural employment, while indigenous manufacturing was growing slowly. North-east Lancashire presented a more extreme case of similar symptoms. Here, total employment actually declined, due mainly to the rapid rundown of the cotton industry; the contribution of industrial mobility was to reduce the impact of this, although the number of jobs created was small in relation to the 1951 manufacturing base.

The third main category comprised the major assisted areas. In all of them industrial movement contributed greatly to regional development, although some care is needed in making this interpretation. It has been noted (Brown, 1972) that, in fact, more jobs have been created in indigenous firms in assisted areas than in firms moving into them. At the same time, however, there has been a rapid loss of jobs in indigenous manufacturing firms. In some cases this more than offset growth in the others, but even where it did not, the net change from indigenous sources was generally very small. In this context the contribution of industrial movement was crucial to their development. For example, total employment in Merseyside grew by about 70,000 during 1951–66, but its net gain from movement amounted to 87,000. Furthermore, the direct job creation resulting from movement must have induced (or, perhaps, preserved) jobs in the region in intermediate goods and business and consumer services via a multiplier effect. Assuming a multiplier of 1·25 (i.e. every four jobs directly created induce one additional job), an extra 21,750 could be attributed to industrial movement. Conversely, in the absence of movement, there would have been a loss of almost 40,000 jobs. The implications of this could be translated in terms of migration, or high unemployment and lower female activity rates, or—assuming wage flexibility—lower incomes or—more likely—some combination of these. The only assisted area not to be in the position of relying on industrial movement to offset indigenous losses (or slow down the decline) was the South West, where the growth in service industries upheld the indigenous sector. However, this situation changed after 1966, and the South West joined the other assisted areas in relying heavily on industrial movement.

CHAPTER 3

Time Series

3.1. Introduction

Industrial movement has two major attributes. One, the geographical distribution of origins and destinations, forms the subject of the next chapter. The other, discussed here, is the temporal distribution of movement. Both are closely related to each other and to the formulation and implementation of policy having, at the same time, a causal and a responsive role. If, for example, the volume and distribution of movement diverge from that desired by government, then new policy instruments will be needed to alter either or both.

The framework of this chapter is as follows. First, the time series of movements are described in as much detail as the available information usefully permits. The source of this data is the unpublished tabulations of the Department of Trade and Industry's surveys carried out in 1968 and 1972 of moves to locations in each standard region. This includes moves between the subdivisions of a standard region, but not within them. Although some data is available for *employment* in moves, for reasons outlined in Appendix C, the discussion here is confined to numbers of moves. With this it is possible to investigate time series at the national level, for "macro-regions" and for standard regions, from 1945 to 1965 and from 1966 to 1971. Unfortunately, the break imposed by a new system of data collection (Appendices A and B) makes it impossible to run straight through from 1945 to 1971. However, the first period is long enough to permit time-series analyses and the second, if short, still presents important temporal variations.

Following this description, the next section discusses the variables which appear to have influenced the volume and fluctuations in the temporal patterns of movement. The argument is put forward that two sets of variables should be expected to play important roles. One can be described as an economic set, containing parameters which describe the continuous evolution of the national economy. The other set can be described as structural, and consists of variables relating to the strength of regional policies. This hypothesis is tested in the third section, using multiple regression analysis to identify the relationships between series of national and regional movement and a number of quantifiable economic and structural variables. The conclusions, broadly, are that there is significant support for the hypothesis, allowing policy-makers to conduct meaningful forecasting exercises, with some qualifications, on the possible outcomes of changes in policy instruments. The qualifications lie in the need to predict, over several years, the level of non-policy variables.

Lastly, we make a digression into another aspect of the time series. Throughout the earlier sections the discussion is based on the recorded numbers of annual movement. However, a substantial proportion of mobile firms is subsequently closed. Due account should be paid to this for its own interest, but it is also important to relate closures to regional policy.

Without doubt, the temporal variations in industrial movement are as important as the geographical distributions. Each complements the other in leading to an understanding of a national system of mobility. In this respect we are fortunate in having an increasing body of data which allows hypotheses to be tested and, ultimately, regional policies to be improved. Hitherto, time series (like geographical distributions) have tended to be collected and analysed in an *ad hoc* manner, relating to individual regions (Keeble, 1968). A recent study by Lever (1973) goes further than any other by attempting to relate movement to cyclical variations in the importance of location factors within a single region, North-east Lancashire. His analysis suggests that there may be an association. In addition, the present author has related firm's perceptions of the advantages of their locations in East Anglia to the time at which they were established there (Sant, 1970). Although these are valuable, they inevitably suffer from incompleteness, and it is not possible to use them as a guide to national or multiregional variations.

3.2. Description

3.2.1. *The Elements of Time Series in Industrial Movement*

There is no reason to expect flows of industrial movement to be constant. In an hypothetical static equilibrium system free from government intervention, for example, where industrial movement provides an equilibrating mechanism in response to factor price inequalities, the position would be reached when regional disparities would begin to close and the flow of industry between regions would slow down. Introducing dynamic elements and the role of government creates additional reasons for trends and fluctuations to occur in the volume and direction of movement.

In the following paragraphs evidence is sought for relationships which can be deduced from a range of regional economic models. The first has already been mentioned; namely, the relationship between graphs of industrial movement and economic (or cyclical) and structural variables (Fig. 3.1). If the latter is temporarily ignored,

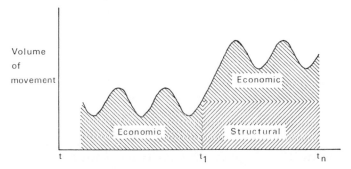

FIG. 3.1. The operation of economic and structural variables in an hypothetical time series of industrial movement.

a national graph might be expected which corresponds generally with that of industrial investment as a whole, because the decision to move is inextricably related to the decision to invest (Townroe, 1969). There may be a lag, due to the greater complexity of the movement process, but the two graphs ought to be parallel, reflecting their response to the same set of exogenous economic conditions.

The same is also true, with qualifications, of graphs of industrial movement into individual regions. Due to disparities in locational attraction, the graphs of industrial movement into declining or slow growth regions located furthest from the main sources might be expected to show greater variability than those of regions located more centrally. This can be illustrated by an adaptation of Smith's (1970) neo-classical model of "spatial margins to profitability" (Fig. 3.2). If the expected revenues resulting from movement become

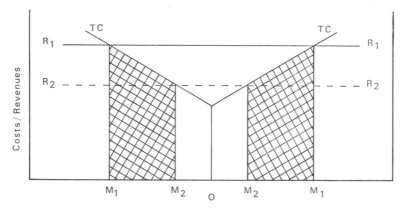

Fɪɢ. 3.2. The effect of temporal variations in revenue on locational attraction in a "spatial margins" model.

higher (i.e. shift from R_2 to R_1)—or the costs become lower—the spatial extent of viable destinations is increased (from M_2 to M_1). In a fluctuating economy, however, the marginal locations (in the absence of subsidies) alternate between profit and loss, while locations closer to the source vary only between different levels of profit.

Having postulated a basic cyclical form for industrial movement, it is now possible to add to this a structural element. That is, by its intervention a government may bring about conditions more (or less) favourable to industrial mobility. This might be achieved simply by improving the flow of information to decision-makers about opportunities in other regions. But this is not likely to be as effective as controls on expansion *in situ* or financial subsidies to move—the two major policy instruments applied in Britain. However, the effectiveness of structural variables can be altered from time to time. The impact can be witnessed in the national graph and also at the regional level. In the latter case intervention may take the form of altering the areas where subsidies are available, rather than altering the level of subsidy to mobile firms, although it is also possible for both changes to occur simultaneously.

The second relationship for which evidence is sought is closely linked to the first. This is the degree to which flows of movement can be created or diverted by intervention. For example, in an hypothetical system of three regions there may be an annual flow of ten firms between regions *A* and *B*. By intervening, the government may succeed only in diverting some or all of these to *C*; or it may leave the size of the flow from *A* to *B* untouched but create a new flow from *A* to *C*. While, in reality, it is not always easy to distinguish creation or diversion—due to economic changes among regions or to unforseen side-effects of alterations in the instruments of policy—it is nevertheless important to seek this relationship. Only by establishing its existence can intervention be carried out in a rational manner.

The preceding paragraphs have implied that industrial movement takes place within an integrated system of regions. If this is the case then it should be expected that flows to one region should be related to flows to another. Moreover, if the system were static, the evidence should show regions to be in competition with each other, so that one region could gain more movement only at the expense of others. Due to the operation of cyclical and structural factors, however, it is more likely that the graphs of some regions will move in unison. This can be tested by carrying out time series intercorrelations.

3.2.2. *National and Regional Time Series*

Evidence of the fluctuating nature of movement time series at the national level is readily available (Fig. 3.3). Total recorded movement between 1946 and 1965 ranged from about 300 moves per annum at its peak to below 100 at the trough. As the graph shows, the immediate postwar period witnessed a high level of mobility; many firms

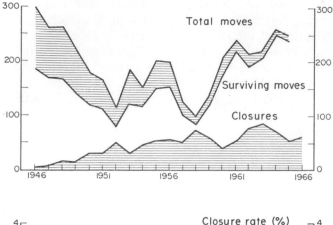

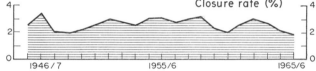

Fɪɢ. 3.3. Time series of industrial movement and post-move closures in Great Britain, 1946–66.

needed new premises and these were most readily available in the peripheral regions (McCrone, 1969). This was followed by a steady fall in numbers to a trough approximately coinciding with a recession in industrial production and employment in the early 1950s. Thereafter, the graph rose to a peak in the mid 1950s, though this was markedly lower than the preceding or subsequent peaks. Another downturn followed, again showing timing similar to the graph of production and investment, only to be superseded by a sharp rise in movement to a new peak in 1961. From this point the graph took on a new form, which can be attributed to a change in the implementation of regional policy. The year 1963 might, following the previous pattern, have been expected to register a very low volume of movement; industrial growth was at, hitherto, its postwar lowest and unemployment at its highest. However, the early 1960s was also a period of rapid growth in expenditure on regional policy (Fig. 3.4),

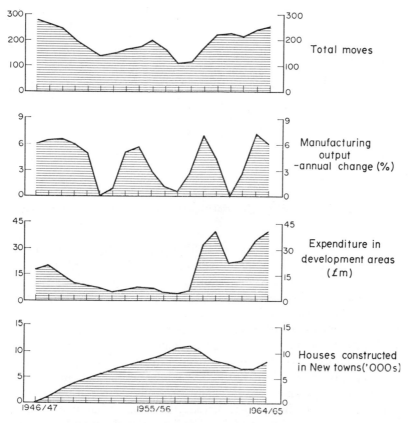

Fɪɢ. 3.4. Time series of selected economic and structural variables, 1946–65.

and there was also considerable construction in new towns. It would appear, therefore, that these were sufficient to prevent a deep trough, though it is necessary to find corroborating evidence in the graphs of movement to individual regions in order to identify the precise effects of these changes (see Figs. 3.6 and 3.7). Thereafter, movement continued its upward course through to 1966.

From 1966 to 1971 the graph (Fig. 3.5) is based on new definitions and, although the reported movement is in line with expectations, it

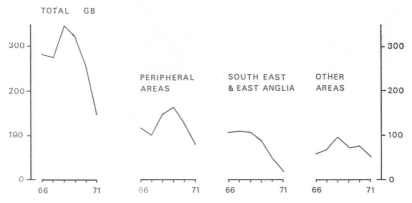

FIG. 3.5. Time series of industrial movement in Great Britain, 1966–71.

is preferable to treat it separately. The period 1966–9 was like the dampened trough of 1963 in so far as it showed a response to structural factors when others would normally have depressed the volume of movement below what was actually recorded. In fact, inter-regional movement continued its upward trend to a peak in 1968, when 350 moves were registered. But throughout this period unemployment was passing through a cyclical upturn, rising sharply through 1966–7, staying on a plateau during 1967–70, and rising very sharply again in 1970. Meanwhile, industrial production changed very little between 1968 and 1972, giving one of the periods of slowest growth in postwar Britain. But, offsetting this, was an accelerated expenditure on regional policy, with the total Exchequer cost rising from about £20m in 1964/5 to £50m in 1966/7 and, following the introduction of investment grants and regional employment premium, to £275m in 1968/9, at which level it remained for the next 2 years. Nevertheless, this high rate of spending on regional policy was unable to preserve the high rate of industrial movement and the graph was eventually forced down by the recession in production and investment in the late 1960s.

In general, therefore, the national graph appears to show that both economic and structural variables have been effective and that regional policy has had some influence in creating movement or, at least, preventing it from falling more dramatically during recessions. But it does not provide any evidence for or against movement diversion or the existence of a regional system. For these it is necessary to turn to the regional graphs.

At the macro-regional level (Fig. 3.6), the three series show distinct differences. Broadly, the series for the peripheral areas between 1945 and 1966 describes a U-shaped curve, cutting through the cyclical fluctuations of the 1950s and early 1960s. The upward trend at the

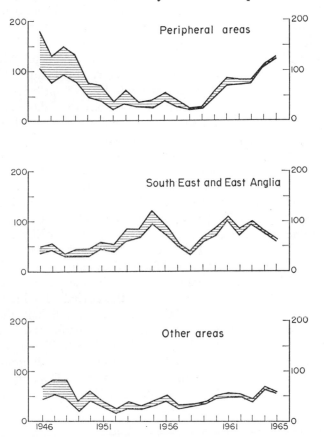

FIG. 3.6. Times series of industrial movement by macro-region, 1946–65.

end of the period continued until 1969/70, when it was curtailed by the latest recession. In contrast, the graph for the South East and East Anglia showed an upward trend through the early 1950s, coinciding with the construction of new towns, before being hit by the cyclical downturn of the late 1950s. It continued to rise again, partly due to the introduction of town expansion schemes in East Anglia (following the Town Development Act of 1952), but suffered a further decline, probably due to the diversionary effect of regional policy, exacerbated, especially after 1968, by the cyclical downturn. There was, therefore, a clear, if imperfect, polarity between these two graphs, indicated by a correlation between them of -0.24; the negative coefficient indicates their tendency to "compete" with each other for a given stock of industrial mobility. In broadly animated terms, this can be described as a struggle by, and on behalf of, the peripheral areas to wrest industry away from the inherently more attractive South East, with the rest of Britain acting as a bystander able, especially after the intermediate areas were created (from 1970) to pick up some of the moves from the metropolis. But it is at the finer scale represented by the standard regions that evidence of the operation of a regional system is most interesting, for it is apparent that considerable "within-group competition" occurred in the macro-regions (Fig. 3.7). Thus, among the peripheral areas, there was considerable similarity between Wales and Northern England (their time series correlation for 1945–66 was 0·87) and between Scotland and North West England ($r = 0.79$), but the two pairs were relatively dissimilar. The first pair gained greatly in the 1940s, while the second accelerated towards the end of the period. But intercorrelations between all the regions (Table 3.1) and the linkage diagrams based on this (Fig. 3.8) also show the East Midlands and Yorkshire and Humberside to be like Wales and the North. To some extent this is due to the role, prior to 1952, of the West Riding and East Midlands as sources of movement, particularly of firms in the predominantly female-employing textile and clothing industries. For most of these it was possible to fulfil locational requirements by relatively short moves to the coalfield regions east of the Pennines, where female activity rates were low.

A third high linkage occurred between East Anglia and the South

West, two regions with different status in regional policy but sharing certain factors in common. The South West contains a substantial development area, but this was chiefly a creation of the 1960s; previously, it had had no more than a few DATAC areas between 1958 and 1960. It also contained, in Swindon, one important town expansion scheme. East Anglia's experience of DATAC areas was so cursory and confined to small rural districts that it was barely

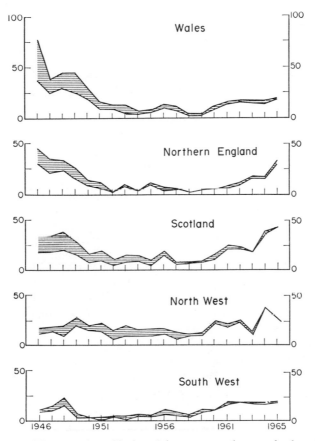

Fig. 3.7. Times series of industrial movement by standard region, 1946–65.

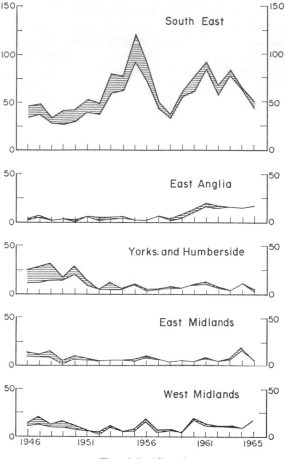

FIG. 3.7. (Cont.)

noticed, but the region achieved a marked upward trend in its graph through the negotiation with Greater London of ten town expansion schemes. Both regions have also come to be recognized as environmentally desirable locations by mobile firms in the South East and have come increasingly to be regarded as part of the metropolitan sphere of influence (Sant, 1970; Spooner, 1972). On the basis of this trend, these regions join Scotland and the North West in the similarity

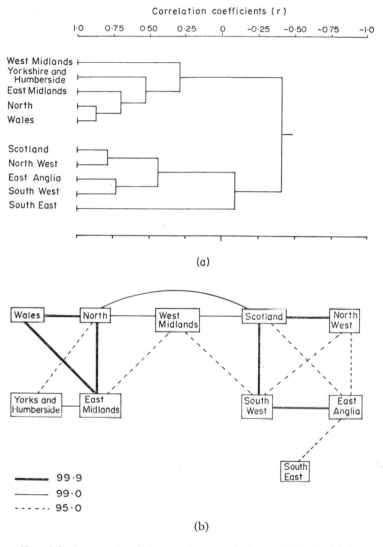

FIG. 3.8. Interregional time series correlations, 1946–65. (a) dendrogram of regional links; (b) main correlation bonds (significant at 95·0 confidence level).

TABLE 3.1. CORRELATION MATRICES OF REGIONAL TIME SERIES, 1945–65

(a) Macro-regions

	1	2	3
1. Peripheral areas	1·00		
2. South East and East Anglia	−0·24	1·00	
3. Rest of Great Britain	0·76	0·05	1·00
4. Great Britain	0·83	0·31	0·87

(b) Standard regions

	1	2	3	4	5	6	7	8	9	10
1. Northern	1·00									
2. Yorkshire and Humberside	0·53	1·00								
3. East Midlands	0·70**	0·61*	1·00							
4. South East	−0·30	−0·34	−0·01	1·00						
5. South West	0·42	0·11	0·38	0·22	1·00					
6. Wales	0·87**	0·58*	0·71**	−0·41	0·14	1·00				
7. West Midlands	0·59*	0·29	0·46	0·26	0·45	0·41	1·00			
8. North West	0·36	0·21	0·18	0·16	0·44	0·19	0·35	1·00		
9. Scotland	0·61*	0·38	0·36	−0·01	0·68**	0·32	0·60*	0·79**	1·00	
10. East Anglia	0·01	−0·26	−0·09	0·47	0·73**	−0·25	0·28	0·46	0·47	1·00
11. Great Britain	0·78**	0·48	0·76**	0·27	0·64*	0·61*	0·70**	0·59*	0·70**	0·36

d.f. = 20.
Significance levels: 99·9% **; 99·0% *.

of their graphs if not in the reasons for accelerating their greater attractiveness.

With one exception, and that only marginal, the South East had little in common with any other region. This is to be expected because the peripheral areas compete with the non-metropolitan South East and the rest of the country tends to rely most heavily on the smaller conurbations for their inward moves. The positive link which did occur, however, was with East Anglia, where inward movement was largely a spill-over from the South East. The West Midlands was only marginally more connected, reflecting this region's role as the secondary source of industrial movement, subject to the same competitive relationships.

3.3. Temporal Models of Movement

3.3.1. *The Pressures for Movement*

The operations of businesses are continuously surrounded by risks and uncertainties (Horowitz, 1970). Many of these become institutionalized through experience, and businesses proceed with confidence that most actions will be met by particular responses. In certain situations, however, the individual business has to make decisions and take actions for which it has little or no precedent. Industrial movement is one such situation: for the majority of firms the location decision is made with relatively little prior strategic planning (Krumme, 1969a). They strive to function efficiently within their given geographical conditions rather than to seek new ones; that is, in Pred's (1967) classification they tend to be adapters rather than adopters. Most, in fact, attempt to carry out expansion at the same site; Holmans (1964) has shown that at least half of the manufacturing jobs created in London and the South East during 1952–61 were either in small-scale expansions, not requiring an industrial development certificate (i.e. less than 5000 ft^2), or required no new building at all. Nevertheless, there are occasions when, in response to internal or external pressures, firms find it necessary to review their locational parameters and to carry out some form of adjustment.

First, over their lives the growth patterns followed by firms include a number of processes (Channon, 1973; Skene-Smith, 1966), such as a diversification from a single product to several or many, internalization of services previously provided by other firms, acquisition of additional productive capacity (possibly by take-over), departmental reorganization, and so on. Each of these has implications for the location of the firm as a whole and for the distribution of functions among its parts. Whenever a change is planned, the firms become potentially mobile. Secondly, firms may come against external pressures on their locations, where the decision to move is initiated elsewhere, to meet the requirements of local planners or central government. The latter, for example, played a major part in the movement of large parts of the British motor industry in the 1960s. Thirdly, pressures may result from exogenous changes in costs of inputs, sources of supply, or distribution of markets, without the firm attempting to carry out internal changes.

The evidence from a number of surveys (House of Commons, 1973; Luttrell, 1962; Keeble, 1968) indicates that expansion is the main motivation for movement, and it is around this that a model to explain temporal variations should be built. Every new firm (assumed for the present to occupy a single establishment) has a ceiling on the size to which it can grow without making changes in its locational conditions. The ceiling may be imposed by a variety of constraints; different factors will apply to different firms. But, what is conducive to movement is not so much that a ceiling exists, but that firms should want to grow beyond that level. Once that decision has been taken, there follows the chain of decisions which lead eventually to the transfer of the entire firm or the setting up of a branch plant.

Now it can be asked under what broad conditions a constant, non-fluctuating flow of industrial movement could be expected. These can be set out in several groups. The first is stable economic conditions, free from business cycles or random changes. Secondly, there should be no changes in the structure and characteristics of industry. Next, regional disparities should be constant. Fourthly, there should be a constant rate of urban renewal. Fifthly, policy instruments should remain unchanged, giving a constant set of assisted areas, controls on industrial development, and inducements to move. Moreover, not only should all of these actually be constant but decision-makers should also expect them to remain constant since movement, like other investment decisions, is based not only on past experience but also on expectations. None of these conditions have existed or can be expected to exist in Britain.

3.3.2. *Problems of Analysis*

But to proceed from a recognition of the volatility of national and regional time series to the specification of quantifiable variables which explain them, requires considerable care. Ideally, we would be able to use any variable which might be considered relevant. Unfortunately, some variables are unquantifiable, while others have only been enumerated over short periods. It is also valuable to have variables which could be disaggregated to the regional level but, while this can be done for some, it is not possible for all. Finally, because it has been hypothesized that regions form an integrated system, it is important to use a single set of variables. This may involve loss of accuracy in explaining a region's series, but it does enable comparisons to be drawn between the responses of different regions to changes in a single set of conditions.

Time-series analysis, using correlation and regression techniques, is not without methodological problems. Autocorrelation, the degree to which values at one time are attributable to values at the time immediately preceding tends to be the most intractable. However, although it poses problems in all economic time series, these tend to be less severe in the case of fluctuating series than with trend series. At least as far as the dependent variable, industrial movement, is concerned, there is no theoretical reason why one year's level of movement should directly influence the next year's. A second problem concerns the nature and significance of lags. The relationship between movement and cyclical and structural variables need not be contemporaneous. Rather, it should be expected that there will be lags between the decision to move, which may be prompted by external changes, and the move itself, which may occur a year or more later. Thirdly, lack of ideal data necessitates the use of "second-best" sources. For example, it would be desirable to have information about the real costs and returns from movement on a year-to-year basis. But these cannot be calculated, and the next-best substitutes are variables which act as general indicators of economic change. Fourthly, problems are posed by the hypothesis that regions form an economic system. This requires some variables to be specified in two parts; one relating to conditions within each region and the other to conditions in the remaining regions. For example, the volume of movement to Wales, we hypothesize, is influenced by the designation of assisted areas in Wales; but it is also influenced (negatively) by assisted area status designated in other parts of the country. However, this assumes that every other such designation has an equal impact on Wales. In fact, it may be that the designation of neighbouring regions, such as Merseyside or parts of the South West, has more influence than the designation of Scotland. If this were the case, it would be necessary to apply appropriate weights to each region. But at this point the limits of practicability have been exceeded. All that can be done is to admit the dilemma and regret that at least one interesting analytical exercise cannot be carried out. Lastly, it is important to be aware that the analysis has, perforce, to be at the aggregate level whereas each firm has its own response to internal and external conditions which may deviate considerably from the average behaviour of the group.

3.3.3. *Specification of Variables*

Although these problems limit the number of usable series, those that remain include several which can be expected to influence the amount and distribution of movement (Table 3.2). Firstly, there are four which act as indicators of economic conditions. These are: (i) changes in the index of manufacturing output at 1964 prices, V_1; (ii) the average annual levels of bank rate, V_2; (iii) the level of undistributed company earnings, V_3; and (iv) annual average levels of unemployment, V_4. Of these, the first is straightforward: faster industrial growth, it is hypothesized, means that more firms are likely to reach their expansion ceilings within a given period and, hence, give rise to a greater volume of movement. The second and third relate to possible sources of financing the investment of a move. If it is done from borrowing, then higher rates of interest will tend to inhibit movement (and other investment as well). On the other hand,

Table 3.2. Independent Variables used in Time-series Analysis
of Industrial Movement, 1945–65

(i) *Economic variables*

V_1 Percentage change in manufacturing output[a] 1964 prices

V_2 Bank rate (annual average)[a]

V_3 Undistributed company earnings (£m)[a] 1964 prices

V_4 Numbers unemployed (June plus December average) ('000)[b]

V_{4a} Region i V_{4b} Great Britain less region i

(ii) *Structural variables*

V_5 Government expenditure on DAs: total (£m)[c] 1964 prices

V_6 Government expenditure in DAs: factory buildings and industrial estates (£m)[c] 1964 prices

V_7 Government expenditure in DAs: loans and grants (£m)[c] 1964 prices

V_8 Employment in DAs ('000)[b]

V_{8a} Region i V_{8b} Great Britain less region i

V_9 Houses constructed in new towns ('000)[a]

V_{9a} Region i V_{9b} Great Britain less region i

V_{10} Town expansion schemes in operation (East Anglia only)

---

[a] *Annual Abstract of Statistics.*

[b] *Employment & Productivity Gazette* (formerly *Ministry of Labour Gazette*).

[c] Annual reports on the Local Employment Acts.

it may be done from retained profits, in which case, if these have been high, the ability to invest will be enhanced.

The fourth variable, unemployment, is more difficult to interpret in terms of its causal relationships with movement. The availability of labour has been cited as a key variable in industrial movement, but this tends to presume static conditions. In a dynamic time-series analysis the situation becomes more complex. Interregional movement is not simply a function of national unemployment levels; it depends also upon the existence of disparities in labour supply among regions. Moreover, in Britain these disparities tend to increase when the national rate increases and a rising rate of unemployment generally reflects a recession. Hence, it is difficult to establish a precise relationship on *a priori* grounds, although this can be partially circumvented by specifying the unemployment variable in terms of (a) its incidence in each region, and (b) its incidence in the rest of the country.

The second set of variables are structural ones, relating to policy instruments. From time to time controls and inducements have been altered (McCrone, 1969; Moore and Rhodes, 1974), introducing new measures, replacing old ones, and changing the intensity of regional policy. Thus, for example, the 1945 Distribution of Industry Act made available loans, provided for industrial estates and advance factories, and exercised control on location through building licences. Towards the end of the period, the 1963 Local Employment Act allowed a tax incentive in the form of accelerated depreciation. Quantifying such disparate policy instruments can only be done adequately in terms of their financial value (V_5, V_6, V_7). Although a given sum spent in different ways may have a different impact on industrial movement, this approach does permit some comparison from year to year of the willingness of central government to promote regional policy. Moreover, it is possible to specify as separate variables the expenditures on (i) factory buildings and industrial estates, and (ii) loans and grants. There are, however, some minor difficulties to be faced. One is that expenditure reflects past decisions to move; the more firms want to move to assisted areas, the higher the expenditure. Another is that part or all of the expenditure on major items prior to 1966 was recoverable; the values are Exchequer costs rather than real costs. This makes it necessary to assume that the recoverable proportion was constant.

Of the two sets of expenditure used here, it is arguable that the more influential has been that on advance factory building and industrial estates (European Free Trade Association, 1971). The origin of this role as provider of sites for industry lies in the attempts of the commissioners for the Special Areas set up under the 1934 Act to attract firms. Early lack of success was attributed to an absence of suitable modern premises; trading estate companies were set up in 1936 to meet this need, and by 1939 the three main estates at Team Valley, Treforest, and Hillington had over 10,000 people working in them. After 1945 such estates proliferated in the development areas, though not many were as large as these three, and by 1969 there were 1166 factories administered by the industrial estates corporations (the successors to the earlier commissioners). In addition, there were about 100 premises under construction. The advantages of industrial estates and advance factories lie in their engendering of external economies, provision of space for expansion, variety of factory layout, and—most important—rapid occupancy at rentals which may be lower than for similar factories in the same area. Expenditure at current values in this category ran at a fairly high level in the late 1940s (about £9m per annum), but fell in the 1950s (to around £4m) before rising slightly in the early 1960s and more substantially after 1964.

Expenditure on loans and grants was negligible before 1960 when the Local Employment Act gave new powers to the Board of Trade. Prior to that the average sum was no more than £1m per annum, but after the Act it jumped to over £20m and tended to increase steadily. In addition, the 1960 Act introduced building grants and discretionary grants which tended to be given to labour-intensive industry investing in areas of high unemployment. These inducements were not geared solely to industrial movement, however, but were available also to firms expanding or investing *in situ*. Also, they tended to be quite complex, and many firms had only an imperfect knowledge of the way in which grants, loans, and other financial inducements operated (Townroe, 1971). Nevertheless, per job created in a development area, the sums provided by the Board of Trade in loans and grants were quite substantial, amounting to about £600 in the early 1960s. Added to the attraction offered by industrial estates, this should have acted as a further inducement compared to the position before 1960 when this category of incentive was almost absent.

While these variables provided a good indicator of the strength of policy in the country as a whole, they are less adequate at the regional level. Here they need to be augmented by a measure describing the proportion of each region in which inducements were available, V_8. Assuming all such areas to have an equal chance, *pro rata*, of attracting industry, the variable identifying attractiveness can be defined as the amount of its employed population living in assisted areas. At the same time, the ability of a region to attract industry would be negatively related to the designation of assisted areas in other regions. An example of the operation of these measures occurs in the South West. Before 1958 it had no parts with development area status. Then, following the Distribution of Industry Act, areas containing almost 100,000 employees were designated. At this time about 4·1 million employees lived in development areas in other regions. Under the 1960 Local Employment Act, however, the South West's status was marginally reduced (80,000 in development districts), while the number in the rest of the country fell to about 3·0 million. In absolute terms, during 1945–65 the position in the South West was altered twice, but in relation to the rest of the country it underwent no less than nine changes. In other regions the frequency of absolute and relative changes was equally great.

The second structural factor is the construction of new towns which were associated with the planned dispersal of people and jobs from the main conurbations, V_9. These developments influenced the volume of movement at the national level but, perhaps more significantly, they added an extra element of interregional competition for industry. New towns in the South East, for example, provided a diversionary effect, reducing the attraction of the assisted areas. Unfortunately, it is not possible to derive a variable which relates directly to the potential attraction for industrial movement to the new towns, but an indirect measure exists in the number of houses completed in each year. As with assisted area status, the relevant values are those for construction in each region and construction in the rest of the country, giving an absolute and a relative indicator of potential attraction. However, it is necessary to augment this variable since no account is taken of construction in town expansion schemes which, though small in the country as a whole, were highly significant in East Anglia. To overcome this it is expedient to introduce a variable, V_{10}, to represent town expansion in the East Anglian models only; this region is sufficiently small for the effect of this change on the other regional models to be insignificant.

3.4. Multivariate Analysis, 1945–65

To explain the national and regional time series, this short list of economic and structural variables had been subjected to a set of statistical experiments. Each of the series has been regressed against (a) economic variables alone, (b) structural variables alone, and (c) economic and structural variables together. Also, the movement series have been (a) unlagged, and (b) lagged by one year against all the independent variables. The introduction of lagged experiments has only a marginal effect on coefficients of correlation, although they do provide better regression equations in the majority of cases.

Before describing the results of multivariate analyses of each of the fourteen series, it is valuable to identify relationships between pairs of variables. This allows us to see (i) which factors appear to have been important in each region, and (ii) which pairs of independent variables have been significantly intercorrelated and, hence, may possibly lead to multicollinearity in the regression models. The first is illustrated in Table 3.3, which contains the lagged correlation coefficients r between each regional series and the variables listed in the previous chapter. The second is partially covered in Table 3.4, which refers to the intercorrelations of nationally based independent variables.

The correlations in Table 3.3 show a degree of consistency which we might expect on the basis of previous observations about the grouping of regional series and the likely response to economic and structural changes. Thus, while the annual changes in the index of manufacturing production (V_1) lack significance in all cases except Scotland, the correlations, with only one exception, exhibit a positive association; industrial growth tends to encourage movement. High interest rates (V_2) tend to discourage movement, particularly over long distances to the peripheral areas, where it can be inferred that the perceived risks are greater. The peripheral areas gained from the expenditure carried out under the various Distribution of Industry and Local Employment Acts $(V_5$ and $V_7)$, while in the remainder of the country the effects were negative or unimportant. (The high correlation in East Anglia is spurious; there was a close correlation between this expenditure and the growth of town expansion schemes; in the multiple regression analyses the former are therefore excluded.) Unemployment within a given region (V_{4a}) tended to be important only within the peripheral areas (especially Scotland, Wales, and Northern England), but unemployment elsewhere (V_{4b}) carried no significance for any region. The assisted area weight within a given region (V_{8a}) underwent a major systematic

TABLE 3.3. CORRELATION COEFFICIENTS r BETWEEN REGIONAL SERIES AND INDEPENDENT VARIABLES (LAGGED MODELS, 1945–65)

Variables
V_1 Index of manufacturing production (1964 prices)
V_2 Bank rates
V_3 Undistributed company earnings (1964 prices)
V_4 Unemployment (total numbers)
    (a) in region i (b) in Great Britain less region i
V_5 Expenditures on regional policy £m (total) (1964 prices)
V_6 Expenditures on regional policy £m (factories, etc.)
V_7 Expenditures on regional policy £m (loans and allowances)
V_8 Assisted area weights
    V_{8a} Region i V_{8b} Great Britain less region i
V_9 New Town weights
    V_{9a} Region i V_{9b} Great Britain less region i
V_{10} Town expansion schemes (East Anglia only)

	V_1	V_2	V_3	V_{4a}	V_{4b}	V_5	V_6	V_7	V_{8a}	V_{8b}	V_{9a}	V_{9b}	V_{10}
(a) Standard regions													
North	0·38	−0·37	−0·15	0·58	0·08	0·51	0·59	0·28	0·03	−0·60	−0·70	−0·65	N.A.
Yorkshire	0·28	−0·68	−0·51	−0·17	0·02	−0·05	0·65	−0·32	−0·06	−0·29	N.A.	−0·80	
East Midlands	0·27	−0·34	−0·17	−0·07	0·03	0·17	0·38	−0·03	−0·10	−0·23	−0·25	−0·56	
Scotland	0·50	−0·17	0·19	0·57	0·23	0·68	0·36	−0·54	−0·52	−0·37	0·13	−0·58	
Wales	0·34	−0·63	−0·47	0·68	−0·18	0·27	0·83	−0·04	−0·01	−0·56	0·71	−0·88	
North West	0·32	−0·11	0·28	0·17	−0·30	0·62	0·24	0·54	−0·06	−0·01	N.A.	−0·30	
East Anglia	0·10	0·55	0·71	0·07	0·44	0·74	−0·08	0·86	0·53	−0·31	N.A.	0·38	0·91
South West	0·18	0·38	0·44	0·19	0·31	0·71	0·14	0·73	0·70	−0·11	N.A.	0·04	N.A.
South East	−0·14	0·40	0·24	0·33	0·25	0·02	−0·47	0·27	0·46	−0·31	0·48	0·53	
West Midlands	−0·26	−0·04	0·01	−0·19	−0·13	0·49	−0·42	0·37	N.A.	−0·31	N.A.	−0·27	
(b) Macro-regions													
Peripheral areas	0·47	−0·41	−0·10	0·39	−0·17	0·56	0·64	0·32	N.A.	N.A.	−0·46	−0·76	N.A.
South East and East Anglia	−0·01	0·32	0·24	0·31	0·18	0·14	−0·35	0·33	N.A.	N.A.	0·41	0·49	
Other areas	0·33	−0·22	0·01	0·04	0·33	0·38	0·37	0·25	N.A.	N.A.	−0·22	−0·50	
Great Britain	0·42	−0·19	0·08	0·31		0·59	0·37	0·49	N.A.	N.A.	−0·42		N.A.

Significance level (95%) with 17 degrees of freedom = 0·45.

TABLE 3.4. INTERCORRELATION MATRIX r OF INDEPENDENT VARIABLES IN THE NATIONAL SERIES, 1945–65

	V_1	V_2	V_3	V_4	V_5	V_6	V_7
V_1	1·00						
V_2	−0·32	1·00					
V_3	0·22	*0·63*	1·00				
V_4	−0·27	0·16	0·11	1·00			
V_5	0·22	0·23	*0·54*	0·22	1·00		
V_6	0·23	−0·53	−0·31	−0·22	0·40	1·00	
V_7	0·08	*0·48*	*0·69*	0·32	*0·94*	0·09	1·00
V_9	−0·28	*0·86*	*0·64*	0·12	−0·06	−0·72	0·24

Significance level (95%) with 17 degrees of freedom = 0·45.

change only in the South West, and, in consequence, this was the only region to have responded significantly, though Scotland also gained considerably from the enlargement of its designated area. On the other hand, there was a consistent negative response in all but two regions to change in the combined assisted area weight in the remainder of the country (V_{8b}). Likewise, where regions contained new towns (V_{9a}), their growth tended to attract movement although the effect was not so strong as the diversion caused by new towns to other regions (V_{9b}). In the major peripheral areas and in Yorkshire and Humberside and the East Midlands, this was a leading factor in determining the number of moves which they attracted.

If many of these simple correlations appear as expected, there remain others which give rise to some interest because of their insignificance or unexpectedness. The West Midlands was the only region whose movement series was not significantly correlated with any of the variables, although it might have been expected to respond to changing economic and structural conditions in a similar way to the South East. Secondly, within the system the South East appeared to be unaffected—in a systematic way, at least—by what was happening elsewhere. In contrast, most of the peripheral areas responded negatively to the growth of new towns in other regions (in practice this meant in the South East). Thirdly, there is an unexpected difference between the response of the main assisted regions to the types of expenditure under the various Acts. Wales, Northern England, and Scotland all had industrial estate companies, with similar rates of progress, from the 1930s, but Scotland's movement series was not systematically correlated with expenditure on factories and estates. Movement to the other two regions was strongly related to this factor, but had weak correlations with expenditure through loans. The latter might be expected, since loans, even when repayable without interest, are not as likely to be such a strong inducement to move to development areas as measures which bear more directly on costs.

Intercorrelations between the nationally based independent variables, the subject of Table 3.4, show that most were relatively poorly associated with each other. There were only a few links at even moderate levels of significance (above the 5% level), and these tended mainly to involve the structural variables. The development of new towns was almost diametrically opposed to expenditure on government-financed industrial building in assisted areas ($r = -0.72$). These and several other high correlations mean that regression equations have to be treated with care in order to identify cases where collinearity has led to significant variables being suppressed. To some extent this can be guarded against by using a stepwise regression procedure (King, 1969), which provides a sequence of "best" models, adding one variable at each step.

The purposes of the multiple regression experiments described in this section are chiefly to investigate the degree to which regional movement series responded to economic and structural changes acting in combination to indicate the partial effects of certain variables (i.e. when others are held constant) and, ultimately, to provide some statistical guide to the forecasting of short-run levels of interregional movement. Ideally, to meet these aims, we should have carried out analyses with every possible combination and alignment of variables, but it is obvious that such a course is impractical. Attention has been concentrated upon what are considered to be potentially the most useful models.

3.4.1. *General Patterns*

Beginning with an overall view, Table 3.5 shows the coefficients of multiple correlation r^2 obtained in the "best" lagged models in each region. No account is taken, at this stage, of the variables contained in those models, and the intention is simply to identify the degree to which the series were related to combinations of variables.

TABLE 3.5. COEFFICIENTS OF MULTIPLE CORRELATION r^2 OBTAINED IN THE BEST LAGGED REGRESSION MODELS, BY REGION, 1945–65

Region	(i) All variables	(ii) Economic	(iii) Structural
Great Britain	0·64***	0·37**	0·50***
Peripheral areas	0·90***	0·66***	0·76***
South East and East Anglia	0·20	0·09	0·20
Other areas	0·51***	0·27*	0·38**
Northern	0·76***	0·49**	0·62***
Yorkshire and Humberside	0·71***	0·46**	0·71***
East Midlands	0·67***	0·12	0·55***
Scotland	0·92***	0·50***	0·77***
Wales	0·91***	0·58***	0·88***
North West	0·61***	0·32*	0·49**
East Anglia	0·92***	0·50***	0·92***
South West	0·78***	0·19	0·66***
South East	0·23	0·16	0·23
West Midlands	0·45**	0·18	0·07

Significance levels: 95%*; 99%**; 99·9%***.

The most important finding in these results is the consistently high significance levels obtained in the main lagged models (column (i)). Only two standard regions (the South East and the West Midlands) failed to reach a high coefficient, but in several the proportion of variance explained exceeded nine-tenths. Bearing in mind that these are cyclical series, often with marked sudden shifts rather than simple trends, these are satisfactory levels of explanation. Even so, there was a considerable range of values. The national coefficient ($r^2 = 0·64$)

lay near the mean of the standard regions; there was a rough division between most of the peripheral areas and East Anglia, with coefficients close to or above the mean, and the South East, the Midlands, and the North West falling below it.

The two subsets, economic and structural, of the main lagged regression model also show interesting variations. In the economic subset the significance level obtained for the national series was only moderately high ($r^2 = 0.37$); but the structural subset accounted for half of the variance. This pattern is repeated in most of the regional series with structural factors contributing rather more in every case but the West Midlands, where neither subset was significant. Interestingly, and somewhat surprisingly, a clear division occurred in the economic subset where it appears that only the peripheral areas responded in a significant manner. The element of surprise comes not from the fact that this relationship existed among the peripheral areas (McCrone (1969) recognizes the same pattern) but that most other regions failed to show a similar relationship. Structural factors, on the other hand, affected nearly all regions significantly although their impact was often negative due to changes in other regions having indirect effects on the rest of the system.

3.4.2. *Regression Parameters*

In considering the regression models for each region the purpose is not only to identify the responses of individual cases but also, and perhaps more importantly, to uncover a linked system of relationships. In an hypothetical system, where the national annual total was unchanging, one region's positive reaction would be reflected in another's negative response to a given variable. Whether this relationship can be uncovered depends on whether it exists in reality and whether the analytical approach is sufficiently incisive. Doubts are bound to occur on both counts, but the search for an integrated system remains a *raison d'être* for the analysis; even if it is not fulfilled, this aim provides a "benchmark" with which the results can be compared.

The question whether any statistical approach can show precisely the nature of a dynamic system is important, if not critical, in this analysis. The problems of regression analysis have been listed earlier and it was admitted that the data used here are far from perfect. More importantly, however, there must be questions about the choice of model to represent a series. In a stepwise analysis variables are added, and possibly subtracted, at each successive step, but the decision about which is the "best" model still contains a large element of subjectivity. It may be preferable, for example, to accept a lower level of explanation in which all variables behave exactly as expected, rather than one with a higher level, in which one variable appears to have an atypical role. In the present analysis the models described as "best" only contain variables for which some rationale can be expressed. Furthermore, in formulating regression equations, the convention adopted here has been to standardize the coefficients. The new regression coefficients can then be compared directly as measures of the relative importance of different variables in accounting for the variation in the dependent variable (King, 1969).

For a number of reasons, the national series presents the greatest problems of explanation. As it consists of many separate series, each with its own parameters, it is to be expected that alternative models might be derived, and to justify any one of them as "best" would be difficult. For example, the national model might be influenced by an inexplicable amount of movement in a single year to just one region. Also, with conflicting regional series (e.g. between the peripheral areas and the South East) the result which might be expected is a model for the national series which is weaker than those for its parts. A further example of the difficulties which can arise involves the role of new towns. By itself, the growth of new towns correlated inversely with the volume of interarea movements in the national series and continued to exert a negative influence in most of the multiple regression experiments. On the surface it might have been expected that as another element in the planning of the distribution of resources the partial correlation of this variable would have been positive. However, it appears that while new towns stimulate movement within regions they also have had a depressing effect on inter-regional movement.

The leading variable in the national series is expenditure on regional policy (V_5), accounting for more than a third (36%) of the variance in annual movement. Subsequent steps in the analysis added the negative influence of new towns (V_9), taking the proportion of explained variance up to 50%, while the volume of unemployment (V_4) and changes in the index of production (V_1) both had positive effects leading finally to almost two-thirds of the variance being accounted for. Interpretation of the first variable is relatively simple, as a significant positive influence from regional policy is to be expected. A difficulty might have arisen if the series had continued beyond 1965 when expenditure rose sharply, making it necessary to take account of the possibility of diminishing marginal returns from industrial movement. Prior to 1965, the level of exchequer costs was comparatively low and their relationship with movement was approximately linear. The positive effect of unemployment on movement contradicts the evidence found at the microeconomic level (Keeble, 1968; House of Commons, 1973) that labour shortages stimulate movement. Here it appears that the opposite is true. However, at the aggregate level it is likely that this variable ought to be regarded as an adjunct to the policy variables; the higher the level of unemployment in the assisted areas, the stronger the controls on location within the South and Midlands.

At the macro-regional level (Table 3.6), the elements of an integrated system begin to emerge. The leading variables in both the peripheral areas and the "other areas" show the negative effect of the growth of new towns elsewhere, while in the model for the South East and East Anglia the development of the metropolitan new towns was the only significant factor with a modest positive influence. A further interpretation of these models appears to suggest that the key to explaining the full interregional system might lie in the position of the South East and, more particularly the political treatment of that region. Possibly the inclusion of a variable expressing the stringency of controls on development in the region would have added to the explanation.

In the peripheral areas, the negative influence of new towns elsewhere was offset by a number of variables. The rate of growth, nationally, in manufacturing output had a positive effect; following the relationship between growth, investment, and movement, this is expected. Less easily explained, rates of interest also had a positive partial correlation. Some multicollinearity may lie behind this, but

TABLE 3.6. BEST LAGGED REGRESSION EQUATIONS (STANDARDIZED) FOR TIME SERIES OF MOVEMENT: MACRO-REGIONS, 1945–65

Region	Independent variables					r^2
	(i)	(ii)	(iii)	(iv)	(v)	
Great Britain	$+0·42\ V_5$ (2·5)	$-0·35\ V_9$ (2·1)	$+0·35\ V_4$ (2·0)	$+0·32\ V_1$ (1·8)		0·64
Peripheral areas	$-0·83\ V_{9b}$ (4·8)	$-0·36\ V_1$ (3·7)	$+0·55\ V_2$ (3·6)	$+0·25\ V_{4a}$ (3·5)	$+0·28 V_6$ (2·2)	0·90
South East and East Anglia	$+0·45\ V_{8a}$ (2·1)					0·20
Other areas	$-0·84\ V_{9b}$ (3·4)	$+0·54\ V_3$ (2·2)				0·42

Note: figures in brackets refer to values of Student's *t*. With 15 d.f. the approximate values for the 95 and 99% confidence levels are 1·7 and 2·1.

it may have been the case that firms wishing to move when rates were high were able to defray part of the investment cost by making use of incentives in the peripheral areas. Significant partial relationships were also afforded by unemployment in the peripheral areas and the level of expenditure on factories and industrial estates by the government. The other areas were negatively affected, like the peripheral areas, by the growth of new towns. The only variable offsetting these was the level of company liquidity. In a region where movement seems to consist largely to the transfer of smaller-than-average establishments, involving a large proportion of internal finance, this relationship is not unexpected.

If the macro-regional models appear to support the existence of an integrated system, albeit indistinctly defined, the same is also true, but in a more complex form, at the level of standard regions (Fig. 3.7). Here the competition for movement occurs more specifically between particular areas. For example, where once most firms leaving the West Riding went to other parts of Yorkshire and Humberside, this flow was replaced by one to the North East. Another example is found in the changing position of the South West *vis-à-vis* the other regions. Over time, an increasing proportion of the South West was granted development area status, while in other peripheral areas the proportion stayed fairly level or even dropped.

Among the five regions containing assisted areas, all but one (Northern England) displayed the same leading variable in their models, namely the negative influence of new towns elsewhere. (However, the Northern region, too, in a highly significant "second-best" model, was influenced by this variable.) Comparing the standardized regression coefficients across these models, although an insecure procedure, indicates that Wales, the region closest to the main generating areas, was the one most influenced (negatively) by the growth of new towns. Scotland and Northern England, being further away, had lower coefficients and were possibly insulated by their distance.

This was practically the limit of the common features in these models. The only other variable to appear with any regularity was growth in industrial production which exerted a positive influence in Scotland and Northern England, but in each case was the least

TABLE 3.7. BEST LAGGED REGRESSION EQUATIONS (STANDARDIZED) FOR TIME SERIES OF MOVEMENT: STANDARD REGIONS, 1945–65

Region	Independent variables				r^2
	(i)	(ii)	(iii)	(iv)	
Northern England	$-0\cdot59\ V_{8b}$ (4·7)	$+0\cdot36\ V_{4a}$ (3·5)	$+0\cdot42\ V_1$ (2·6)		0·76
Wales	$-1\cdot07\ V_{9b}$ (5·3)	$+0\cdot39\ V_6$ (3·2)	$+0\cdot49\ V_{9a}$ (2·8)	$+0\cdot19\ V_7$ (2·0)	0·91
Scotland	$-0\cdot98\ V_{9b}$ (7·0)	$+0\cdot71\ V_{9a}$ (5·3)	$+0\cdot29\ V_{4b}$ (2·7)	$+0\cdot29\ V_1$ (2·6)	0·92
North West	$+0\cdot94\ V_3$ (4·3)	$-0\cdot91\ V_{9b}$ (4·2)	$+0\cdot37\ V_{4a}$ (2·2)		0·61
South West	$-1\cdot00\ V_{9b}$ (4·3)	$+0\cdot64\ V_{8a}$ (4·5)	$+0\cdot30\ V_2$ (3·8)		0·78
South East	$+0\cdot48\ V_{9a}$ (2·3)				0·23
East Anglia	$+0\cdot83\ V_{11}$ (10·8)	$+0\cdot31\ V_{8a}$ (4·0)			0·92
Yorkshire and Humberside	$-0\cdot84\ V_{9b}$ (6·2)	$+0\cdot29\ V_{8a}$ (2·0)			0·71
East Midlands	$-1\cdot82\ V_{9b}$ (3·9)	$+1\cdot13\ V_{9a}$ (2·7)	$+0\cdot72\ V_3$ (2·0)	$-0\cdot62\ V_7$ (1·8)	0·67
West Midlands	$-0\cdot76\ V_{4a}$ (2·8)	$-0\cdot72\ V_{8b}$ (2·7)	$+0\cdot69\ V_3$ (2·4)	$+0\cdot62\ V_{4b}$ (2·4)	0·45

Note: figures in brackets refer to values of Student's *t*.

important in their models, and regional unemployment (also positive) in the North West and the North. In Wales, the activities of the industrial estate companies (and, after 1960, by the Industrial Estates Management Corporation) showed up in the strong positive influence of the expenditure on factories by the government. Likewise, the development of a new town in the region (at Cwmbran, designated in 1949) also attracted movement. Scotland's new towns, at East Kilbride (designated in 1947), Glenrothes (1948), Cumbernauld (1955), and Livingstone (1962), also proved to be highly important in their influence on the flow of industry into parts of the region. By contrast, the main positive factor in movement to locations in the North West, only part of which was a development area, was the level of company liquidity. The designation of the region's three new towns came too late to affect the series, and since most moves into the region were relatively short-distance, it is expected that they should have been related to economic conditions. The South West, on the other hand, was almost entirely controlled by structural factors. The reduction in the growth of new towns in the South East and the progressive increase in the development areas designated in the South West were both beneficial to the region.

The model for the South East was closely similar to that for the South East and East Anglian macro-region, but that for East Anglia bears evidence of the very strong influence of the region's town expansion schemes. With a small basic population, the region's series was bound to reflect the impact of these developments, even though they are minor when compared with most new towns. In addition, the region gained small but significant amounts during the years when parts of it had assisted area status. In the remainder of the country regional models again tended to show the effect of new town developments elsewhere, although the East Midlands gained from the growth of Corby (designated in 1950). The West Midlands, most of whose moves came from the Birmingham conurbation and the Black Country, showed a close relationship with unemployment; low numbers out of work tended to push firms out into the rest of the region in search of a labour supply. Offsetting this, the extension of development areas tended to divert movement away from West Midland locations.

3.4.3. *Regional Shares*

The assertion has been made that movement to the peripheral areas reflects the general volume of industrial mobility. Taken to one extreme, this can lead to the view that the solution to the problems of assisted areas lies in rapid industrial growth which will spill over into an increased amount of long-distance movement. However, the analysis of the annual movements described above only partially supports that assertion. Although industrial growth did influence the volume, it was not the only relevant factor, nor was it the most important. Movement to the assisted regions depends heavily upon the diversionary effects of policy.

This is further shown by the relationship between the shares of the national total going to different regions and the total volume of movement. In only two of the peripheral regions, Scotland and Northern England, was the share related to the total and in those the association was weak ($r^2 = 0.48$ and 0.41 respectively). Over the full array of regions adequate explanations only come from the addition of policy variables. Even so, there were regions which lacked any marked trend in the shares which they attracted and which, therefore, did not respond to any model (Table 3.8).

3.4. Post-move Closures

The data used in the time series analysis described total recorded annual movement. However, these contain a substantial number of establishments which had closed by the end of the data collection period. More than 4000 moves were recorded for 1945–65, but of these about 1000 had closed by the end of 1966; of the 1600 moves (excluding those within the same regional subdivision) during 1966–71, about 140 had closed by 1972. It is important, for two reasons, to investigate the temporal and regional incidence of closure. The first is that non-survival clearly nullifies some of the efforts put into regional policy. The second is that the analysis of geographical distributions of movement, reported in the next chapter, is based upon survivors only; hence it is valuable to have an indication of the degree to which the results are affected by this disparity in definitions.

A detailed description of post-move closure is reported elsewhere

TABLE 3.8. COEFFICIENTS OF MULTIPLE CORRELATION (r^2) OBTAINED
IN BEST REGRESSION MODELS OF TIME SERIES OF REGIONAL SHARES
OF TOTAL MOVEMENT, 1945–65

Region	Total moves (i)	Total moves plus policy variables[a] (ii)
	Independent Variables	
Peripheral areas	0·38**	0·55***
South East and East Anglia	0·23	0·36**
Other areas	0·05	0·27*
Northern	0·48***	0·81***
Scotland	0·41**	0·55***
Wales	0·11	0·85***
North West	0·10	0·10
South West	0·05	0·63***
South East	0·26*	0·56***
East Anglia	0·01	0·90***
West Midlands	0·01	0·01
East Midlands	0·00	0·00
Yorkshire and Humberside	0·00	0·63***

Significance levels: 95%*; 99%**; 99·9%***.
[a] See Table 3.2.

(Sant, 1975), but there are a number of features which are relevant
here. The first is the actuarial probability of closures during the life
of a cohort of mobile establishments. Secondly, there are questions
about the incidence of closure in relation to the type of move.
Thirdly, there is the issue of the effectiveness of regional policy, not
only in creating and diverting movement but also in supporting
post-move establishments.

3.4.1. *The Incidence of Closures*, 1945–66

Closures occur for several reasons, not all of them associated with
failure. For example, a firm may close an establishment for the
purpose of rationalization; or exogenous, non-economic factors may
force a closure followed by relocation elsewhere. Failure can also be

subdivided. Cases have occurred where relocated establishments, having incurred higher unit costs immediately after the move, have failed to reduce costs to break-even levels sufficiently quickly (Luttrell, 1962). In other instances, sudden shifts in demand (e.g. following a change in product trends, or a cyclical fluctuation) have caught what might otherwise have become a profitable firm. Often the fault lies less in productivity than in liquidity. However, it should be emphasized that closure is a problem not confined only to mobile firms. The Committee of Inquiry on Small Firms (1971), for example, reported that in its sample study of 1251 manufacturing firms employing 200 or fewer workers, 23% had gone into liquidation, ceased trading, or been taken over during 1963–70; of the sample, about 20% were described as failures. In other sectors (e.g. the distributive industries) the proportions were higher. Thus Beesley's description (1955) of mobile plants "marching stolidly into ambush" is an exaggeration when applied to all movers, though it may be appropriate for some.

Figure 3.3 (p. 72) identified total recorded movement and closures per annum during 1945–66 and the number of survivors from each cohort. From the data on which these are based it is possible to extract a number of properties relating closure to movement. These are: (i) annual closure rates, (ii) cohort closure ratios per annum, and (iii) age specific closure rates.

The annual closure rate is calculated by expressing closure in a given year as a percentage of all movers in previous years still in existence at the start of that year. These are graphed using a two-year running mean (Fig. 3.9). To give some insight into the relationship between this curve and other cyclical changes, the peak years in

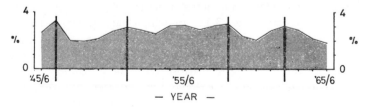

FIG. 3.9. Annual closure rates of mobile establishments, 1945–66.

national unemployment are also indicated. Although by no means a smooth curve, the closure rate fluctuated with a similar rhythm to that of unemployment, from a low of 1·5% in 1949 to peaks of over 3% in 1947, 1958, and 1963. Clearly, therefore, mobile industry, like any other, is vulnerable to cyclical change.

Secondly, the cohort closure ratio (Fig. 3.10), describing the proportion of each year's moves which had closed by the end of 1966, shows an expected fall as the existence of cohorts became shorter. Thus about 40% of the 1945 cohort had closed by 1966; 25% of the 1955 cohort and 5% of the 1964 cohort had also closed. The fall is approximately linear, though there are fluctuations around the best-fit line. Dividing the ratios of each cohort by its age gives, on average, a "whole-life" closure rate of about 1·9% per annum. Unfortunately, there are no exactly comparable figures for British industry as a whole, but this rate is unlikely to differ radically from that for non-mobile plants of similar age, size, and structure.

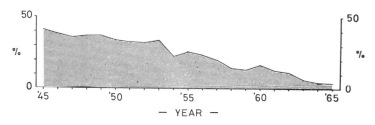

Fig. 3.10. Cohort closure ratios, 1945–66.

But the average annual cohort closure rates mask an important variation in vulnerability against pressures to close at different times in the life of an establishment. This is expressed in terms of age-specific closure rates (Fig. 3.11) in which each point in the graph describes the mean closure rate in the cohort's first, second, . . ., nth year. Because the series is truncated in 1966, each year of cohort-life has a smaller number of observations than the preceding one; so to avoid too small samples, we have ignored the closure rates for cohorts moving after 1961. Also, to dampen the changes in the graph, a two-year running mean has been applied. The result is a curve

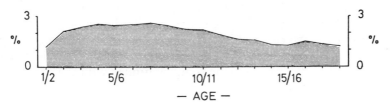

Fɪɢ. 3.11. Age specific closure rates, 1945–66.

which indicates that closure is relatively uncommon in the earliest years of a cohort's life, but increases sharply to reach a plateau at about the fifth year. High rates (above 2·5%) last until about the ninth year, after which the incidence of closure diminishes steadily. The longer a plant stayed at its location, therefore, the greater became its life expectancy.

3.4.2. *The Effect of Regional Policy*, 1945–71

The creation of higher and more stable levels of employment in the assisted areas carried an implicit condition that closures should be minimized or at least brought into line with the rates in non-assisted areas.

Broadly, regional variations stem from two causes: (i) differences in the kinds of establishments and industries attracted by the regions, and (ii) disparities in locational costs. The first tends to lie outside the direct control of regional policy in that little can be done to determine the character of mobile industry or of the types of industry going to different regions except in a negative way. It is not possible, for example, to ensure that only firms in growth industries should relocate in the assisted areas or that the same areas should receive a lower proportion of branch plants. On the other hand, the second factor has been the primary concern of regional policy, and a variety of measures giving different levels of subsidy has been enacted since 1945 (Brown, 1972).

Despite the need for a cautious interpretation imposed by imperfections in the data, it is perhaps one of the most striking features of industrial movement that variations in cohort closure rates (adjusted for size of cohorts) have, indeed, altered markedly. As Table 3.9

shows, between 1945 and 1960 the peripheral areas suffered from rates well above the national average, with an index of 117 (United Kingdom = 100) compared with only 83 in the rest of the country. Through 1960–5, however, the rates in the two regions were equal, and between 1966 and 1971 the trend continued with the peripheral areas becoming less vulnerable to closure.

TABLE 3.9. ADJUSTED CLOSURE INDICES IN THE PERIPHERAL AREAS AND THE REST OF THE UNITED KINGDOM, 1945–71 (UNITED KINGDOM = 100)

Destination	1945–60	1961–5	1966–71
Peripheral areas[a]	117	100	91
Rest of United Kingdom	83	100	107

[a] Peripheral areas defined as Northern Ireland, Scotland, Northern England, North West and South West standard regions.
Source: unpublished DTI tabulations.

In so far as it is possible to generalize about comparative locational advantages in different regions since 1945, it appears that the balance lay, initially, against the development areas. Taking into account the then existing scale of subsidies, Hague and Dunning (1954) concluded that, compared with the London area, the development areas had slightly higher costs and the new towns slightly lower, and that the differences were greatest in the early years in the life of a new establishment. However, these costs related only to the static position and ignored the effects of dislocation upon the firm's links with suppliers of materials and services and with former markets. On each of these counts it is reasonable to conclude that while all moves were likely to incur some disadvantages, those going to development areas (and thereby usually having the greatest spatial dislocation) suffered most and found it most difficult to reduce the disadvantages.

But the 1950s were years of very low regional incentives; in particular, there was little, if any, help to firms in overcoming the initial costs of movement. In comparison, the 1960s saw a progressive strengthening of inducements, with the total outlay on various policy instruments increasing from around £5m per annum in the late 1950s to £50m in 1966–7 and about £350m in 1970–1 (at current values). These increases reflected the demands of new inducements, most of which were geared to improving the liquidity of firms, especially in the initial years of their investment. Under the Local Employment and Finance Acts of 1963, these included investment grants for plant and machinery and "free depreciation", which allowed firms, if they wished, to defer tax payments until their investment had been written off. In 1966 the latter was abolished, but investment grants were increased, as they were again in 1967, giving greater bonuses to firms which might not see a profit on their investments and hence not benefit from free depreciation. Another, more massive, change also occurred in 1967, namely the introduction of the regional employment premium which, although intended as a subsidy on the employment of labour, also has the side-effect of increasing the cash flow to firms in assisted areas. These, together with other forms of assistance, have been estimated (Wilson, 1973) to contribute a cost subsidy in the assisted areas of about 2·5–5% of net value added. At this level they ought to do much to remove inter-regional cost disparities and probably account for most of the change in closure ratios in the peripheral areas.

In the process of this turnabout in the viability of firms moving to different regions, there appear to have been two important side-effects. The first is that the distance involved in industrial movement has a less direct effect on closure. The second relates to a new differentiation between branch plants and transferred establishments.

Evidence prior to 1960 indicates the longer moves sustained the higher incidence of closure. This may be inferred from Table 3.9: moves to peripheral areas, with a median distance of about 150 miles, had closure rates about 50% higher than moves to other regions, which had a median distance of about 50 miles. This is supported by Keeble's (1968) findings. Of firms moving from north-west London between 1940 and 1964, those locating in the provincial zone (more than 100 miles from London) had closure ratios twice as high as those staying within the metropolitan zone (20% compared with 9%).

The picture during 1966–71 was substantially different, as Table 3.10 shows. Classifying moves according to whether the destination

TABLE 3.10. CLOSURE RATIOS BY CATEGORIES[a] OF ORIGINS AND
DESTINATIONS, 1966–71 (UNITED KINGDOM = 100)

Origin and destination	Destinations		Total United Kingdom
	Peripheral areas	Other areas	
(a) Within same subdivision	90	88	89
(b) Within same standard region (excluding category (a))	88	150	132
(c) In different regions	102	102	102
Total	91	107	100

[a] Data for 1966–71 relate to the eleven standard regions and sixty-two statistical subdivisions of the United Kingdom. For a description, see Appendix A.

Source: unpublished DTI tabulations.

lay in the same subdivision as the origin, in the same standard region (but a different subdivision) or in a different region, and differentiating between peripheral and other areas, we can see that only one group was markedly different from the rest. This was the non-assisted middle-distance movers, relocating within the same region, with a closure index of over 150 compared with between 88 and 102 in the other five groups. In practice, it appears that this category places itself at greatest risk. By moving as far as they do the firms in it (predominantly single-plant transfers rather than branch plants) lose many of the advantages of a wide range of beneficial linkages with their former locales. At the same time they have not moved far enough to gain the assistance available in the peripheral areas. In comparison, the equivalent group within the peripheral areas, nurtured by greater financial assistance and, almost certainly, by careful advice from government agencies, had a very low rate of closure.

It is also possible to infer from the data prior to 1960 that branch plants were more vulnerable than transferred establishments; the former contributed over 80% of moves to peripheral areas but only about 55% of moves to the rest of the country. Again, Keeble (1968) provides support, showing that branch closure rates were almost one and a half times as high as transfer closure rates (15% and 11% respectively), with the worst performance being experienced by branches in the provincial zone and the best by transfers in the metropolitan zone. The evidence for 1966–71 (Table 3.11) shows major differences. Branches generally had become more viable in the peripheral areas, but had lost ground, relatively, in the other areas.

TABLE 3.11. CLOSURE INDICES FOR BRANCH PLANTS AND TRANSFERRED ESTABLISHMENTS, 1966–71

Destination	Branch plants	Relocated establishments	All moves
Peripheral areas	80	100	91
Other areas	121	102	107
Total United Kingdom	94	102	100

Source: unpublished DTI tabulations.

Although forced by lack of sufficient data to rely upon inference, it appears to be safe to conclude that each of these changes (closures by region, by distance moved, and by industrial organization) is largely the result of alterations in the balance of regional advantages brought about by the greatly increased level of incentives and financial support available in the assisted areas. The only other major factors which could, in theory, have been effective, are the characteristics of industrial movers. However, these tend to change slowly and, compared with the position before 1960, there had been little change in size of firm or ratio of branch plants to transfers going to different regions. There may, however, have been some change in the industrial composition of movers to different regions. Before 1960 the peripheral areas tended to take a significantly worse mixture than the rest of the country with over a third of their movers coming from declining industries. In comparison, the proportion in the other regions was less than one-fifth. Recent incentives, with considerable benefits to profitable capital-intensive firms, may have altered the balance, but this is not yet supported empirically.

CHAPTER 4

Geographical Distributions

4.1. Introduction

In turning from temporal patterns to geographical distributions we change the scale and scope of the analysis. In this chapter the areal base is the subregion or statistical subdivision of standard regions. These, and the definitions used in recording movement, are given in Appendices A and B. For brevity, however, we shall use the term "regions" to mean either standard regions or their subdivisions; the context will provide the sense in which it is used.

The change in scale consists of having forty-nine regions for which movement was recorded during 1945–65 and sixty-one during 1966–71; as before, Northern Ireland is excluded. Movement into and out of each region has been recorded for four periods, 1945–51, 1952–9, 1960–5, and 1966–71. However, origins tend to be less easily identi-fied, especially in the case of multiplant companies, so that there is a residual of moves with unallocated origins (less than 1% of those recorded during 1945–65). In addition there was a substantial number of moves from abroad (over 8% of the 1945–65 total). Finally, the geographical distribution is based upon recorded survivors. This means that all regions can be expected to have been understated but, more seriously, as the analysis in the previous chapter indicates, there was a bias in this. The greater discrepancies are among the peripheral areas in the earliest periods. It is quite possible, for example, that the moves shown for Wales or Scotland during 1945–51 are only half the number which actually occurred, while those to the South East are unlikely to be understated by more than a third. But, ignoring these problems, we still have a description of the broad patterns of interregional movement which can be subjected, with necessary qualifications, to a multivariate analysis.

As in the previous chapter, the main aim here is to seek evidence of a systematic pattern of movements responding to disparities in the character of regions and the implementation of regional policy. In the following sections, therefore, the procedure is to describe the geographical distribution of movement, to bring together variables to explain the distributions, and, finally, to present the results of a multivariate analysis.

4.2. Generation and Attraction

As the time series described above showed, movement tended to fluctuate and to respond to the implementation of regional policy. The four phases into which the postwar period has been divided roughly correspond with the timing of the major changes in the series. The first relates to the late 1940s when planning controls and the availability of sites and labour favoured the peripheral areas. In contrast the 1950s saw the demise of regional policy and its replacement by structural planning, especially in the South East through the construction of the metropolitan new towns. This, in turn, was replaced by a shift in emphasis back to the development areas in the early 1960s following the start of a new phase of substantial contraction in their basis industries. The fourth period starting in 1966 was marked by a rapid increase in the level of assistance.

These changes are reflected in alterations, between one period and the next, of the magnitudes of movement from and (more especially) to each region. But equally important are the cross-sectional variations between regions in their roles as origins and destinations of movement. These are differences which are expected to reflect the regional pattern of disparities among social and economic indicators and their status in regional policy. Although most regions tended to keep the same role as net generators or attractors of movement, the scale at which particular regions operated was subject to wide fluctuations. This is illustrated in Figs. 4.1 and 4.2. Greater London, as is well known, was by far the greatest generator of movement in every period, giving rise during 1945–71 to more than 1700 surviving moves to other regions. But although it was the leading region at all

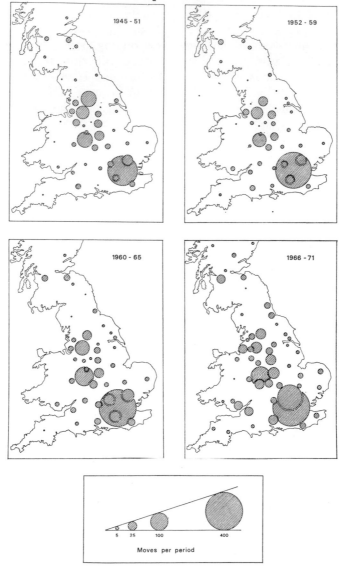

FIG. 4.1. Generation of industrial movement by area and period, 1945–71.

FIG. 4.2. Attraction of industrial movement by area and period, 1945-71
(See Fig. 4.1. for key.)

times, the share of total movement with sources in Britain originating in London fluctuated from 43% in 1945–51 to 55% in 1952–9 and only 34% in 1966–71. Meanwhile, other areas also rose and fell as sources of movement. The most dramatic among these was the West Yorkshire textile region which in 1945–51 generated almost 10% of all moves, but in 1952–9 was responsible for only 3% and continued to decline thereafter. In contrast, the South East, excluding London, increased from supplying 8% of moves in 1945–51 to 18% in 1966–71, and in the latter period appeared to be partially taking over the role of London. The two other major conurbations, Birmingham and Manchester, tended to supply fairly constant shares, with respectively about 10% and 6%, though the latter registered a slight fall in 1966–71. The only other sources of any significance lay in the Midlands and included Nottingham, Leicester, and Coventry, which together generated a fairly constant share of about 5%. Thus, throughout the postwar period the overwhelming majority of moves have come from within the industrial axial belt of Britain; the rest of the country never supplied more than 20% of the total.

The distribution of destinations was both more widespread and more volatile. For example, South Wales began by taking 13% of the moves in Britain during 1945–51, but only 3% in the two subsequent periods before increasing to 10% in 1966–71. In contrast the non-metropolitan South East took 24% of the 1945–51 moves, but 54% of those in 1952–9, before falling rapidly to take only 20% in 1966–71. These two present a picture of countervailing attractions. A third example, Devon and Cornwall, shows a continuous upward trend from less than 2% before 1959 to 5% after 1966, while a fourth, the Yorkshire coalfield region, tended to take a continuously falling share (although intermediate area status in 1970 may have halted this trend). The first three reflect changes in regional policy, but the fourth was due mainly to the drying up of its local source of movement in the West Yorkshire textile region.

4.3. Interregional Movements

The explanation of the distribution of origins and destinations is aided by a description of the interaction between regions. By looking at the paths taken by the major flows and the resultant pattern of interregional dominance, the elements of an interregional system can begin to be identified.

Three categories account for the greater part of the interregional flows (Figs. 4.3 and 4.4). The two largest, both originating in Greater London, were to the non-metropolitan South East and East Anglia and to the more populous development areas. The third consisted of flows from the major provincial sources to nearby reception areas. The main ones in this category were to adjacent regions, with firms moving to less congested overspill sites or to pockets of female labour. Where provincial sources supplied development areas these tended to be the ones closest to them (e.g., Manchester to Merseyside, the West Riding to the industrial North East, Birmingham to South Wales). The patterns of interaction for 1966–71 are generally similar to these, but with a finer regional breakdown they uncover other significant flows, of which the most important were from coastal South Wales to the nearby central and eastern valleys and from the South West into South Wales.

In general, these flows indicate an influence from two sets of factors. The first begins with a "distance decay function"; the further apart a potential origin and destination the smaller, other things being equal, the flow between them. The distance decay function is the first step towards a gravity model (Olsson, 1965) which would predict that movement was not only an inverse function of distance but also was directly influenced by the size of the origins and destination. However, care should be taken before stating that industrial movement is like other forms of spatial interaction. If size is defined identically for both origins and destinations (e.g. by using population or employment) then, clearly, this is going to have a poor explanatory power. For example, Greater London and the West Midlands conurbation, the two largest regions, had a smaller flow than Leicester and the industrial North East which are further apart and have smaller populations. Furthermore, most interaction models are designed to predict two-way movements, whereas industrial movement clearly tended to be one way.

This invokes the second set of factors, the disparities that exist between regions among economic and policy variables. Mobile

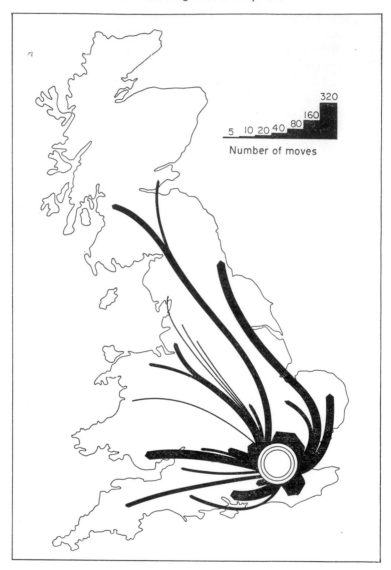

Fig. 4.3. Flows of industrial movement from Greater London, 1945–65.

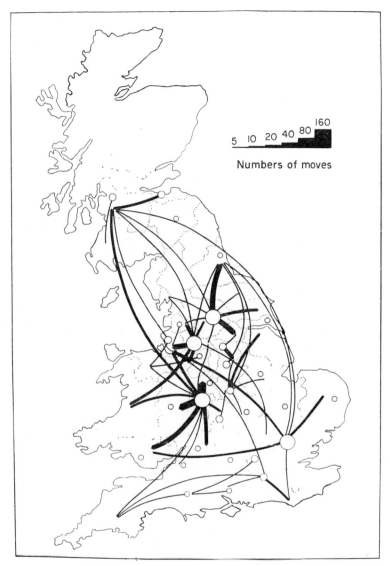

Fig. 4.4. Major flows of industrial movement from provincial sources, 1945–65.

industry tends to seek advantages not found at the parent or original site. The majority of firms meet their requirements by short moves, but there is a substantial number for whom longer-distance movement is feasible and attractive. But this tends to preclude movement between similar regions; for example, between regions of equally high or low unemployment. Hence, the negligible flow between different parts of the South East (excluding London) and between one development area and another. Conversely, the flows were substantial between regions of low and high unemployment, between areas of high- and low-cost sites, and between non-assisted and assisted areas. The result is a curve of movement which does not fall to zero at some predictable distance but which has minor subsidiary peaks where disparities in factor supplies and policy inducements create attractions.

These flows give rise to a well-defined system of supply areas (Fig. 4.5). Allocating each region to the sphere of influence of its main source of movement, the pattern which emerges shows a number of regularities. First, supply areas tend to be contiguous, surrounding the source. It was uncommon for any source to supply a substantial volume to reception areas located beyond another source. Indeed, only London was able, on a significant scale, to leapfrog other sources, becoming the largest supplier for the North East and parts of Scotland. Manchester's dominance over the greater part of Wales is due to the boundaries used before 1966; after that date it was seen that the West Midlands dominated Central and South West Wales, and Manchester was the main source for North Wales. This leads to a second observation: that supply areas were related to the size of the source. Greater London had by far the largest sphere of influence, while that of the West Midlands conurbation was bigger than, for example, Sheffield's. Thirdly, the configuration of supply areas can be investigated further by calculating the proportion of inward movement originating in each major source (Fig. 4.6). This shows that reception areas closest to a given source were most heavily dependent upon it. More remote regions and areas located between two sources formed "shatter belts". The system can be pictured as a series of intersecting supply cones, with the height of each cone dependent upon the volume from each source. Thus London's cone,

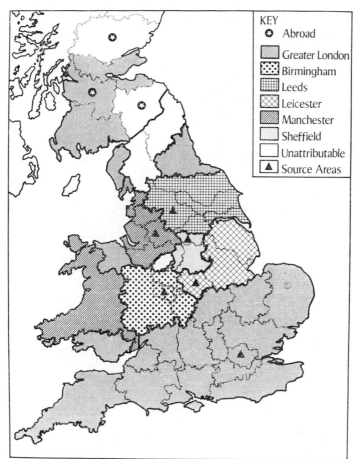

KEY
- ⊗ Abroad
- Greater London
- Birmingham
- Leeds
- Leicester
- Manchester
- Sheffield
- Unattributable
- ▲ Source Areas

Fig. 4.5. Main source areas, 1945–65.

the highest, dominates over all of England south of the line from the
Wash to the Severn, where it meets the cones from the West and
East Midlands (the latter based on Leicester), which, in turn, meet
the cones from Manchester and Sheffield. Eventually, London's cone
again dominates in Northern England and Scotland, but at a much

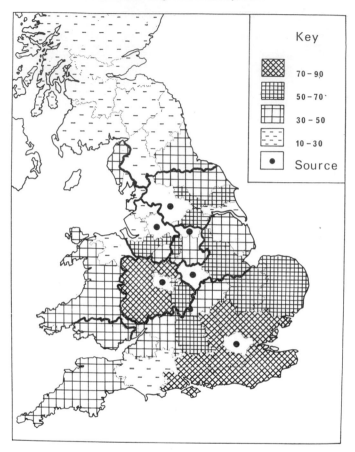

FIG. 4.6. Inter-area dominance, 1945–65 (Percentage of immigrant establishments in each area originating at its dominant source.)

lower level than in the South East. Changes over time in these patterns tended to be minor, and there were few cases of one region replacing another as the main source for a third. The most important exception was Merseyside which received more in total from Manchester but looked increasingly to London after 1960.

4.4. Movement from Foreign Sources

About 8% of the recorded surviving moves had origins outside the United Kingdom. The majority of these were branches or subsidiaries of American companies. By any measure this proportion, giving rise to about 100,000 jobs during 1945–66, was a significant addition to industrial capacity. What adds to its importance, however, is the size, character and distribution of these establishments. The average employment of foreign-owned establishments was about 420, compared with 275 for an indigenous mobile establishment. Moreover, as Forsyth (1972) has recorded, the US-owned establishments in Scotland grew more rapidly, had higher rates of investment, and were more productive (by all measures) than their indigenous counterparts. It should be noted, however, that this comparison does not distinguish between mobile and non-mobile British firms. It would almost certainly be found that similar establishments of British and American origin locating in Scotland had less-marked differences. Nevertheless, it is clear that foreign-owned establishments make a significant impact on regional economies especially through their demand for labour and the diffusion of business practices.

The impact tended to be regionally concentrated, and in certain regions foreign-owned establishments provided a large proportion of inward movement (Fig. 4.7). This was particularly the case in West Central Scotland, where 28% of in-moving firms had foreign sources, providing 47% of the region's employment resulting from industrial movement. No other region had a higher level of dependence, but several other assisted areas attracted significant numbers; South Wales (12% of inward moves), the industrial North East (10%), Merseyside (15%), East Central Scotland (23%) were the main beneficiaries. To a considerable degree this distribution can be attributed to the working of regional policy (foreign-owned firms being most easily steered to assisted areas), but the evidence put forward by Forsyth (1972) and by the ILAG survey (House of Commons, 1973) both suggest that this was no more important than the availability of labour and accessibility to transport facilities.

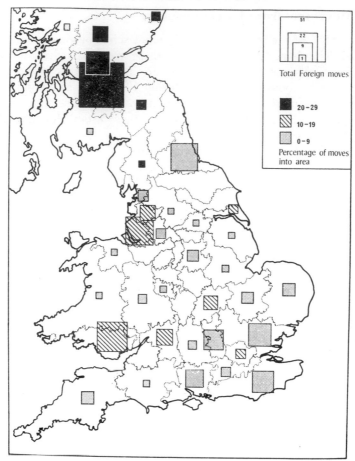

Fig. 4.7. Industrial movement originating abroad, 1945–65.

4.5. Geographical Models of Movement

The requirements of geographical models of interregional movement differ from those of the time series discussed in the previous
chapter. On the one hand, by dividing the postwar period into
discrete phases the problems associated with time series analysis are
avoided. On the other hand, a new set of difficulties is imposed by the

method of enumeration of movement. That is, in order to be counted, a move had to cross a regional boundary. Immediately this requires all variables to be area-based. No account is taken of conditions applying to individual firms and therefore none can be taken of conditions at individual locations. Instead the variables must apply to populations of firms and the general character of regions. In addition, since the existence of a "distance decay function" has been noted, it is important to take account of the form of regions; that is, their shape and size. It should be readily apparent that a change in the size of regions or a new alignment of their boundaries would alter the enumerated movements, especially if this involved lines being drawn through, or close to, conurbations rather than at the fringe of their spheres of influence.

It is useful to represent industrial movement as occurring along a path. In this scheme a move is regarded as starting in the urban core of a region. This is realistically portrayed as being located near to the geographical centre of the region. Some of the enumeration areas were irregular (Appendix A), but most had their boundaries passing through rural zones. The path then passes through a zone contained within the region's boundary in which there may be features conducive to relocation and whose effect is to reduce the number of moves crossing into another region. These "intervening opportunities", together with the size of the region (which determines the distance from the urban core to the boundary), exert a negative influence on movement. Finally, the path crosses the boundary, the generated move is enumerated, and the establishment seeks a new region in which to locate.

What follows can be described in the same terms. The probability of the path terminating in a given region depends on four sets of factors: (i) the distance between the region and the source of the move; (ii) the size of the region; (iii) factors which tend to attract moves; and (iv) factors which tend to repel moves. The first of these follows from the distance decay function noted earlier. The second factor arises because once an establishment's path has "entered" a region, the chance of its "leaving" will vary inversely with the size of the region. The third and fourth factors are made up of socio-economic parameters. Thus, for example, a high level of urbanization (implying high site costs and constraints on expansion) will act as a repellant, while a low level will be an attraction.

Problems arise when the path is retraced and, starting at the source, specific quantifiable variables are sought to explain generation and attraction. First, the variables that might be chosen must be accurately related to the regions used in the enumeration of moves. For the most part, this is easily achieved, since the regions correspond exactly to local government boundaries (prior to reorganization in 1974) and almost perfectly to employment exchange boundaries. Secondly, since the analysis is concerned with four discrete periods, it is necessary for the variables to approximate conditions in each period as closely as possible. Ideally, the variables would take account of the conditions and changes which occurred in each region during a period, but in the absence of such detail for either set it was decided to use, wherever possible, data relating to the start of each period. Thus, for 1952–9 most of the independent variables relate to 1951 and for 1960–5, to 1961.

4.5.1. *The Distribution of Origins*

The simple notion of a movement path tells something of the hazards and opportunities encountered by an establishment between origin and destination. However, it tells little about how many moves are likely to be generated by a region. From experience it can be postulated that this is most likely to be associated with some measure of the "mass" of the area; that is, its weighted or unweighted population. Some ambiguity in the definition of mass is inevitable at this stage because there exists a variety of possible methods of measuring it, each with a different interpretation (Olsson, 1965; Isard, 1956). The preferred definition in the present case would be based on the number of manufacturing establishments in an area at the start of a period weighted by their industrial composition and size structure. Unfortunately, it is impossible to proceed along these lines since there is no available information, at this scale, on establishments. It is necessary, instead, to use cruder measures related to employment in manufacturing (X_1).

If experience points to the mass factor as a starting point in migration studies, it also leads to the observation that it is unlikely to provide more than a moderate proportion of the explanation in this case, where industrial movement is related not only to the mass of the region but also to its socio-economic characteristics and planning constraints. Thus, it has been noted that several of the more massive areas also had characteristics which were hardly likely to encourage outward movement and vice versa.

There is evidence to show that it is not the size of the manufacturing sector alone that is important, but also its composition. Certain industries have a higher propensity to generate movement than others (Howard, 1968). This arises chiefly from a close relationship between movement and growth in employment, though other factors such as productivity, size of plant, and transport costs are also important (Townroe, 1973). The conclusion, therefore, is that account should be taken of the industrial composition of regions. This can be done by calculating an index (X_{13}):

$$I_i = \sum \frac{e_{ij} \times m_j}{E_i},$$

where e_{ij} is employment in industry j of region i, E_i is total manufacturing employment in region i, and m_j is moves per 1000 employees in industry j as a ratio of moves per 1000 employees in all manufacturing industry in Great Britain.

Thus, if industries behave regionally as they did in the country as a whole, a region with a high index (i.e. greater than 1·0) may be expected to generate more movement than the volume of its manufacturing employment alone would predict (Fig. 4.8).

Ex hypothesi, labour costs are expected to exert a positive influence on the number of moves, assuming these to be real costs taking account of levels of productivity and the labour component of value added. In Britain, however, levels of earnings (X_6, X_7) and, probably, also of productivity, vary little between regions, so that this factor achieves little apparent prominence although it becomes important when account is taken of other variables. Unfortunately, this is the least satisfactorily presented variable, having several shortcomings. The figures available in the *New Earnings Survey*, which is the only data on an areal basis compatible with the industrial movement matrix, were collected only from 1967 (Fig. 4.9): it is necessary,

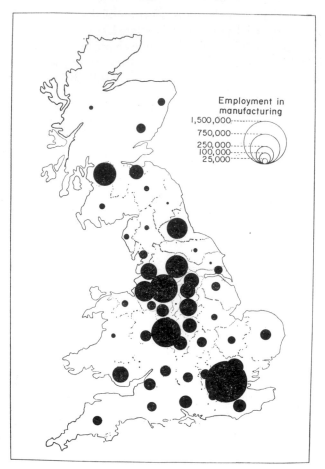

Fɪɢ. 4.8. Employment in manufacturing, 1951.

therefore, to assume the same distribution for 1945–66. Moreover, the figures are based on workers in all sectors rather than just manufacturing. Also the survey's areas correspond with those used in enumerating industrial movement during 1966–71; they differ from those used in 1945–66 and it is necessary to interpolate the values for some regions.

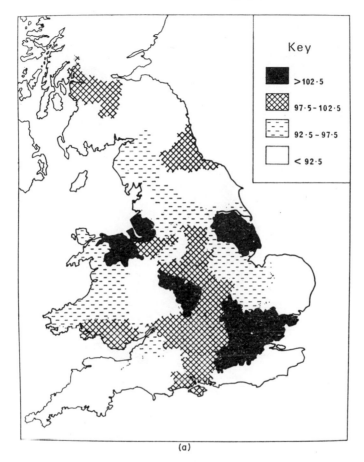

FIG. 4.9. Average gross weekly earnings for male manual workers,
1968 (GB = 100).

Labour supply has been considered to be more crucial; areas with
surplus labour are most likely to generate below-average volumes of
movement and vice versa. There are two main indicators of potential
labour supply; activity rates and unemployment (Figs. 4.10 and 4.11).
The former (X_5) shows greater areal variation among females, with
rural areas and some urban ones where opportunities for women

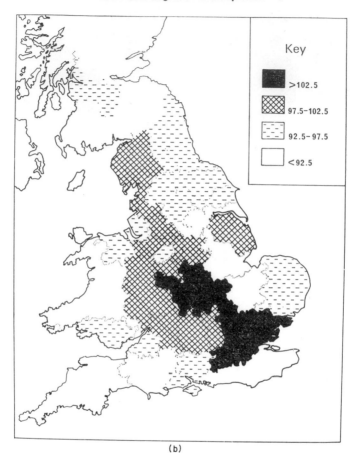

(b)

FIG. 4.9. Average gross weekly earnings for female workers, 1968
(GB = 100).

have traditionally been lacking having rates far below those of the larger conurbations (especially Greater London). The estimation of activity rates has been discussed by Taylor (1968) and by Gordon (1970), and it is clear that no foolproof method exists since the effective supply may not be the same as the number of inactive women of working age. Thus the crude unadjusted rates used here

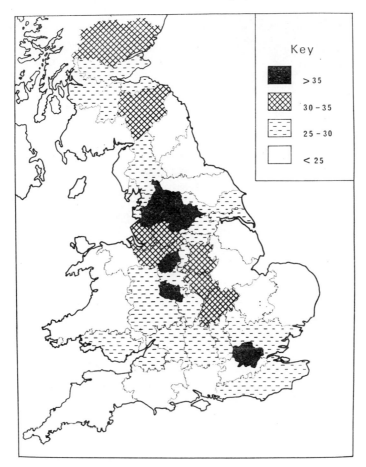

FIG. 4.10. Female activity rates, 1951 (unadjusted).

are regarded only as close indicators of relative female labour supply.

The same observation applies to unemployment rates (X_8, X_9, X_{10}); in a series of studies of the characteristics of the unemployed (Ministry of Labour, 1962 and 1966) it was shown that a large and regionally variable proportion was difficult to place in jobs due to age, personal disabilities, lack of training, or spatial immobility. The

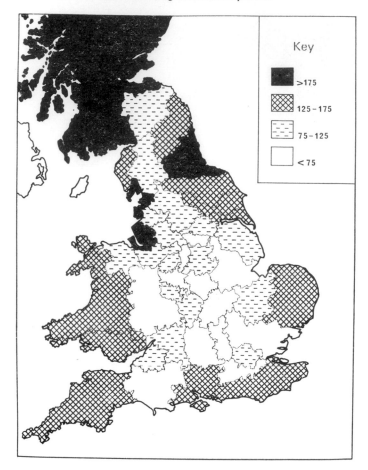

Fig. 4.11. Rates of unemployment, 1961 (GB = 100).

third of these, skills, has been given attention in the setting up of industrial training centres, and the fourth can be alleviated to some degree by special transport provided by firms (Moseley, 1973), though in rural areas with low population densities and relatively poor public services, the effect is limited. Little can be done about the other characteristics. Even when this proportion is taken into consideration, however, there remain significant variations in the rates of unemployment and numbers out of work in different parts of Britain. Both variables are included in the analysis because each plays a role in influencing movement. However, numbers unemployed correlate highly with total manufacturing employment, and, since the latter provides the best mass factor, the former is kept out of the model. Given low rates of unemployment, on the other hand, it is likely that industry in a region will face a major constraint on its expansion, particularly in the short run. Moreover, low rates, regardless of the numbers out of work, signify a tight labour market in which earnings are likely to be bid up by competing firms, which is desirable for the region but is also likely to encourage growing firms to look to locations with higher rates of unemployment and lower labour turnover in which to set up new establishments.

The next two variables in this group are urban employment densities (X_2) and the urbanized proportion of each region (X_3). The former (Fig. 4.12) is expressed in terms of the number of economically active persons per acre in urban administrative areas in each region, while the latter is the percentage of each region contained in such places. This, of course, ignores peri-urban development in rural districts adjoining major urban centres, but in explaining the generation of movement it is reasonable to direct attention to the older urban zones where pressures to move arising from congestion and high land values, both likely to be positively associated with employment density, are greatest. Peri-urban areas tend to be recipients of industry rather than generators. For this reason it is valuable to include a measure of the space within each area which is urban (Fig. 4.13), since this provides a possible influence on the volume of movement; the smaller the non-urban area, the greater will be the volume generated and vice versa. In Greater London, for example, it is impossible (by our definition) for peri-urban movement to occur since there is no non-urban space; by contrast, in East Anglia urban places account for only 6% of the total area, and establishments forced out of city centres because of congestion alone are less likely to look beyond the region for a new location.

It was postulated earlier that movement was most likely to occur when an enterprise reached a ceiling on development *in situ*. This is a

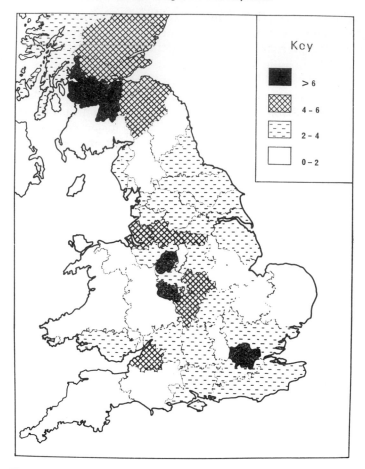

FIG. 4.12. Urban employment density, 1961 (employment per urban acre).

concept which can most easily be handled in terms of the individual establishment, but it can be considered that, assuming other factors to be constant, a faster growth rate implies that more firms are likely to reach their ceiling in a given period. However, the specification of a variable to express this poses problems since it is not possible, on *a*

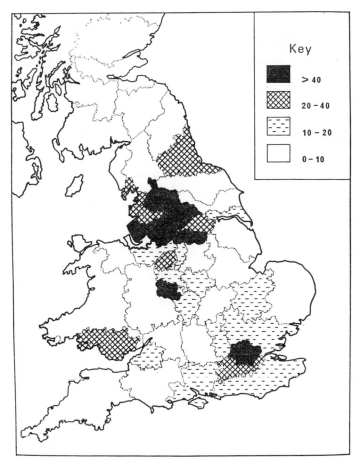

Fig. 4.13. Levels of urbanization, 1961 (percentage of area with urban status).

priori grounds, to decide over what period growth is relevant, how large should be the lags, and whether the relevant variable should be growth in total employment or only in manufacturing. A partial solution has been derived statistically by analysing movement in 1960–5 against employment changes (X_{14}) concurrently and in 1951–

61. The latter proved most satisfactory but the relationship was a weak one.

The next set of variables consists of regional policy measures, which raise problems peculiar to themselves. The implementation of regional policy is expected to have negative effects on the volume of movement generated by regions in which assisted areas and new towns are designated. However, in order to analyse their effects it is necessary to devise a systematic measurement based upon the assumption that the policy will be pursued with equal vigour wherever it applies; for example, that *pro rata*, all assisted areas will be treated alike at all times, and that each new town has the same chance of attracting industry as every other. Given these assumptions, which may be untenable but are essential, it is possible to quantify policies. To arrive at values for assisted areas (X_{11}) a calculation is made of the proportion of each region's population residing in zones where this status applied, weighted by the duration of that status (Fig. 4.14). Thus, for example, if in a five-year period half the population of a region lived in an assisted area and the designation lasted for the whole of the period, the value would be 50; if, however, the designation lasted for only two years, the value of assisted area status to that region would only be 20 (the figures are expressed as percentages). The calculation of new town and town expansion scheme weights (X_{12}) are made on a similar basis, taking the target population expressed as a percentage of the region's base year (1951, 1961, or 1966) population, weighted by the number of years between the designation and the end of the period (Fig. 4.15).

Lastly, the path of a generated move must cross a boundary to be enumerated, making it desirable to include a definition variable, namely the estimated radial size of each area (X_4), calculated as if each area were circular and each move originated at the centre. Other things being equal, it is expected that the generation of movement and the size of areas would be inversely related.

In this description of variables the influence of each has been discussed as if all others were held constant. No statement was made about the probable significance of any of them in reality, but analysis indicates that most of them could contribute to a satisfactory explanation of movement. However, experiments with different models

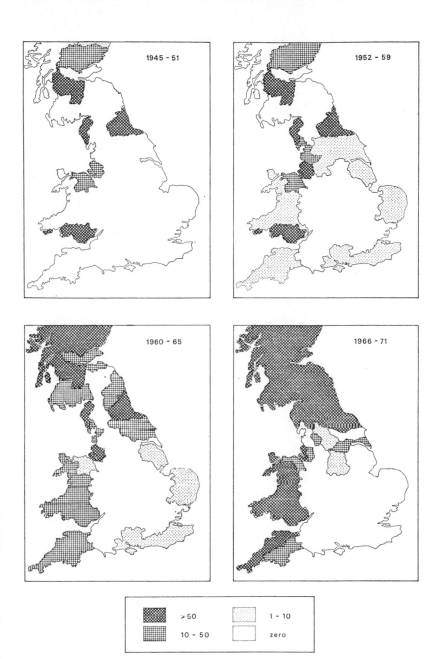

FIG. 4.14. Assisted area weights, by period.

135

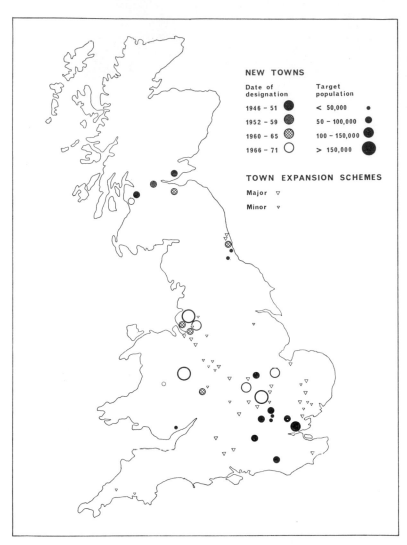

FIG. 4.15. New town and town expansion schemes 1946–71.

(described below) all pointed to one outstanding feature; the main variable is the mass factor. The regional distribution of the origins of movement depends primarily on the stock of industry in each area. But, equally important, the addition of variables from each of the other sets in Table 4.1 gives not only a significant increase in the level of explanation, but also takes it close to perfection in some instances.

4.5.2. *The Distribution of Destinations*

The same cannot be claimed for the explanation of the pattern of destinations. Like generation, the attraction of movement into a region depends upon the interaction of many variables, most of which can be treated summarily because they are, in fact, the same as those used in analysing generation patterns. They differ only in that their relationship with movement is inverted. Where a variable was previously seen to exert a negative influence on the volume of outward movement (e.g. the regional policy variables), it is expected now that its influence on the volume of inward movement would be positive. However, although attraction and generation have in common the greater part of the list of variables in Table 4.1, there are two major differences concerning (i) the role of the mass factor, and (ii) the use of a modified gravity measure. It was argued above that the volume of outward movement depends strongly on the stock of industry in each area; the existence of a close relationship between them ensures a high overall explanation of generation patterns. But there is neither logic nor experience to indicate that inward movement should be equally well related to the same definition of mass. Although some movers are drawn to large concentrations of industry and markets, these tend not to have been major attractions in Britain. Where firms have moved to industrial regions it has been for other reasons of which the chief has been labour supply. Other things being equal, recruitment is easier in larger centres or, more precisely, where the volume of unemployment is greater. Using numbers unemployed as a measure of mass (Fig. 4.16) in models of attraction has certain dangers, however. It ignores the latent supply of female workers who are neither employed nor registered as unemployed and it also takes no account of occupational mobility among workers of

TABLE 4.1. INDEPENDENT VARIABLES USED IN THE ANALYSIS OF MOVEMENT
GENERATION AND ATTRACTION

A. GENERATION
  (i) *Mass factor*
    X_1 Numbers employed in manufacturing, 1951, 1961, 1966 ('000)

  (ii) *Areal spatial structure*
    X_2 Urban employment density, 1951, 1961, 1966 (employees per
         urban acre)
    X_3 Per cent of region with urban status, 1951, 1961, 1966
    X_4 Size of region (estimated radius, miles)

  (iii) *Labour factors*
    X_5 Female activity rates, 1951, 1961, 1966
    X_6 Male earnings (average), manual workers, 1968
    X_7 Female earnings (average), manual workers, 1968
    X_8 Male unemployment, 1951, 1961, 1966–70 (average June +
         December)
    X_9 Female unemployment, 1951, 1961, 1966–70 (average June +
         December)
    X_{10} Total unemployment, 1951, 1961, 1966–70 (average June +
         December)

  (iv) *Regional policy factors*
    X_{11} Per cent employment in assisted areas
    X_{12} Target population of new towns and town expansion schemes
         as per cent of base year population

  (v) *Others*
    X_{13} Industrial composition, 1951, 1961 (estimated)
    X_{14} Employment change, 1951–61 (used only in moves in period
         1960–5)

B. ATTRACTION
  Variables as above, except:
    X_{1a} Total numbers unemployed, 1951, 1961, 1966–70 (average
         June + December)
    X_{15} Total employment in development areas
    X_{16} Total target population in new towns and town expansion
         schemes
    X_{17} Modified gravity measure

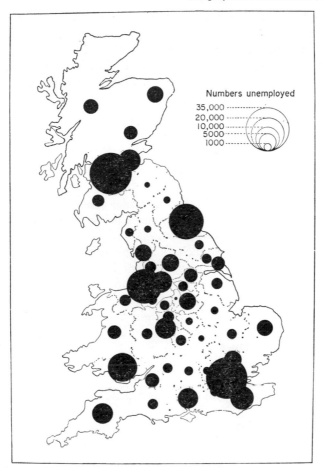

Fig. 4.16. Numbers unemployed, average 1951.

both sexes. But, more seriously, it is a relatively unstable measure of mass. Although the pattern of unemployment may remain similar, one year's volume may be markedly different from the next.

Secondly, we would expect there to be a greater attraction into areas located close to the main sources of movement. This can be supported empirically by the distance decay function described above but it could, in any case, be postulated on *a priori* grounds. To measure "distance" from sources requires more than just a map of routes, however. The sources vary in their importance and it is therefore necessary to use a set of weighted measures; or what is, in effect, a modified gravity model (X_{17}). This is based on the formula

$$G_i = \sum_{j=1,7} \frac{O_j}{D_{ij}},$$

where the attractive power of a given region (G_i) is derived from a summation of the moves generated (O_j) by each of the major sources (defined in Fig. 4.5 for the period 1945–65), divided by the distance (D_{ij}) between the source and the area under consideration. Where the attractiveness of one of the seven sources is itself concerned, only the other six are used in the calculation.

In addition to these we include as alternative measures of policy variables, the absolute number resident in development areas per region (X_{15}) and the total target population of new towns (X_{16}). These differ from the variables listed in the generation models only in that they relate to numbers and not weighted percentages. Their introduction is for the purpose of experimenting with models containing regional policy variables alone.

4.6. Multivariate Analysis of Geographical Distributions

4.6.1. *The Generation of Movement*

Of the cross-sectional analyses conducted in this study, the experiments to find explanations of the pattern of movement generated by the sets of regions yield the best results. In practice it seems that we can predict more accurately where moves will originate than where they will terminate. This presents an interesting juxtaposition with theories of industrial location. The greater proportion of these concentrate on destinations, selected by hypothetical enterprises in a simplified world, where rational choice leads (except in certain cases) to clearly predictable locations; this is true whether the theory deals with individual cases (Weber, 1929; Smith, 1971) or with industrial patterns (Losch, 1954). In reality, however, it appears that factors of location are less powerful than factors of dislocation, though it should be noted that both provide very good explanations of the aggregative movement patterns investigated here.

The procedure adopted in this section is a stepwise one. It begins with a discussion of the effects of individual variables on movement and continues with experiments on different multivariate solutions. At each step the analysis deals separately with movements in each period.

Correlation coefficients between the number of moves generated per area and individual independent variables are contained in Table 4.2. Three variables each showed consistently high correlations.

TABLE 4.2. CORRELATION COEFFICIENTS *r* BETWEEN NUMBERS OF SURVIVING MOVES GENERATED BY AREAS AND INDEPENDENT VARIABLES

Variable	1945–51	1952–9	1960–5	1966–71
1. Manufacturing employment	0·90***	0·87***	0·89***	0·89***
2. Urban employment density	0·63***	0·63***	0·63***	0·56***
3. Area with urban status	0·72***	0·67***	0·70***	0·56***
4. Size of area	−0·20	−0·17	−0·19	−0·04
5. Female activity rates	0·45**	0·37**	0·42**	0·49***
6. Male earnings	0·33*	0·32*	0·37**	0·38**
7. Female earnings	0·23	0·21	0·43**	0·50***
8. Male unemployed (%)	−0·12	−0·08	−0·11	N.A.
9. Female unemployed (%)	−0·23	−0·17	−0·21	N.A.
10. Total unemployed (%)	−0·15	−0·10	−0·15	−0·30*
11. Assisted area weight	−0·11	−0·09	−0·14	−0·19
12. New town weight	0·00	−0·02	0·01	−0·05
13. Industrial composition	0·34*	0·34*	0·35*	N.A.
14. Employment change, 1951–61/1961–6	—	—	−0·04	−0·09

Significance levels: 95%*; 99% **; 99·9% ***.
Numbers of observations: 1945–65, 49; 1966–71, 61.

Manufacturing employment (X_1) with 0·90, 0·87, 0·89, and 0·89 (coefficients easily significant at the 99·9% level) provides, as expected in an economy where the process of industrial dispersion dominates, the closest explanation of postwar movement. That the coefficient was not higher was attributable chiefly to the below-par generation of movement by the heavily populated industrial development areas. The two other variables achieving highly significant coefficients are both indicators of congestion. Urban employment density (X_2) had three values of 0·63 and one of 0·56, and the proportion of each area with urban status (X_3), had coefficients of 0·72, 0·67, 0·70, and 0·56. These confirm most strongly the findings of those who have suggested that lack of space is the major factor pushing firms out of urban regions.

By contrast, the variables relating to conditions of labour supply, though often quoted by management and researchers alike, showed very little correlation with the generation pattern at this level of analysis. Female activity rates (X_5), with 0·45, 0·37, 0·42, and 0·49, was the best of this set. Conforming to the changing structure of industry, with an increasing demand for female operatives to carry out light tasks, the mobile firms tended to leave areas where proportions of women in work are high. This was particularly so in the first period when quite a large number of mobile establishments came from the textile industry, traditionally associated with very high female activity rates. The average wages of male manual workers (X_6) and, latterly, of female workers (X_7) also appeared fairly important, but rates of unemployment (X_8, X_9, X_{10}) held no significance although they did possess the expected negative sign in their correlations.

In view of the nature of many of these variables, it is not surprising that many of them should have, superficially at least, low powers of explanation. Research in recent years has increasingly indicated the need for multivariate explanations, with succeeding variables being used to mop up the residuals left by previous ones. Variables which seem to carry little weight when seen individually may become more significant when the effect of others is accounted for. However, for this to be so it is necessary that the intercorrelations between the independent variables should be relatively small; that is, the different variables must not have the same distributions.

In fact, the independent variables do tend to be weakly related, as is shown in Table 4.3. Here the independent variables used in analyses of generation and attraction are all contained in a single matrix, relating to the period 1960–5; the matrices for 1945–51, 1952–9 and 1966–71 were similar to this. Only the coefficients exceeding 0·50 (where $p = 0·999$) are presented.

It is interesting to note, in passing, that these matrices, besides containing information integral to the present analysis, also present a useful description of the postwar British regional economic system. Through the matrices it is possible to trace interrelationships which are important in other contexts besides that of industrial movement.

The highest intercorrelations occur, not surprisingly, among those variables dealing with rates of unemployment. Male and female unemployment normally show very similar patterns and, of course, their likeness to total unemployment rates are equally great. Slightly lower coefficients occur between these variables and the development area weight (X_{11}) in the period 1960–5 and between the volume of manufacturing employment (X_1) and the urbanized proportion of each area (X_2). Few of the remaining coefficients exceeded 0·70. The values found between female wages (X_7), female activity rates (X_5), and female unemployment (X_9) at no time exceeded 0·63.

In moving on to consider these variables in the context of multiple regression analysis, the procedure adopted is to carry out a series of cross-sectional experiments, the results of which are contained in Table 4.4. Analyses have been conducted separately for each period with and without the mass factor. The purpose of this is not to present a definite single set of results, but rather to investigate some of the numerous possible sets of relationships in different ways. Nevertheless, there were certain consistencies which permit firm statements of a more general nature and, possibly, to predict movement generation patterns under varying conditions.

The first experiment (Table 4.4, model 1) contains all the specified independent variables but, as suggested above, the one which dominated throughout each period was manufacturing employment (X_1). In the stepwise regression analysis it was always the first variable to enter, and retained its primary position while other significant variables were added. In many respects, however, it is these other

TABLE 4.3. MATRIX OF INTERCORRELATIONS BETWEEN INDEPENDENT VARIABLES IN GENERATION AND ATTRACTION ANALYSES, 1960-5

Variable	1	1a	2	3	4	5	6	7	8	9	10	11	12	13	14	15	16	17
1																		
1a	0·67																	
2	0·71	0·62																
3	0·87		0·51															
4																		
5	0·55		0·61	0·55	−0·57													
6					−0·51													
7							0·63											
8					0·54													
9					0·58				0·87									
10					0·57				0·99	0·93								
11									0·89	0·81	0·89							
12																		
13								0·53		−0·50								
14																		
15		0·72							0·68	0·54	0·66	0·71						
16									0·59	0·56	0·60		0·79					
17														0·53	0·82			

Notes: Only *r*-values > ±0·50 are shown. For list of variables, see Table 4.1.

variables which contain the greater interest. What they show is a system in which the influence of size is offset by the form and character of regions. The volume of manufacturing employment alone tends to over-predict movement from the older industrial development areas and from regions containing important intervening opportunities. Hence there was a corrective influence applied by the regional structure variables. In addition, the effect of labour and regional policy variables can also be seen; in each case they further dampened the generative power of regions.

Even without a mass factor (Table 4.4, model 2), it is still possible to achieve high levels of explanation; the average coefficient of multiple correlation (r^2) in model 2 was 0·67 (compared with 0·86 in model 1). Moreover, through each period the same five variables dominated the regression equations. The first two, urban employment density (X_2) and urban area (X_3), alternated in significance, but their very close complementarity means that their precise order is not important. Of greater relevance, their standardized regression coefficients show the degree to which they led over the other variables. On the basis of these values, it can be inferred that they had about twice the power of the other significant variables. Adding further support to these was a third expression of spatial structure, namely the estimated radial extent of the areas (X_4). Thus, excluding the mass factor, it is possible to derive a sound explanation of movement generation patterns simply on the basis of urban density, the amount of each region covered by places of urban status, and the size of each region. At a somewhat lower level of significance, the next factor in this set of models was industrial composition (X_{13}). As noted earlier, there appeared to be considerable interregional homogeneity in the propensity of industries to generate movement. This is, again, shown to hold, with considerable consistency; the regression coefficient of this variable barely changed throughout two decades (1945–65). But against expectation, following the studies which have noted, the importance of labour supply as a major influence on the attraction of industry, the set of variables representing this factor barely made an impression, even in the multivariate analysis. Male unemployment rates (X_8) provided a slight inverse influence and appeared to become increasingly significant as time progressed, and female activity rates

TABLE 4.4. MOVEMENT GENERATION MODELS: 1945–71

MODEL 1. *All variables included*

	1945–51			1952–9			1960–5			1966–71		
	(i)	(ii)	(iii)	(i)	(ii)	(iii)	(i)	(ii)	(iii)	(i)	(ii)	(iii)
	$+1{\cdot}47\,X_1$	10·0	***	$+1{\cdot}32\,X_1$	9·7	***	$+1{\cdot}26\,X_1$	9·7	***	$+1{\cdot}14\,X_1$	10·2	***
	$-0{\cdot}49\,X_3$	4·1	***	$-0{\cdot}19\,X_{11}$	3·1	***	$-0{\cdot}38\,X_3$	2·8	***	$-0{\cdot}15\,X_5$	1·8	*
	$-0{\cdot}21\,X_{11}$	3·8	***	$-0{\cdot}39\,X_3$	2·9	***	$-0{\cdot}17\,X_{12}$	2·7	**	$-0{\cdot}15\,X_3$	1·5	*
	$-0{\cdot}17\,X_2$	2·1	**	$-0{\cdot}16\,X_5$	2·1	**	$-0{\cdot}17\,X_8$	2·4	**	$-0{\cdot}11\,X_6$	1·5	*
	$-0{\cdot}16\,X_{12}$	1·7	*	$-0{\cdot}09\,X_{12}$	1·5	*	$+0{\cdot}15\,X_{13}$	2·1	**	$-0{\cdot}11\,X_4$	1·3	
							$+0{\cdot}13\,X_4$	1·7	*			
	$r^2 = 0{\cdot}89$			$r^2 = 0{\cdot}85$			$r^2 = 0{\cdot}86$			$r^2 = 0{\cdot}82$		

$X_1 - X_{13}$ as in Table 3.3.

Column (i) regression coefficients; (ii) value of Student's t; (iii) significance level: 90% *; 95% **; 99% ***.

TABLE 4.4 (*cont.*)

MODEL 2. *Excluding mass factor* (X_1)

	1945–51			1952–9			1960–5			1966–71		
	(i)	(ii)	(iii)	(i)	(ii)	(iii)	(i)	(ii)	(iii)	(i)	(ii)	(iii)
	$+0.56\,X_3$	5·2	***	$+0.61\,X_2$	5·2	***	$+0.54\,X_3$	5·3	***	$+0.46\,X_3$	3·9	***
	$+0.47\,X_2$	4·7	***	$+0.55\,X_3$	4·7	***	$+0.52\,X_2$	5·2	***	$+0.36\,X_4$	3·4	***
	$+0.26\,X_4$	3·2	***	$+0.31\,X_4$	2·6	**	$+0.42\,X_4$	3·8	***	$+0.30\,X_2$	2·9	**
	$+0.21\,X_{13}$	2·1	**	$+0.22\,X_{13}$	2·1	**	$-0.29\,X_8$	2·5	**	$+0.26\,X_7$	2·6	**
	$-0.19\,X_8$	1·7	*	$-0.26\,X_5$	2·0	**	$+0.21\,X_{13}$	2·2	**	$-0.15\,X_{11}$	1·5	*
				$-0.23\,X_8$	1·7	*						
	$r^2 = 0.71$			$r^2 = 0.69$			$r^2 = 0.72$			$r^2 = 0.57$		

Note: All regression coefficients have been standardized (see King, 1969) p. 140.

briefly achieved some significance in the 1950s, but with these exceptions (noting that female unemployment would have been suppressed due to its high correlation with male rates), there was no evidence of their having importance on the generation of movement.

4.6.2. *The Attraction of Movement*

In most respects generation and attraction of industrial movement can be regarded as opposite sides of the same problem, many of the factors encouraging one act to the detriment of the other, so that comparison between Tables 4.2 and 4.5 shows that most variables common to both tables have opposite signs. However, a number of important differences arise when considering attraction. The most important changes occur in the specification of the mass factor (X_{1a}); the exclusion of industrial composition (X_{13}), which has no relevance for attraction; the addition of a weighted gravity measure (described above) to the list (X_{17}); and new forms of the policy variables $(X_{15}$ and $X_{16})$ which are introduced for a separate experiment.

As Table 4.5 indicates, the fundamental distinction between the correlates of generation and attraction is the lack of a single dominant variable to explain the latter. The new mass factor is capable of accounting for no more than a minor part of the pattern of destinations. Total numbers wholly unemployed (X_{1a}) had correlation coefficients (r) of 0·58, 0·21, 0·46, and 0·35 respectively for the four periods. On the other hand, the role of policy factors—assisted areas $(X_{11}$ and $X_{15})$ and the new and expanded towns $(X_{12}$ and $X_{16})$—took on much greater significance, proving to be the best correlates of attraction.

The weakness of the mass factor is attributable chiefly to the existence of large numbers out of work (but low rates of unemployment) in the major English conurbations, where every other factor militates against location. However, it was not accompanied by any marked rise in the coefficients of the various indices of labour supply and cost. Female activity rates (X_5) had an expected negative relationship but were far from significantly related to attraction; conversely and unexpectedly, wage levels (X_6, X_7) were related positively but with low coefficients. Only unemployment rates (X_8, X_9, X_{10}) approached statistical significance and that for just the first period.

TABLE 4.5. CORRELATION COEFFICIENTS *r* BETWEEN NUMBERS OF SURVIVING
MOVES ATTRACTED BY AREAS AND INDEPENDENT VARIABLES

Variable	1945–51	1952–9	1960–5	1966–71
1a. Total numbers unemployed	0·58***	0·21	0·46**	0·35**
2. Urban employment density	−0·06	−0·10	−0·03	−0·08
3. Area with urban status	0·19	0·05	0·03	0·07
4. Size of area	0·02	0·11	0·16	0·10
5. Female activity rate	−0·17	−0·06	−0·12	−0·12
6. Male earnings	0·21	0·25	0·16	0·30*
7. Female earnings	−0·01	0·09	0·07	0·20
8. Male unemployed (%)	0·35*	0·02	0·15	N.A.
9. Female unemployed (%)	0·35*	0·02	0·15	
10. Total unemployed (%)	0·37*	0·04	0·21	0·01
11. Development area weight	0·64***	0·04	0·18	0·21
12. New town target weight	0·33*	0·78***	0·58***	0·28*
15. Development area employment	0·75***	0·12	0·53**	0·44***
16. New town target population	0·47**	0·88***	0·74***	0·67***
17. Modified gravity weight	0·12	0·63***	0·27*	0·29*

Significance levels: 95% *; 99% **; 99·9% ***.
Numbers of observations: 1945–65, 49; 1966–71, 61.

Neither, to make up for these, was the combination of variables expressing congestion (X_2, X_3, X_4) anywhere near significant.

Of course, these results could have been obtained in a system where industrial movement is unhampered by political constraints. However, the coefficients for the planning variables (0·64, 0·04, 0·18, and 0·21 for the assisted area weight; 0·33, 0·78, 0·59, and 0·28 for new and expanded town target) provide strong circumstantial evidence of the degree to which patterns of location have been diverted by government action. That is, given the policies of dispersion from congested cities, and regional equality of opportunities, the simple act of designating areas for special treatment was enough to ensure a flow of movement above that warranted by other factors.

As before, the approach to multivariate analysis taken here is an experimental one, investigating different combinations of variables. In addition to tests with and without the mass factor, however, the experiments also include one where the only variables are those relating to indices of labour cost and availability (model 2), and another which contains unweighted measures of assisted area and new town targets (model 3). The results of these four sets of analyses are presented in Table 4.6. The general level of explanation among the various attraction models, though quite significant, is considerably lower than that found in the generation models; coefficients of multiple correlation in model 1 were approximately 0·71 compared with 0·85 found in the corresponding generation model. Nevertheless, the explanation of almost three-quarters of the variance in the distributions occurring in each of the four periods, considering the complicated interaction of "natural" and political pressures exerting influences upon location decisions, denotes a fairly consistent response by mobile industry to conditions in different parts of the country. Moreover, by juxtaposing the attraction models (Table 4.6) against the generation models (Table 4.4) it is possible to distinguish the elements of a dynamic system.

Among the attraction models, that dealing with indices of labour (model 2) can be dismissed. With the exception of the first and last periods, when male wages (X_6), male unemployment rates (X_8) and female activity rates (X_5) in concert wielded a significant influence on the pattern of destinations, this group of variables was extremely weak. The reasons for this are found in the growth of movement to new towns in the South East (i.e., to areas with high wage levels and low unemployment rates); in the tendency for many mobile enterprises to be relatively labour intensive; and in the weak correlation between rates of unemployment and absolute measures of labour supply.

In contrast, the two new variables created for model 3, namely the volume of employment in designated assisted areas (X_{15}) and the total target population in new and expanded towns (X_{16}), were much more effective. Between 1945 and 1951 new towns, which had barely had time to start attracting industry, played a minor role, but during the 1950s they came to dominate the distribution of movement. In the early 1960s, however, the more valuable set of incentives for the assisted areas is reflected in the more balanced regression model for that period. The later 1960s saw a return of new town targets as the dominant variable despite the massive rise in expenditure on regional policy. This apparent anomaly is at least partly explained by the designation of new towns in the assisted areas, the revised targets for those in the South East and the success of town expansion schemes, especially in East Anglia. (Nevertheless, in model 1, which incorporates all variables, regional policy in its weighted form(X_{11}) wields a markedly stronger influence.) Although it concentrates only upon these two variables, the model provides an important indicator of the role of interventionist policies designed to influence destinations chosen by mobile enterprises. It can be inferred that when such policies are in operation the pattern of location can be predicted with some confidence by observing where they apply.

In model 1 the striking feature is the consistency with which the same set of variables dominated. Except in the 1950s the mass factor led, increasing its power considerably after 1960. The new towns policy, as expected from earlier observations, provided the main force during the 1950s. Thirdly, a consistent positive influence was exercised by proximity to the main sources of movement (X_{17}). The fourth member of the set was urban employment density(X_2), which provided a negative influence. The regional policy weights (X_{11}), which were partly subsumed within the mass factor were significant only when accompanied by high levels of expenditure, a finding consistent with the results of the time series analysis. Thus in these we have the main elements of locational attraction at the regional level, namely labour availability, regional incentives and land availability and costs (the last being implied by urban employment density), and the ability to satisfy the preference for short distance movement.

4.6.3. *Residual Distributions in Generation and Attraction*

So far the discussion of generation and attraction has concerned

TABLE 4.6. MOVEMENT ATTRACTION MODELS: 1945–71

MODEL 1. *All variables (excluding X_{15}, X_{16})*

	1945–51			1952–9			1960–5			1966–71		
	(i)	(ii)	(iii)	(i)	(ii)	(iii)	(i)	(ii)	(iii)	(i)	(ii)	(iii)
	$+0.60\ X_{1a}$	5.4	***	$+0.50\ X_{12}$	6.1	***	$+0.90\ X_{1a}$	6.8	***	$+0.54\ X_{1a}$	4.3	***
	$+0.42\ X_{11}$	4.4	***	$+0.56\ X_{17}$	6.1	***	$-0.41\ X_{3}$	3.7	***	$+0.50\ X_{17}$	3.8	***
	$-0.39\ X_{2}$	4.2	***	$+0.30\ X_{1a}$	3.2	***	$+0.38\ X_{12}$	3.7	***	$+0.47\ X_{11}$	3.5	***
	$+0.28\ X_{17}$	2.8	***	$+0.18\ X_{10}$	2.0	**	$-0.29\ X_{2}$	2.4	**	$+0.19\ X_{12}$	2.1	**
	$+0.18\ X_{12}$	2.0	**	$-0.17\ X_{6}$	1.9	*	$+0.21\ X_{17}$	2.0	**	$-0.30\ X_{2}$	2.0	**
										$+0.20\ X_{6}$	1.7	*
										$-0.22\ X_{5}$	1.6	
	$r^2 = 0.76$			$r^2 = 0.80$			$r^2 = 0.69$			$r^2 = 0.60$		

MODEL 2. *Labour indices only* $(X_5 - X_{10})$

	1945-51			1952-9			1960-5			1966-71		
	(i)	(ii)	(iii)	(i)	(ii)	(iii)	(i)	(ii)	(iii)	(i)	(ii)	(iii)
	$+0\cdot43\ X_8$	$3\cdot1$	***	Not significant			Not significant			$+0\cdot46\ X_8$	$3\cdot4$	***
	$+0\cdot30\ X_6$	$2\cdot9$	***							$-0\cdot34\ X_5$	$2\cdot5$	**
	$r^2 = 0\cdot21$									$r^2 = 0\cdot18$		

MODEL 3. *Regional policy variables* $(X_{15}$ and $X_{16})$

	1945-51			1952-9			1960-5			1966-71		
	(i)	(ii)	(iii)	(i)	(ii)	(iii)	(i)	(ii)	(iii)	(i)	(ii)	(iii)
	$+0\cdot67\ X_{15}$	$7\cdot5$	***	$+0\cdot89\ X_{16}$	$12\cdot4$	***	$+0\cdot89\ X_{16}$	$6\cdot7$	***	$+0\cdot58\ X_{16}$	$5\cdot6$	***
	$+0\cdot31\ X_{16}$	$3\cdot4$	***	$-\quad X_{15}$	$0\cdot9$		$+0\cdot32\ X_{15}$	$3\cdot4$	***	$+0\cdot19\ X_{15}$	$1\cdot8$	*
	$r^2 = 0\cdot66$			$r^2 = 0\cdot77$			$r^2 = 0\cdot64$			$r^2 = 0\cdot48$		

$X_{1a} - X_{17}$ as in Table 3.3.
Column (i) regression coefficients (standardized); (ii) value of Student's t; (iii) significance level: 90% *; 95% **; 99% ***.

only the parameters obtained from series of regression analyses. However, it is valuable to inquire to what degree the different areas conformed to conditions predicted by the movement models, to identify anomalies where they occurred, and to suggest reasons for these.

Basically, anomalies (residuals) arise either from deficiencies in the statistical analysis (measurement errors or poor specification of variables), or from the exclusion of important variables, some of which may not be quantifiable. As far as statistical deficiencies are concerned, we can be reasonably confident that measurement errors are small apart from those due to the closure of firms after movement. Also, experiments with different specifications of the same variables have produced results which are no better, and often worse, than those described above. On the other hand, it is possible to suggest that greater differentiation within some of the variables might have yielded better results. For example, it might have been preferable to use finer categories in defining industrial composition, or distinguished between categories of non-urban land, some of which would not be usable for industrial development.

These, however, would give marginal improvements, whereas the role of variables hitherto not considered is almost certainly fundamental. This assertion is made because, in confining attention to the variables listed above, we are conscious that a large part of modern location theory has been underrepresented. For example, no direct attention has been given to behavioural constraints, the role of industrial linkage, or the influence of regional markets and supply areas. In reviewing the residual patterns (Figs. 4.17 and 4.18) there seem very strong grounds for considering all of these.

Behavioural constraints can be grouped into two categories on the basis of whether they apply to management or to government. In the previous chapter it was stated that homogeneous behaviour on the part of management and unbiased treatment of development areas by governments would be assumed. Clearly, neither of these assumptions is realistic, though it is impossible to measure how far they deviate from practice. Management behaviour, investigated in detail by Townroe (1971), varies widely. Professional expertise is often lacking in the decision process, the range of alternatives investigated

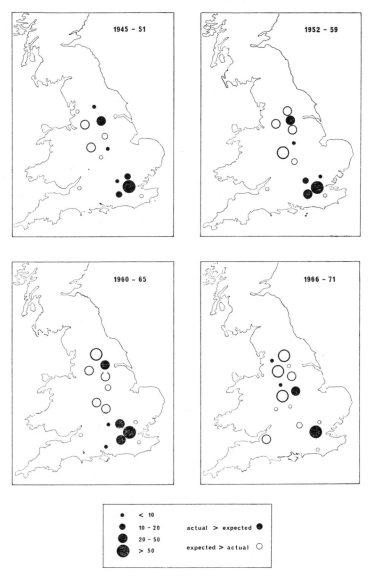

Fɪɢ. 4.17. Residual distributions of movement generation, by period.

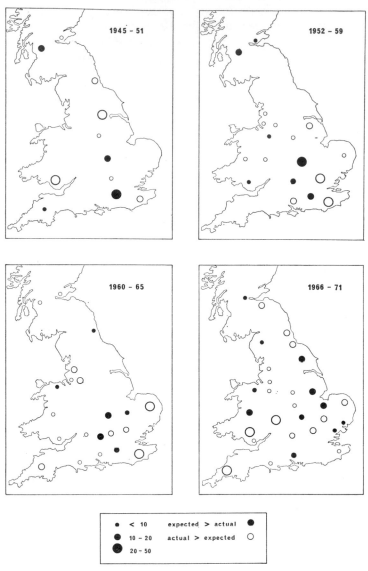

FIG. 4.18. Residual distributions of movement attraction, by period.

tends to be small, and judgements are often subjective. Given this background of partial ignorance, plus the effect of social and psychological factors asserted by Eversley (1965), it is not surprising that the overall pattern of movement should not be perfectly predictable. Regions may generate more movement than expected when there are opportunities for relocation nearby, easily perceived by potential movers and giving ready access to old business and personal contacts. Likewise, some regions possessing marked environmental qualities may attract more and generate less than expected.

The second category, regionally selective government behaviour, is not possible to identify. At this point, however, we are more interested in d scrimination between the assisted areas, some of which have fared much better, other things being equal, than others. There have been occasions (e.g. the 1963 reports on Scotland and the North East) when a "new deal" has been announced for particular regions, and there may have been directives to promote these rather than other regions. Also, closures on a massive scale threatened by a concentrated declining industry might warrant special attention, whereas less spectacular but no less intransigent problems might not.

While it is impossible to explain every residual, it appears that many of them have their causes among these factors. In each map residuals are expressed as the surplus or deficit number of establishments generated or attracted by each region. Regions with large residuals (e.g. Greater London) may be associated with low ratios and vice versa. However, while the ratio may be important as an indicator of accuracy with which movement to or from an area has been predicted, there is greater interest in the numbers by which actual and expected moves differed. Many regions were consistently over- or underpredicted in the generation models, having negative or positive residuals. In the latter group there is evidence of the efforts to disperse industry from Greater London, leading to movement which exceeded the amount which the area's parameters would have justified and to suggestions (Eversley, 1973) that too much pressure has been exerted, creating a danger of metropolitan poverty amidst affluence in the Home Counties. By contrast, the next two largest conurbations, the West Midlands and Manchester, produced many fewer moves than expected. Neither of these areas exported disproportionately large establishments to make up for their small numbers of moves; so it would appear that over a long period they have been favoured by policy makers. In part, also, the negative residual in the West Midlands conurbation may be attributable to the strong degree of industrial linkage in the region (Smith, 1970).

Residuals from the attraction models tended to be less stable, possibly because the factors contributing to locational choice are geographically more variable than the ones determining the need for movement. As a result, the four sets (Fig. 4.18) show important shifts; for example, the major positive residuals (i.e. attracting more moves than expected) in the 1945–51 period, South Wales, and the South Yorkshire Coalfield, lost this position later. By contrast, of the assisted areas, Scotland and Cumberland could fairly claim to have been neglected, while Merseyside, possibly through proximity to Manchester, was able to attract movement roughly as expected. In the early 1960s the Scottish, Welsh, and North-eastern residuals were generally reversed. In the case of South Wales, this marks the success of earlier policies giving, despite a few resistant pockets in the valleys, a much healthier economic framework; in the North East the redevelopment of Teesside was equally impressive. However, West Central Scotland remained the main problem region of the early 1960s, with few intrinsic attractions for industry and a clear need for special attention.

In the South East, with the exception of Greater London, the general pattern was one of positive residuals. To a large extent this is attributable to proximity to the metropolis, producing the gravity effect noted above. However, there were important variations within the region. The southern half, though receiving the smaller number of moves, had the larger residuals, which appear to be related to environmental values. The same factor probably accounts for the increasingly large positive residuals found in the South West and East Anglia. Greater London, by contrast, shows evidence of exceptionally tight control on location in the area. Having a potential labour supply, judging from numbers unemployed, larger than almost every other area in the country, plus access to the biggest market in Britain, it is expected that in the absence of controls London would have gained several dozen more moves than it actually did.

Ideally, one would find improved models to reduce these residuals still further. At this stage, however, there are too many "unknowns" to justify the inclusion of dummy variables to represent behavioural and other factors. Also, the present models, though leaving some residuals which are large in absolute terms, tend to give fairly low residual ratios for the most important areas in both generation and attraction models. The greatest inaccuracy comes in predicting flows to and from the minor areas. Many of these would be likely to reappear as "random" movements, whatever the nature of the model.

CHAPTER 5

The Prospects for Industrial Mobility

IN HIS introduction to a volume of essays on forecasting and the social sciences, Young (1968) states four propositions: "First, that all decisions are decisions about what should happen in the future; second, that all decisions are based at any rate implicitly on forecasts of what will happen in the absence of any decision, and in the event of a variety of possible decisions being taken; third, that on the whole the more thought that can be given to forecasts in the time available before the decision has to be taken, the better; and fourth, and above all, that however much thought is given to forecasts, they should always be treated with scepticism."

The final point is worth emphasizing: "The margins of error in the forecasting . . . will not usually be small, and, what is worse, it will seldom be possible to say just how large they are" (Young, 1968). The near inevitability of error in such forecasts stems from a variety of sources. Some can best be described as "strategic", arising from shortcomings in model design. Ayres (1969), discussing technological forecasting, includes such possibilities as "lack of imagination", "failure to recognize convergent trends", and so on, all of which apply equally in the social sciences. Among statistical sources of error we might be faced by basic faults in the data used in deriving models, or we might find that models themselves are inadequate. However, as Young has stated, while we might be suspicious, we still will not be able to say where perfection lies and, therefore, will not be able to do more than make rough estimates of the size of errors.

Nevertheless, there remain strong grounds for experimenting with forecasts. If nothing else, they play a major role in the proper conduct of a decision-making process by providing a rigorously derived set of conditional statements about what might happen (or is likely to happen) in given circumstances. More than that, however, properly derived forecasts need a sound theoretical background and, in turn, they provide the most effective tests of theories. Perhaps this is less evident in the social sciences than in some physical sciences, where factors can be isolated with greater ease, especially in laboratory conditions. By comparison, the social scientist operates in more complex, open systems, of which the main elements tend to be relatively unstable. This has the effect of demanding either a greater level of abstraction for most theories in the social sciences, or, if more realism is desired, more complex theories. In either event, as in the physical sciences, the test of acceptability in the social sciences is "repeatability". That is, the theory or model which explains one set of conditions at one time or place must be able to predict or adequately explain conditions among the same factors at another time or place. One might argue on this basis that as long as the raw material of the social sciences, human attitudes and behaviour, remains so complex and variable, no theory will ever be perfect. However, while this is undeniable, it does not mean that efforts to theorize and forecast are misplaced: by striving to achieve even a lower level of acceptability the social scientist inevitably increases his knowledge and understanding of human systems and improves his theories and forecasts.

In this chapter the objective is to make some progress towards an ability to forecast industrial movement. The approach is discursive rather than statistical because, firstly, we are aware of certain shortcomings in the models described in the two previous chapters, and, secondly, before forecasting movement it is necessary to have accurate predictions of all the relevant independent variables. The latter is a problem which has exercised the analytical skills of business cycle economists for decades (Burns and Mitchell, 1946; Bronfenbrenner, 1969), and progress towards accurate forecasts of even short-term economic movements has been erratic. Since regional policy should deal with at least the medium-term, the requirements are far from being met. Nevertheless, there is value in discussing those elements of industrial mobility and economic change which are amenable to prediction as well as those which constrain our ability to make accurate forecasts.

The following sections concentrate upon two crucial issues; the ability to make short- and medium-term forecasts and the long-term prospects of industrial mobility. In the first, interest centres upon identifying as clearly as possible the way in which the regional system operates before investigating the way in which changes in various elements of the system influence the volume and direction of movement. The second requires an examination of the conditions influencing the overall level of movement and asks what limits they might impose over the long term; whether, for example, the 350 moves recorded in 1968 represents maximum mobility. Of course, there can be no absolute answer to this, but the question remains a vital one for policy-makers since the answer to this, coupled with the needs of the assisted areas, must ultimately determine the nature of their policies.

5.1. Short- and Medium-Term Forecasts

5.1.1. *Requirements*

The first practical step towards making usable forecasts is to test our models against past conditions. The outcome is a set of "retrospective forecasts" made from the standpoint of an omniscient being. For example, this hypothetical person would have had perfect knowledge of the course taken between 1960 and 1965 of all the economic and structural variables listed in Tables 3.2 and 4.1. His problem in forecasting moves in this period on the basis of previous models would, therefore, have been made much more simple than that of the conventional forecaster, who would have lacked such omniscience and needed to project the independent variables prior to taking any other step. We could have placed the same constraint upon our man, but there seems little to be gained from doing so at this stage. The assumption of perfect knowledge about the independent variables allows us to indicate how well forecasts might perform under the best of all possible conditions. It is a simple matter to drop the assumption and carry out additional sets of experiments.

Basically, short-term forecasts are concerned with two major questions:

(i) Given projected trends, what will be the volume and distribution of movement over a specified period?

(ii) Given a new set of conditions (e.g., the designation of new towns or extra incentives in the assisted areas), what impact will these have on the volume and distribution of movement over a specified period?

Having identified these questions, the next steps are to ensure that the data to be used for the exercise are free from major shortcomings and to decide upon methods by which the forecasts will be derived.

The data problems which need to be surmounted have been listed by Lowry (1966) in his study of population migration and comprise:

(i) Stability in the parameters of the movement models with small randomly spread errors.

(ii) Estimates of (a) the independent variables to be used in projecting the pattern of movement, and (b) the volume of movement to be distributed over the specified period.

(iii) Applicability of past parameters to future conditions.

The first of these has already been partly discussed in previous chapters. Comparing the cross-sectional models of interregional movement in Chapter 4, it was shown that these tended to change only marginally between one period and the next. Similarly, analysis of time series over different periods indicates that they, too, were relatively stable. However, the fact the differences did occur is significant, for we have an immediate source of error, albeit a small one. This is augmented by errors inherent in the movement models, none of which contained perfect correlations; residuals in one model would be passed on in a forecast. The second item is crucial, requiring known future values for dependent and independent variables. Retrospectively this poses no problem, but when the question concerns the pattern and volume of future movements the number of variables about which justifiable assumptions can be made is strictly limited. Likewise, major difficulties could be posed by the third. However, the factors of greatest importance in interregional movement in Britain were substantially the same throughout 1945–71, though they may have altered marginally in their influence from time to time. For short- and medium-term forecasts, therefore, it could confidently be assumed that similar relationships would continue.

5.1.2. *The Regional System*

From what has gone before it is possible to abstract a system in which changes in the volume and distribution of interregional movement are integrated through a set of simple relationships (Fig. 5.1). No doubt this scheme could be augmented and subdivided but, for the present at least, it serves to identify the main elements.

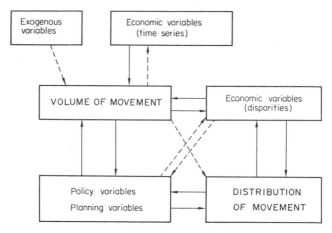

Fig. 5.1. A systematic view of changes in the volume and distribution of interregional movement.

Expressed in the language of general systems theory (Kast and Rosenzweig, 1970) this can be defined as an open system. It is also a contrived system because the bonds which secure it are social rather than physical or biological. The openness of the system goes without saying; inputs are received into the transformation system (i.e. industrial mobility) and converted into outputs which, via a feedback mechanism, in turn influence the inputs. It is, therefore, a system in continual interaction with its environment, tending towards a dynamic equilibrium with it. Consequently it is possible to predict or at least to give indicative estimates of the effect of changes in the inputs of the system.

The key to the system is that most of its relationships can be, and generally are, two-way linkages. Policy variables, for example, both influence and are influenced by the distribution of movement; the same is true of regional economic disparities. Only the effect of exogenous variables (e.g. industrial movement from foreign sources) can strictly be regarded as one way; it cannot be argued on any logical grounds that these variables are influenced by the volume and distribution of industrial movement within the national system. The links between regional disparities and policies have also been shown as indirect ones; disparities affect policies only when they conflict with social objectives and, conversely, policies influence disparities only when they succeed in diverting resources or creating new ones. It may appear surprising that a two-way linkage is postulated between the volume of movement and economic (time-series) variables, such as growth in industrial production. However, as Moore and Rhodes (1973) have demonstrated, where industrial movement brings into operation resources which would otherwise remain unemployed, there is a net gain to GDP. Their estimate of the effect of movement to the development areas during 1963–70 is that the benefit to the national economy lay between £400m and £500m per annum by 1970, or approximately 1% of GDP. They also considered that, on balance, this had a stabilizing effect, dampening down the fluctuations which we have shown to be influential on the time series of industrial movement.

With what is basically a circular system it might appear possible to break into it at any point. However, our reasoning hitherto has been that, given an evolving structure of industry, it is only necessary for there to be regional disparities for industrial movement to occur. This can be supported by recourse to urban land use models in which activities able to pay higher rents and demanding central locations are able, over the long term, to displace activities already located at the centre. Thus from the start it can be expected that the system generates a given volume and distribution of movement. It is not possible to make a precise calculation of this component, but it may be noted that when both policy inputs and economic inputs were at their lowest, in 1951/2 and 1957/8, the system generated about 100 interregional moves per annum. Some of these may have been directly attributable to development in the new towns, but generally it appears that the effect of that input was to divert movement rather than to raise the overall volume.

Above this base there was a fluctuating number of moves. Again with reference to the 1950s, when there was a very low expenditure on regional policy, a minor peak of about 200 moves was recorded in 1954/5 following a substantial rise in the rate of industrial growth. One might therefore conclude that an annual increase in manufacturing output of about 6–8% (the fastest recorded during 1945–65) would generate approximately 100 additional moves per annum. Moreover, there is evidence that an increasing volume of movement is associated with longer distance movement and vice versa, and that in an upswing the share going to peripheral areas increases. This is consistent with findings concerning the regional incidence of business cycles (Sant, 1973) which point to remoter areas generally being the more volatile. However, the reasoning behind the changing distribution of movement is not completely clear. It may be due to greater confidence following industrial growth, which in turn offsets the perceived risks of movement to more distant locations. The linkages in the system continue to the next major input, the role of policy. Given the existence of regional objectives (arising from welfare disparities or strategic planning) the options to the government, as far as industrial mobility is concerned, are to increase the volume, alter the distribution, or, most likely, a combination of the two courses. As already noted, the influence of new towns has tended to be to divert movement rather than to create it. The other policy inputs appear to have had both effects. Their ability to create movement is seen from the failure of the movement time series in 1962/3 to fall back to the 1958 level. In both years the economic inputs were sufficiently weak to have predicted a fall towards 100 moves. Instead the fall was so dampened that recorded movement was about 200. Thus at its peak the effect of policy expenditure before 1965 was probably to create up to 100 per annum more moves than would otherwise have occurred. But this input also influenced the distribution of movement, and there is some evidence of a diversionary effect. In 1960–5, for example, the non-metropolitan South East had a lower volume of movement than it had in 1952–9 (down 30%), as well as a falling share (down

45%). Conversely, the share going to peripheral areas rose faster than the numbers.

The above paragraphs refer to the inputs to the system. Evidence of the output lay beyond the scope of the preceding analysis, but the linkages can be inferred from events. Thus the policy in the 1940s resulted in both a high level of movement and a substantial diversion to the peripheral areas. The regional welfare objectives (i.e. the output) were believed to have been largely achieved, at least in the short term, and there was a justification for a relaxation of policy (McCrone, 1969). The new input from the early 1950s, therefore, was a weaker implementation of policy plus a preoccupation with new towns. Combined with a further, accelerated run-down in certain basic industries in the peripheral areas (e.g. textiles, shipbuilding, coalmining), the conditions were set, by the early 1960s, for a widening of regional disparities. Using the feedback mechanism of general systems theory, this provided a rationale for a strengthening of policy. The outcome of the new input was predictable in that it both raised and diverted movement to the assisted areas.

5.1.3. *Retrospective Forecasting: The Geographical Distribution*, 1960–5

In view of the requirements for usable forecasts outlined above, it is valuable to conduct experiments based on the origins and distributions of movement. This is done by deriving retrospective forecasts based on questions which presuppose differing degrees of knowledge about the system:

(i) What would have been the distribution of movement during 1960–5 on the basis of a simple projection of the distribution of 1952–9?

(ii) Given the statistical models of movement in 1952–9, described above (Chapter 4), what would have been the distribution during 1960–5 assuming that those models had been perfectly stable and that the regional parameters could be perfectly predicted?

Before forecasts can be derived, two adjustments are required. The first is to account for differences in length of period; 1960–5 was 25% shorter than 1952–9. The second is necessitated by the incidence of closure. The 1952–9 models are based on firms surviving to 1966, but these amounted only to 75% of the total number moving during 1952–9. Likewise, only 90% of the 1960–5 cohort survived until the end of 1966. Thus the overall adjustment needed to bring the forecast into line with the actual number of survivors is a downward shift of 10% from the predicted figure. This is applied across all forty-nine areas; although there is evidence that the incidence of closure varied between regions, it is not possible to allocate this accurately among areas.

It is necessary also to resolve which models should be used. The choice has been between those derived from all the identified variables (Table 4.1) and those using a limited number and between a simple model based on all regions and those based on subsets of regions. The first is relatively straightforward; the general models derived from all variables are substantially better at explaining movement. For the second, it has been argued that all regions together constitute an interacting system. However, experiments in the analysis of movement generation, in which areas were divided into two subsets (peripheral areas and the rest of Britain) yielded markedly better models. This arose because the peripheral areas, despite having 20% of the industrial employment in Britain, only gave rise to 5% of moves. On the other hand, the use of subsets for forecasting requires a more careful classification of areas than that implicit in this simple division into two basic categories. For example, there may be other significant subgroups and, over time, it might be necessary to alter their composition. Hence, for simplicity, the approach has been to use single-system models for both attraction and generation.

Firstly, it is clear that a forecast based on a simple projection of movement from one period to the next yields a very poor prediction when conditions are changing as rapidly as they were in the early 1960s. In this case there was an underprediction of about 30%. But although widely off the mark, this forecast deserves some attention, for it depicts roughly what might have been expected in the absence of any change in economic or structural variables.

The greater part of this discrepancy is taken up in the model-based forecasts; the short-fall from the generation and attraction models was, respectively, 6% and 5%. To some extent the extra volume of movement during 1960–5 can be attributed to the designation of enlarged development areas and of town expansion schemes. The residual could be due to computational errors, but equally it should be recalled that 1960–5 witnessed a rapid growth in expenditure on regional policy as well as marginally faster growth in manufacturing output, both of which are excluded from the cross-sectional models. Indeed, the geographical distribution of the residuals from the attraction forecast suggest that the incidence of policy expenditure played a major part in the discrepancies.

This indicates that while movement was created, especially to the

TABLE 5.1. SUMMARY OF 1960–5 CROSS-SECTIONAL FORECASTS BASED ON 1952–9 MODELS

Generation

Forecasting model[a]	Forecast	Actual	% Error
I Projection of 1952–9 moves	716	1008	−29
II Best fit regression model	960	1008	−6

Attraction

Forecasting model[a]	Forecast	Actual	% Error
I Projection of 1952–9 moves	778	1128	−31
II Best fit regression model	1077	1128	−5

[a] Models used in forecasts:

Generation
$$Y = 37 \cdot 1 + 0 \cdot 34\, X_1 - 0 \cdot 43\, X_{11} - 1 \cdot 17\, X_3 - 1 \cdot 88\, X_5 - 0 \cdot 69\, X_5$$
$$r^2 = 0 \cdot 84$$

Attraction
$$Y = 37 \cdot 7 + 1 \cdot 71\, X_{12} + 0 \cdot 44\, X_{17} + 1 \cdot 27\, X_{1a} + 0 \cdot 05\, X_{10} - 0 \cdot 15\, X_6$$
$$r^2 = 0 \cdot 80.$$

peripheral areas, the greater effect was a diversion to areas where the greater financial incentives were available. Whether this was detrimental to areas thus suffering a fall in incoming firms cannot be adequately answered at this point. The total volume diverted, when spread over many areas, may not have been great but in some areas it may have been the case that anticipated movement did not take place.

In the generation forecast the greatest errors of under-prediction were concentrated in South East England. Thus at a time when there was concern at the "drift" to the South East (Chisholm, 1964) and a recurrence of higher unemployment in Scotland and the North East, intervention concentrated on counteracting the drift by tapping the main source of industrial movement. In contrast a number of other major urban-industrial areas which might have been expected to contribute more, were, in fact, over-predicted. This was clearest in the West Midlands, but also occurred in the Nottingham/Derby area, the West Riding, and Bristol. Continued growth of the new towns in the Essex/Hertfordshire/Bedfordshire area was mainly responsible for actual movement generated being less than the forecast.

Regional discrimination appears to have been even more clear-cut in the attraction forecasts. Over-predicted areas occupied the central axial belt from Greater London to the North West and West Riding, under-predicted areas lay around the periphery. All of the development areas gained substantially more than forecast, due to the higher financial incentives. Norfolk and Suffolk and Kent and Sussex, with their town expansion schemes and small pockets designated as DATAC areas, had two of the largest residuals in the country, and central Lancashire—favourably treated to make up for the contraction of the cotton industry—also attracted more than was forecast. At the other end of the spectrum most areas in the South East attracted fewer moves than expected, partly because their new towns had all come close to meeting their initial target populations but mainly because of the diversionary effects of policy. In the East Midlands, Northamptonshire provided the largest single over-prediction in the country. There the main growth centre, Corby New Town, had not only come close to meeting its target in the early 1960s but it was also dominated by a single employer (a major steel company), so that in terms of employment rather than number of moves it had a relatively small residual.

5.2. Long-term Prospects for Mobility in the United Kingdom

The deduction of the future state of industrial mobility, by applying expected long-term trends in selected phenomena to our present understanding of their relationships with movement, is useful in providing a broad scenario against which to plan and act. In the present context the method involves, on the one hand, the relationships between industrial movement and its various correlates and, on the other hand, the extrapolated volume of employment in manufacturing, its organization in establishments and companies, its industrial composition and technological base, its place in regional planning, and so on. The main groups of factors are listed (not exhaustively) in Table 5.2. Many of the items listed there, it must be admitted, are barely foreseeable in the near future, and still less over several decades. Nevertheless, it is useful to continue the discussion in terms of trends and possible new developments up to the end of the twentieth century—the end point for many regional plans and strategies currently being produced.

At the outset, it is valuable to distinguish between changes in the volume or direction of movement associated with a linear trend and changes which are likely to be sharp, bringing about a new trend at a higher or lower absolute level. For example, in Fig. 5.2 we might assume that over time the ratio between movement and employment is stable, with employment growing steadily, giving the curve AA to describe the volume of movement. At a point in time (t_1) a sharp change occurs in, for example, incentives to locate in assisted areas, the curve describing movement shifts to a new plane (BB) and continues with a course parallel to the earlier one. This is, of course, an hypothetical case, but it is analogous with the division of variables in the time-series analysis discussed earlier. There, variables were divided into two sets—structural and economic—to deal with the overall level of movement and short-term fluctuations. Here fluctuations are abstracted, but the lesson is the same.

TABLE 5.2. CLASSIFICATION OF SELECTED SOURCES OF
CHANGE IN LONG-TERM INTERREGIONAL MOBILITY

1. *Growth of manufacturing sector*
    (i)   Employment
    (ii) Output and productivity

2. *Restructuring of industry*
    (i)   Company organization
    (ii) Size of plant
    (iii) Industrial composition
    (iv) Costs of production and distribution
    (v)   Technical change

3. *Environmental change*
    (i)   Regional factor price differentials
    (ii) Urban diseconomies
    (iii) Transport costs

4. *Regional policy and planning*
    (i)   Incentives and controls
    (ii) New town schemes
    (iii) Urban redevelopment

5. *Miscellaneous factors*
    (i)   Trade policy
    (ii) Resource exhaustion and substitution

However, Fig. 5.2 is extremely simplified. There is no reason why
the trend should be a straight line; neither can one necessarily expect
the intervention of a new factor to cause a single, easily identifiable
shift. Nevertheless, it provides a useful basis for classifying the
factors which have an influence upon the shape and level of the graph
and helps to answer questions of major concern. It may be added
that these are intended only to account for the long-term picture,
and no consideration is given to cyclical fluctuations.

It might be argued that the fundamental constraint on the volume
of movement is the size of the manufacturing sector. Certainly there
is circumstantial evidence of this control in the relationship between
(i) movement generated and employment per area, and (ii) movement
generated and the growth of industries (Townroe, 1973). However, it
is equally possible to postulate that even in the absence of any growth

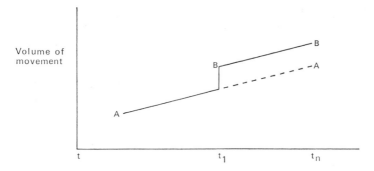

F<small>IG</small>. 5.2.   Hypothetical model of long-term trends in industrial movement.

in the manufacturing sector as a whole, there may be considerable movement resulting from the restructuring of the sector or from the response of industry to changes in regional economic disparities. Likewise, there could be movement without any such changes in industry or in environmental factors as long as changes in regional attraction could be induced through government policy or if shifts in the distribution or use of resources take place.

If the trend in mobility were controlled by the size of the manufacturing sector alone, then it could be predicted with some confidence that the slope of our hypothetical graph would be extremely shallow. Between 1951 and 1971 employment in manufacturing increased by only about 0·5 million, or less than 7%. Forecasts to the end of the century have varied, along with alterations in expected population growth (Department of the Environment, 1971), but it seems reasonable to expect no more than 1 million, and probably not much more than 0·5 million additional manufacturing jobs by 2001. This low rate of increase is attributable partly to the slow population growth found in Britain, but is also due to the tendency for manufacturing to expand less quickly than the service sector. Indeed, the tertiary activities are regarded as increasingly important sources of mobile industry (Rhodes and Kan, 1971), although it is necessary to guard against too much optimism that they will become the main instrument of interregional movement.

The second set of factors, concerned with changes in the structure of industry, is extremely difficult to evaluate. The character of manufacturing as a whole undergoes a continual evolution; new activities replace old ones, productivity increases, factors of production are used in different combinations, and so on. As Townroe (1973) has shown, industries are most likely to generate movement when they are growing fastest; and in Table 5.3, it is shown that the first and last quartiles in the growth ratings of industries (Minimum List Headings) were responsible for 53% and 5% respectively of the total movement. However, the question which must now be asked is whether the industries presently growing most, and hence likely eventually to dominate the British economy, have intrinsic characteristics which differ from those of the industries being replaced. If they do differ, the next step is to draw inferences about whether the new composition is likely to be more or less mobile than the old. At this point, however, very considerable difficulties arise, making it necessary to assume that inferences drawn from a static cross-sectional view of industry derived from the 1963 census of production give a reasonably accurate description of likely long-term trends.

A large number of factors could be included in a list describing the process of industrial restructure. In Table 5.3, however, attention is concentrated on components of industrial inputs and outputs in an attempt to see which items, if any, appear to be changing in importance. The first observation is that few industrial characteristics show a regular shift across the spectrum of quartiles defined by growth rates, although there is a number of major distinctions between extremes. Comparing growth industries with those that were static or declining, it is seen that the former has lower proportions of gross output (i.e. total sales less changes in stocks or inventories) attributable to the cost of inputs and a higher proportion attributable to value added or net output (i.e. processing within the industry plus distribution to customers). Likewise, the composition of net output exhibited broad differences between the groups. The growth industries tended to incur lower transport costs and to spend proportionately less on wages and salaries. Comparing the importance of international trade to the groups, it is also seen that the former exported a greater proportion of net output, but imported less of its

TABLE 5.3. INDUSTRIAL CHARACTERISTICS, EMPLOYMENT CHANGE AND INDUSTRIAL MOVEMENT

	By rates of growth			
	Upper quartile	Second quartile	Third quartile	Lower quartile
1. Per cent of UK employment, 1953	24	26	25	25
2. Employment change (%), 1953–66	47	22	0	−30
3. Per cent movement generated (approximately), 1952–65	53	25	17	5
4. Gross output *per capita*, 1963 (UK = 100)	84	102	128	87
5. Fuel costs, (% gross output), 1963:				
(a) Total	1·5	3·0	2·7	3·2
(b) Coal and coke	0·3	0·7	1·1	1·4
6. Material costs (% gross output)	39·6	44·3	49·8	52·3
7. Net output (% gross output)	47·5	42·3	30·5	36·3
8. Net output *per capita*, 1963 (UK = 100)	103	112	101	82
9. Transport cost (% net output)	3·9	3·9	6·9	6·6
10. Labour costs (% net output):				
(a) Wages	34·1	35·7	36·0	46·3
(b) Total	51·4	50·7	52·8	61·2
11. Per cent employment in small firms (1963)	6·6	5·8	6·9	4·6
12. Mean employment per establishment (1963)	177	268	194	180
13. Exports/net output (UK = 100), 1963	92	132	73	87
14. Imports/primary inputs (UK = 100), 1963	75	75	157	123
15. Per cent sales to consumers and public authorities, 1963	23	23	42	33
16. Per cent sales to intermediate output (two leading sectors), 1963	31	45	44 (34)[a]	57
17. Per cent purchase from leading sectors (two leading sectors), 1963	38	35	40 (50)[a]	47

[a] Excludes tobacco.

Source: census of production.

primary inputs (i.e. materials only; services are not included). In so far as it is possible to identify trends over time, it appears that the proportion of gross output attributable to value added has increased steadily in recent decades (from 33% in 1951 to 43% in 1968) and that the change has been most marked among the growth industries. Conversely, the labour cost component of net output has tended to fall, though relatively slowly (from 55% in 1951 to 50% in 1968). Concurrent with these changes, there appear also to have been shifts in the configuration of sales and purchases, with growth industries having less concentrated markets and suppliers. A lower proportion of total output from this group consisted of sales to consumers and public authorities on current account; by corollary a higher proportion was sold as intermediate products to other industries, for investment, or as exports. At the same time, though geared more closely to intermediate markets, sales from the growth industries tended to be diversified among a greater number of industrial sectors. In this group less than one-third of such sales went to the two main purchasing industries; by contrast, in the group with declining employment the proportion was well over a half. A similar variation is found in the degree to which purchases were concentrated among industries. The declining industries appear to have more specialized sources of supply than the growing industries.

Evidence concerning the size of establishments gives less-clear differences. In terms of numbers employed, establishments in the growth industries were above average size, though the highest quartile (which may have had the greater potential for further concentration) still had marginally the smallest average in 1963. On the other hand, between 1951 and 1963 the faster growing industries tended to have the greater increase in employment per establishment, although only in the most extreme cases, such as motor-vehicle manufacture, were the impact of economies of scale particularly notable. During this time the average employment for all manufacturing establishments (except those with fewer than twenty-five employees) increased from 128 to 144. In addition there appears to have been a marked change in floorspace per worker in recent years. A survey by the (then) Board of Trade indicated average gross figures of 256 ft^2 and 263 ft^2 in 1960 and 1966 respectively for all manufacturing and 247 ft² and 264 ft² for growing establishments. Thus, marginal increments of factory space are used with lower labour-intensity, the difference being about 7%. However, three points should be made about these figures. First, they relate to a very short period over which it is unrealistic to expect a large change in factory size. Second, floorspace and employment figures should be compounded. For example, a 10% increase in both gives rise to an increase in total floorspace required of more than 20% which, for large firms in urban locations, constitutes a major change. Third, these floorspace figures take no account of the configuration of factories and note should be taken of the ratio between floorspace and curtilage (the total land owned or leased by the firm). Thus, new factories have their production almost totally confined to a single floor; a survey by Stone (1962) suggests that this was so in over four-fifths of factories built between 1945 and 1960.

A third source of change in industrial structure is the development of corporate organizations controlling large numbers of plants, often dispersed among several different industries. These, it has been argued (Steed. 1971), are more flexible in their actions and more able to develop locational strategies which reflect regional differentials and opportunities. According to the 1963 census of production, the sales of only 24% of a selected list of 271 products were less concentrated in the leading five firms making each product in 1963 than they had been in 1958, and most of those were only marginally different. On the other hand, among the remainder there were cases of greatly increased concentration. For example, in 1958 the five leading television manufacturers accounted for half the sales; in 1963 they held over four-fifths: in the baking industry less than one-third of bread sales was made by the five leaders in 1958, whereas in 1963 the figures exceeded 70%. Concentration of output within a few companies might be expected to be accompanied by agglomeration of plants, as happened during the development of the motor industry, for example; this requires that economies of scale should outweigh all other considerations. However, there is not sufficient evidence to show that the present trend is overwhelmingly in this direction. What appears to have occurred in recent years is some growth at the upper end of the size distribution of establishments, plus a considerable volume of mergers and takeovers, but also a significant volume of branch establishments. Another effect which might ensue from concentration within major companies has been noted by Parsons (1972), namely the trend towards separation of control functions from operating units.

The third main group of factors affecting mobility consists of environmental changes such as developments in the regional differences of factor supplies and costs, trends in urban economies and diseconomies, and alterations in the structure of transport costs. None of these is easily defined or measured, but superficially there seems to be no reason for believing that their directions of change will be such as to reduce the volume of movement. Regional differences in labour costs (ignoring possible variations in productivity or cost per unit output) and land values do not appear to have been reduced in recent years, but to have slightly widened. Incomes from employment (Schedule E) increased relative to the national mean during 1949–64 in the south of England but tended to decrease in the north and in Scotland, though the pattern was partly reversed in the latter part of the period, testifying to some success in regional policies (Coates and Rawstron, 1971). Commercial and industrial land values are rather more complex, with differential trends within, as well as between, regions. In so far as it is possible to measure the changes, it appears that the gap in values of equivalent sites in different regions has widened (Rhodes and Kan, 1971).

Urban development in recent decades has been described by Hall (1968, 1973) as having two main features. Firstly, areas defined as Metropolitan Economic Labour Areas have held an almost constant share of population and employment in Britain; secondly, within these areas there has been considerable decentralization, especially of population. Among the industrial sectors there appears to have been centralization in the service sector, only partially offset by decentralization in manufacturing. The causal chain behind this process is fairly complicated, and contains sociological motivations as well as economic competition for urban space (Garner, 1967) but, in central place terminology, it appears that much manufacturing has become, for a variety of reasons, a low-order activity neither requiring, nor desired (by planners), to be in central locations. Despite protestations, particularly in London (Eversley, 1973), that the process leads to a danger that cities are losing revenue and character and being laid open to "ghetto"-like problems, it seems realistic to agree with Hall that decentralization is likely to continue in the foreseeable future.

The fourth group of factors consists of possible changes in the content and effect of regional policy. The treatment of assisted areas has been successively strengthened in legislation through the last four decades without either achieving the long-term goals set for it or exhausting the variety and intensity of incentives and controls open to use. It would not be unrealistic to assume that, as long as goals remain unfulfilled, the level of action by central governments will continue to be raised. The same consideration applies to the development of new towns to replace the derelict housing stock of major conurbations and siphon off their projected growth. There is no doubt that their "greenfield" industrial sites and relatively large (at least initially) supplies of labour are attractive levers to induce mobile establishments to locate there and since their designation is usually associated with redevelopment in metropolitan areas supply of industry is virtually assured.

To gain some impression of the likely trend in regional policies or, at least, the trend necessary if present targets are to be fulfilled, it is worth enumerating the targets of some of the more important projects and strategies. Thus, at the start of 1971, the new towns designated by that date had added about 700,000 inhabitants to the areas in which they were located. This population growth was accompanied by an increase in manufacturing employment of about 170,000, or about one job per four persons. At the same date, the additional population planned in the new town schemes in existence amounted to a further 1·4 million. Assuming the same ratio between population and manufacturing employment, this means that about 350,000 jobs will need to be created, mainly through industrial movement. In the assisted areas it is difficult to identify a specific target, but if we assume that one objective is to reduce unemployment to the national average level of recent years, an estimate can be attempted of the number of jobs needing to be created. Between 1959 and 1969 national unemployment averaged about 2·1%; in the four standard regions (Scotland, Wales, Northern Ireland, and Northern England),

I.M.R.D.—G

containing the main development areas, the average ranged from 3·3% to 7·1%. In absolute terms, this difference represents about 100,000 jobs. If, alternatively, some other objectives were to be met (such as raising incomes or activity rates), the figure would be placed even higher. Ridley's (1972) estimate of the needs of three other employment requirements in the main assisted areas (Scotland, Wales, Northern England, Yorkshire and Humberside, and the North West) include the following: (i) to equalize female activity rates with the national average: 250,000 jobs. (ii) To meet the natural increase in labour supply at current (1951–71) rates of migration: 350,000. (iii) To meet the projected run down of basic industries (coal, steel, textiles, shipbuilding, heavy engineering): 300,000. Added to the unemployment objective this gives a total target, which Ridley regarded as necessary for the 1970s, of more than 1 million jobs. To these readily identifiable quantities may be added the objectives of a number of regional strategies and *ad hoc* plans, which may not contribute much to long-distance movement but will influence the intraregional allocation of industry. Thus, the *Strategic Plan for the South East* (South-east Joint Planning Team, 1971) proposed the containment of its expansion within selected major growth areas. Even so, considerable industrial mobility would be required simply to meet the targets suggested for these areas; the Plan concluded that about 30,000–40,000 mobile jobs might be needed each year between 1981 and 1991. Most of these would probably originate in Greater London, but planners in that area have argued in favour of a higher rate of industrial growth (Donnison and Eversley, 1973).

These examples by no means exhaust the list of possible demands on mobility in the United Kingdom for the foreseeable future: most areas, whether or not they benefit from assisted area status or new town programmes, compete in some way for industry (Camina, 1974), and many of them are very active in their search. Together, their total demand for mobile jobs probably exceeds supply by a large margin, so that it is almost certain that many of them will be left with unfulfilled ambitions. Given this situation, it is equally almost certain that legislation to increase mobility will be strengthened. But whether increased expenditure on regional incentives would yield a proportionate increase in industrial movement is another question.

The critical question of what expenditure on regional policy is necessary to induce an extra move to a development area is, unfortunately, impossible to answer in an adequate manner. The answer depends on the nature of the areas generating movement, the character of firms, and the comparative disadvantages of development area locations. However, it might be expected that a condition of diminishing returns to extra marginal inducements operates beyond a certain level. To illustrate this, assume that the opportunity cost of moving every industrial establishment is known and that these are ranked from highest to lowest. With this information, we could then calculate the amount of inducement necessary to make each one relocate. Now if every firm had the same opportunity cost the problem of diminishing returns would not arise; the marginal cost of moving the second and subsequent establishments would be the same as the first. However, establishments vary in many ways, and it must be expected that they present an array of opportunity costs. Thus the most footloose will require the least inducement, and vice versa. Of course, this is a highly simplified situation, taking no account of different ways of supplying inducements to movement. For example, the same sum expended on cash grants or rent-free factories may be more effective than repayable inducements. It is also likely that the absolute sum expended is less significant than the relative differential created between locations. The two measures do tend to be correlated but not so closely that they are interchangeable as measures of inducement. Nevertheless, we can deduce that diminishing marginal returns to a particular instrument of policy are likely to occur at some point.

Evidence of this relationship is not available over a long enough period to be conclusive, but it is possible to estimate the assistance given per job under the Local Employment Act between 1963 and 1973 (Table 5.4). Giving the ten-year average an index of 100, it can be seen that the Exchequer cost fell to 60 in 1966, indicating the effectiveness of the policy in the early 1960s, after which it increased steadily until 1973 when it stood at 148. We should emphasize, moreover, that this expenditure excludes investment grants and the regional employment premium which were introduced in 1967 and which accounted for over two-thirds of the total expenditure thereafter.

TABLE 5.4. ASSISTANCE APPROVED UNDER THE LOCAL EMPLOYMENT ACT AND EMPLOYMENT ESTIMATED TO ARISE FROM ASSISTED PROJECTS, 1963–73

Year	Assistance (£m)	Employment ('000)	Index of cost per job
1963–4	54·16	57·58	94
1964–5	72·81	82·98	88
1965–6	75·86	127·41	60
1966–7	99·38	118·71	84
1967–8	83·26	92·85	90
1968–9	98·46	103·49	95
1969–70	150·34	133·30	113
1970–1	125·84	115·46	109
1971–2	115·73	84·97	136
1972–3	124·15	83·95	148
1963–73	557·75	725·98	100

Source: annual reports of the Local Employment Act.

Finally, the fifth set of factors, though they might have been classified along with environmental changes, have been separated since they represent alterations in the economic landscape which are finite rather than evolutionary. Thus, in this category are included the exhaustion and substitution of raw materials and the creation of new trading conditions; for example, through the joining of the European Economic Community. Changes in the use of raw materials, either through exhaustion of old sources or exploitation of new ones, have been responsible for some mobility in the past, but this appears to be becoming a decreasingly important factor. Fewer industries are now directly concerned with processing raw materials and, in a growing number, more materials are being imported, so that a change in source of supply has little significance for a firm located in the

United Kingdom. One could argue that, in effect, the source of supply is the port of landing, and as long as this stays the same there is little or no incentive for the firm to move.

The creation of a new trade block has, in theory at least, important implications for industrial location (Meade, 1955), since the removal of tariffs within the bloc and their realignment around it lead to a new set of locational conditions and a new set of trading links. Compared with the patterns of trade between other European countries and the rest of the world, that of the United Kingdom can only be described as widely anomalous (due, of course, to its historical connections with the Commonwealth). As described by Alexandersson and Nostrom (1963), the former group have a pattern which fits well to a gravity model of interaction, with trade between pairs of countries closely influenced by size (GNP) and proximity; by contrast, Britain's trade has no such relationship. However, membership of the EEC will almost certainly cause a new British interaction model, more like that of its partners, and in the process it may be that many firms will place a greater value on east-coast locations which, it has been shown by Clark (1969), have a higher market potential. A further factor, investigated by Smidt (1966), concerns the movement of industry into the Community from other countries (especially the United States). In the period 1957–64 there was some evidence that these firms sought locations well situated to serve most, if not all, of the EEC (Forsyth, 1972). If the same pattern continues, the implications for movement into the United Kingdom may be considerable. Peripheral areas within the United Kingdom (which gained most from movement from abroad) are even more peripheral in terms of their relationship to the Community. On the other hand, low labour costs, plus historical ties of language, may make these areas relatively attractive.

In any strict sense it is impossible to make an accurate evaluation of the combined impact of these forces of change. However, it is possible to suggest a range of alternatives within which the most likely long-term trend will be found. Thus there seem no strong grounds for believing that industrial mobility will fall in the foreseeable future (except during short-term cyclical fluctuations) nor that it will increase dramatically. Most of the important changes described above are likely to involve, firstly, a greater intrinsic propensity to move in manufacturing firms and, secondly, fewer barriers and more incentives to interregional movement. Offsetting these, the main factor which may constrain growth in mobility is the possible exhaustion of sources of movement if, for example, the main conurbations have their central population and manufacturing employment so reduced that industry is no longer "pushed" out with such velocity by rising costs and planned redevelopment. Conceivably, a time could come when the only industry leaving such areas is that associated with the natural growth of firms. However, it could be argued that the role of conurbations as industrial seedbeds will continue to be great, and that in order to maintain them at their planned populations there will continue to be a high rate of industrial overspill.

CHAPTER 6

The Impact of Industrial Movement

THE purpose of this chapter is to carry forward the discussion from a review of the impact of policy on industrial movement to an investigation of the effect of industrial movement upon regional development.

Policies are not immutable, even when there is a consensus about their importance. Rather, they are subject to pressures to change from at least two directions. Firstly, the objectives which policies are designed to serve may themselves change; secondly, the instruments which serve a policy may become more or less efficient, or may be seen to be less efficient than first hoped. Thus we are concerned here with the implications of the findings in this study and of current trends in regional development and of possible exogenous forces for the continued evolution of regional policy in Britain. The last is, of course, a most complicated question: objectives, policies, and instruments can all change simultaneously. After the closing of the earlier records (1945–65) on which our analyses are based, there were important changes in the instruments of policy culminating in the Industry Act 1972 (Cmnd 4942), placing greater emphasis on the development of indigenous industry, the movement of non-manufacturing establishments, and increased spending on infrastructure. The position was reached in 1974 where a substantial proportion of the sum expended under the various policy instruments went to projects other than mobile manufacturing firms. This shift is in line with some of the implications of our analysis, particularly in regard to meeting short-term objectives, but there are other implications which deserve further investigation.

6.1. Regional Policy and Industrial Movement

In addition to this study, which treats regional policy variables as part of the input to a general system of industrial mobility, there have been others which estimate the effects of policy on movement more directly. Some of these have been expressed in general terms (Beacham and Osborne, 1970; Keeble, 1971), but a number have attempted to quantify the effect. Among these the two most important are by Moore and Rhodes (1973) and by Brown (1972); in addition, Cameron and Clarke (1966) have provided a survey from which it is possible to abstract an estimate of the effect of policy. An interesting point about all of these is that they employed different estimation techniques, yet at the same time they yield results which are consistent.

Cameron and Clarke, in their survey of firms locating in Scotland, asked whether the decision to move there had been taken in spite of a preference to develop at or near their existing locations. In other words, was long-distance movement made inevitable by the combination of a refusal of an industrial development certificate and an offer of financial inducement by the government? Many firms in their sample did, in fact, fall into this category, accounting in total for 81% of the employment in the sample. The figure for firms locating in other assisted areas closer to the main sources of movement is probably lower, but if we use this proportion to give an upper estimate of employment created in the assisted areas as a result of movement induced by policy, the outcome (based on the Department of Trade and Industry record) is more than 400,000 by 1971. Of these, 140,000 were in moves which occurred after 1960, and were therefore in establishments which were still growing.

Moore and Rhodes (1973) do not differentiate between movement of establishments and other sources of growth in assisted areas because their analysis includes the period, in the later 1960s, when regional policy expenditure was being used to create employment in indigenous firms. However, it can be inferred that movement provided the greater part of the change. Their approach is to establish an association between policy measures and the behaviour of regional manufacturing employment and investment. Firstly, they measure the strength of postwar regional economic policies, identifying periods of passive and active implementation. The year 1963 is identified as the keypoint in the transition from the former to the latter. They next analyse changes in employment in the main development areas (Scotland, Wales, Northern England, and Northern Ireland) and the United Kingdom as a whole, on an annual basis between 1950 and 1971. These are structurally adjusted time series, using a "shift and share" technique to take account of regional differences in industrial composition; all manufacturing industries except shipbuilding and metal manufacture are included. The first received a substantial amount of direct public investment, while the second underwent nationalization in 1967. For the development areas this series provides a good guide to trends during the period of passive policy up to 1963; the structurally adjusted national and regional series almost moved in unison (Fig. 6.1). After 1963 the two series diverged markedly, so that by 1971 manufacturing employment in the development areas was about 12% higher than it would have been if policy had continued to be passive. To corroborate that this

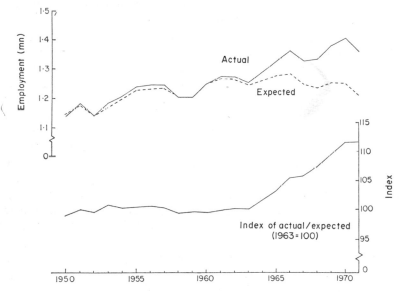

FIG. 6.1. Actual and expected employment in manufacturing industries (excluding shipbuilding and metals), composite development areas, 1951–70.

was the effect of policy, a similar analysis was carried out for manufacturing in the South East and Midlands and for non-manufacturing activities in the development areas. The first showed these two source areas to have had structurally adjusted falls in manufacturing employment after 1963. The second indicated that while structurally adjusted changes in the non-manufacturing sector (which was barely touched by regional policy) had a very minor upward divergence in the development areas, this is consistent with the multiplier effect of growth in manufacturing. On this evidence, Moore and Rhodes concluded that the net employment created in manufacturing during 1963–70 in the main development areas amounted to 150,000 jobs. To this can be added employment generated in shipbuilding and metal manufacture (estimated to be less than 10,000 jobs), the regional policy effect in Merseyside and South West England, the two development areas excluded from the analysis (33,000), and the indirect, or multiplier, effects on non-manufacturing. Assuming an employment multiplier of 1·15, the last item contributed a further 30,000. Thus the total for 1963–70 comes to about 220,000.

Brown (1972) derived an estimate of the benefit to development areas from a series of simple calculations. Employment in development areas in establishments for which an industrial development certificate was necessary rose from about 20,000 per annum in the late 1950s to 70,000 in the late 1960s. The increase (50,000) then has to be adjusted for the upward national trend which, *ex hypothesis*, amounted to about 12,000 jobs, giving a direct effect of the intensification of policy on employment in the development areas of 38,000 per annum, which is consistent with the Moore and Rhodes estimate of 220,000 jobs induced by policy during 1963–70. Brown also estimates that less than half the increase was attributable to industrial movement (15,000 jobs); the remainder was expansion and new investment carried out by firms already located in the development areas.

These estimates are roughly consistent with those which can be derived from our time-series analysis described in Chapter 3. In the national series the estimated regression coefficient indicates about 2·5 moves per additional million pounds (at 1963 costs) of exchequer cost prior to 1965. By the mid 1960s, therefore, policy-induced movement accounted for an estimated 100 establishments per annum, leading to employment of about 15,000–20,000. Thereafter, the situation became more complex as a result of new types of inducement (e.g. the regional employment premium) and the possibility of diminishing marginal returns from movement, but it is likely that the policy-induced component continued to rise.

6.2. Regional Indicators and the Impact of Industrial Movement

Increasingly, it has come to be accepted that there is no single individual criterion by which to assess progress towards regional objectives, just as there is no single criterion by which to measure regional welfare. Indeed, the Hunt Committee, in its analysis prior to recommending the designation of intermediate areas (1969), investigated twelve different criteria of regional disparities. Although it could be claimed that some in that list were of dubious quality and difficult to justify, if considered individually, their interpretation as a set provided a valuable picture of social and economic conditions. A similar set can be used to investigate the trends in different regions to see whether differences are narrowing or increasing. Those selected here are: incomes, unemployment, activity rates, migration, and industrial composition. The general picture described by these is a mixed one: some factors indicate improvement but others do not. The latter group contains the main welfare indicators: incomes, unemployment, and migration, all of which show little relative change. To some degree it is possible to hold that the changes so far brought about in industrial composition presage further improvements in the position of the assisted areas, but in view of the quantity of jobs created (about 440,000 between 1945 and 1965 and 80,000 in 1966–71) through industrial movement, it is important to ask why disparities still remain.

Of course, the simple direct answer is that industrial development has been insufficient to create the demand for labour necessary to remove them. Much of the extra employment found in mobile and growing firms has, in any case, been offset by closures in declining industries (Lloyd, 1970). However, while acknowledging these reasons, there are others of great significance arising from the nature of the impact of new firms in assisted areas.

6.2.1. *Regional Indicators*

Data on *per capita* earned incomes show that in the early 1970s the gap between less and more prosperous areas was as large as it had been in the late 1940s. Care is needed in explaining this, since it might be due to the creation of new, lower paid jobs (e.g. for women), but overall the most likely reason has been the continued failure of effective demand for labour to match supply. Excluding Merseyside, the peripheral areas contained the whole or the greater proportion of thirty-four British counties or sets of counties on which the Inland Revenue published sources are based (Coates and Rawstron, 1971). The distribution does show some improvement which coincides with the increase in expenditure on regional policy since 1960. The figures for 1959–60, compared with 1964–5, show that sixteen counties improved their position and only fourteen actually lost ground. The unweighted average index of the thirty-four areas at these two dates shows that the earnings in the peripheral areas were 87% and 89% of the national average. Also they appeared at least to gain further ground between 1965 and 1970; nineteen counties improved their standing, while only nine fell back. However, these gains have been marginal and do not offset the earlier relative decline. In 1964–5, twenty-six counties were further behind the national mean than they had been in 1949–50 when the unweighted index stood at 90% of the national average. Of these, seven were in Wales, which had gained proportionately more through industrial movement than any other major assisted region.

The second key indicator is unemployment rates. In particular, interest lies in the ratio and differences between assisted areas and the rest of the country. If job creation through industrial movement reduces unemployment substantially, then there ought to be a marked fall in the ratio between the two groups of regions. However, this can be offset by the supply of labour being disproportionately increased, either by new workers coming on to the market or by a higher rate of closure or labour shedding among existing industries. Over the long period, despite a rate of natural increase of population

in the assisted areas near or equal to the national average, the net
effect has not been a closing of differentials. As Fig. 6.2 shows, the
changes which have taken place have been cyclical and there is an
absence of a significant trend. When the national rate has been high,
the ratio has tended to be low (Spearman $R = -0.80$). Similarly,
there is a high correlation, this time positive ($R = 0.85$), between the
national rate and the difference between development areas and the
national rate.

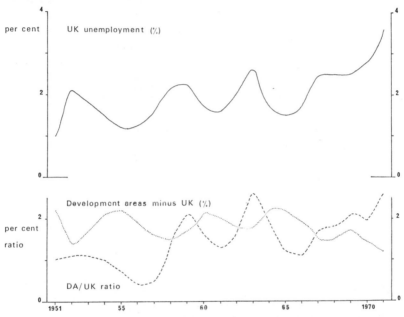

Fig. 6.2. Unemployment rates, differences and ratios in the development areas and the United Kingdom, 1951–70.

On the other hand, activity rates present a different picture. Here
disparities have been reduced substantially (Bowers, 1970), due
mainly to regional variations in the growth of female labour forces.
Lower-than-average female activity rates have been a characteristic
of most development areas. Compared with a national rate of 36·3%
in 1954, the figures in the North, Wales, and Scotland were, respect-

ively, 29·6%, 25·0%, and 36·3%. By 1964, Scotland (38·8%) still had about the national average (39·2%), but the North (33·2%) and Wales (28·9%) had each caught up a percentage point. By 1970 the disparities had closed even more and Scotland had overtaken the national average (40·9% compared with 40·0%). Male activity rates, however, remained fairly static in all regions.

Migration patterns are difficult to identify due to their relatively infrequent collection and the occurrence of movements from abroad; patterns reported during censal years may differ from the norm by substantial amounts. Nevertheless, the overall figures of estimated net migration do provide a good indicator of differentials in regional welfare. Between 1951 and 1969 the development areas, almost without exception, continued to lose population through migration (Table 6.1), and there was no tendency for the loss to slow down, taking all areas together. Wales gained population in the early 1960s, but had reverted to a net loss in the second part of the decade, while the South West registered a net gain, especially after 1966. In these two instances, however, the gains were associated less with economic opportunities than with retirement. A second useful synopsis is provided by the net balances of interregional migration to and from the South East and West Midlands of persons of working age (i.e. men aged 15–64 and women aged 15–59) in the 12 months before the 1966 census (Table 6.2). Both regions lost marginally more than they gained; 132,000 left the South East against 126,000 who entered, and in the West Midlands a gain of 46,000 was more than offset by a loss of 49,000. However, this was regionally selective; the South East lost to East Anglia, the South West and East Midlands, but gained from all the development areas, especially Scotland. The West Midlands had a similar distribution of gains and losses. These migration patterns largely account for the differences in growth of total population. Between 1951 and 1969 the development areas increased their numbers by about 3·4% compared with about 14·1% in the rest of the country. If there had been no migration, a differential would still have occurred, due to the slightly slower rates of natural increase in most development areas as a result of their above-average age structures and the distribution of overseas immigrants, but it would have been considerably smaller.

TABLE 6.1. NET INTERNAL MIGRATION AND NATURAL INCREASE IN POPULATION, BY STANDARD REGION, 1951–70

| | Net migration | | | Natural increase | Total change as per cent of 1951 population |
| | Annual average change ('000) | | Total ('000) | | |
	1951–61	1961–70	1951–70	1951–70	
North	−8·0	−5·6	−130·4	+353·2	7·1
Yorks	−9·6	−7·3	−161·7	+435·3	6·1
East Midlands	+3·9	+6·1	+93·9	+358·7	12·4
East Anglia	+2·7	+13·1	+144·9	+140·1	20·1
South East	+43·8	+3·8	+472·2	+1578·4	13·4
South West	+9·9	+21·3	+290·7	+243·6	16·4
West Midlands	+4·7	+6·1	+101·9	+636·9	16·7
Wales	−4·9	+0·5	−44·5	+174·0	5·0
North West	−12·4	−8·6	−201·4	+544·6	5·3
Scotland	−28·2	−35·4	−600·6	+655·8	1·1

TABLE 6.2. NET MIGRATION TO THE SOUTH EAST AND WEST MIDLANDS, 1965–6 (MALES AGED 15–64; FEMALES AGED 15–59) ('000)

A. *South East*

	Net gain	Net loss
Northern	1·08	
Yorkshire and Humberside	0·84	
East Midlands		2·30
East Anglia		7·33
South West		7·10
Wales	1·16	
West Midlands	1·84	
North West	1·38	
Scotland	4·44	
	10·74	16·73

B. *West Midlands*

	Net gain	Net loss
Northern	1·14	
Yorkshire and Humberside		0·44
East Midlands		1·13
East Anglia		0·07
South East		1·84
South West		2·37
Wales	0·46	
North West		1·08
Scotland	1·77	
	3·37	6·93

Source: Sample census 1966.

Changes in employment include a number of facets. Aggregate employment grew slowly in the development areas through the 1950s, falling considerably behind the rest of the country (Table 6.3). After

TABLE 6.3. EMPLOYMENT CHANGES[a], IN THE UNITED KINGDOM
AND SELECTED STANDARD REGIONS 1950–72 (1950 = 100)

	United Kingdom	Scotland	Wales	North
1950	100·0	100·0	100·0	100·0
1954	101·8	101·7	101·7	101·7
1958	105·4	101·0	104·1	105·0
1962	110·8	102·8	106·9	105·2
1966	114·8	103·6	111·0	107·9
1969	112·7	102·3	106·9	105·8
1972	109·1	100·0	111·8	105·0

[a] Estimated numbers of employees (employed and unemployed).
Source: Department of Employment.

1966 the disparity closed, but both sets of regions suffered a slight contraction in employment. But behind these aggregates there lay important variations among the behaviour of different industrial sectors, leading ultimately to a changed industrial composition. The chief cause of the downturn in the 1960s, despite the greater volume of industrial movement, lay in the accelerated contraction of a number of industries which were relatively concentrated in the development areas (Table 6.4). At the same time there was a slowing down of the rate of growth of service industries. While both of these trends also occurred in the rest of the country, there remained a disparity in their favour in the performance of both sectors. Without the positive effects of industrial movement, seen in the growth of the "general manufacturing" category, the position of the development areas would have been much worse.

Despite the apparent lack of positive effects on total employment, the selectivity in the incidence of change has had a marked impact on industrial composition. A comparison of coefficients of concentration covering nearly two decades shows that individually and as a whole the development areas became more like the nation in their industrial compositions, especially after 1960. Bearing in mind that they have increased their total employment very slowly, this implies a process of replacement, with new sectors taking the place of old. It is possible to

TABLE 6.4. EMPLOYMENT CHANGES[a] BY SECTOR IN DEVELOPMENT AREAS[b] AND NON-DEVELOPMENT AREAS, 1951–63 AND 1963–70

Employment sector	Percentage share of employment total in 1963		Changes in employment, 1951–63 (% per annum)		Changes in employment, 1963–70 (% per annum)	
	DAs	Non-DAs	DAs	Non-DAs	DAs	Non-DAs
Selected declining industries[c]	22·3	13·3	−1·93	−0·59	−4·06	−1·71
General manufacturing[d]	23·9	33·6	0·50	0·69	1·68	−0·18
Services other than transport[e]	35·9	37·6	1·40	2·04	0·70	0·77
Construction and residual[f]	17·9	15·5	0	−0·17	−0·18	−0·88
Total	100·0	100·0	0·09	0·83	−0·16	−0·11

[a] After making adjustment for changes in the Standard Industrial Classification in 1958, 1964, 1966, and 1968.

[b] Scotland, Wales, Northern Region, and Northern Ireland.

[c] Agriculture, mining and quarrying, shipbuilding, linen, metal manufacture, and transport.

[d] General manufacturing industries are defined as the manufacturing order number of the 1958 Standard Industrial Classification excluding shipbuilding and metal manufacture.

[e] Professional and scientific services, insurance, banking and finance, distributive trades, miscellaneous services, and public administration and defence.

[f] Construction, gas, electricity and water, self-employed, and armed forces.

Source: Moore and Rhodes (1973).

recognize three general factors at work. The first was the faster contraction of employment in most declining industries in the development areas than in the country as a whole. For example, the primary sector (agriculture, fishing and forestry, mining and quarrying) fell from about 14·5 to 4·4% in the development areas, but only from 9·0 to 3·8% nationally. Among manufacturing industries metal manufacturing and shipbuilding also decreased employment at faster rates, and in the service sector, transport and communications and distributive trades followed suit. The only major anomaly, over the period 1951–69, occurred in textiles, where the development areas had an increased share, while the proportion employed nationally fell sharply, due to the contraction of the cotton industry in the North West.

The second factor causing concentration coefficients to converge was the national trend favouring the growth of some service industries at faster than average rates. In this the development areas almost managed to keep pace with the rest of the country, the small disparity being due to the market orientation of most services. Since the development area markets generally were growing slowly, this was to be expected. The third factor, jobs created by industrial movement, was the counterpart to the first—employment lost by industrial contraction. The importance of both is that they provide basic or export sectors on which the region depends. Industrial movement has contributed towards creating new economic bases. By 1969 the share of development area employment in the "growth" industries of the manufacturing sector (26·5%) was not much less than that in the same industries in the rest of the country (28·1%), whereas in 1951 the gap had been considerably wider (18·3 against 25·2%). Indeed, by 1969, employment in this sector was greater than that in the primary and declining manufacturing sectors together in the development areas. The contribution of industrial movement is shown by the fact that over 80% of jobs created were in the growth sector.

The position in the early 1970s, therefore, was a mixed one. Income disparities showed little trend between 1949–50 and 1964–5, but there was a slight improvement in the last years of that period. Similarly, there was no trend in unemployment or migration. On the other hand, there were major changes in the structure of employment. Female activity rates rose markedly and industrial composition altered to become more like that found nationally. This position has been described as a "holding operation" (North-east Development Council, 1971); that is, differentials were not allowed to increase and some fundamental improvements (in infrastructure as well as industrial composition) took place. Of course, it is possible to do no more than conjecture what the situation might have become, but since we have certain facts about the movement of industry and the jobs created by it, the rest can be made to follow.

Between 1945 and 1971 these moves gave rise to about 540,000 jobs in the peripheral areas, of which 60% were taken by men. Let us assume that all of the men and all of the single women in these jobs would have migrated from their region of residence if industry had not moved in. If 80% of these men were heads of households and if each of these households contained three persons, then the population thus supported was about 778,000. Adding the single men (65,000) and assuming that about half the women (say, 108,000) employed in these jobs were single, we have around 950,000 persons who would have migrated. But, had these left, there would also have been a contraction of demand and a further number would have been induced to leave. Assuming a negative employment multiplier to be 1·15, this additional number would have been around 140,000. Therefore, on these assumptions, well over a million people were supported in the development areas who might otherwise have migrated. Some might have left Britain, but by far the greater proportion would almost certainly have moved to areas providing the mobile industry, predominantly the South East and West Midlands, where another multiplier, this time positive, would have operated to create demand for even more immigrants. The magnitude of this movement can be gauged from the fact that, in reality, the South East and West Midlands had a total net gain of 625,000 from migration between 1951 and 1966, and that this represented almost 30% of their total population increase. The addition of an equivalent amount might have led to faster industrial growth in these regions, but it would also have created major pressures on housing and public services. It would, in addition, have left the development areas with lower consumer demand and a less-skilled workforce, both of which would tend to depress *per capita* incomes relative to the prosperous regions. But we could reverse the assumption and hypothesize that none would have left the development areas despite the absence of industrial movement. The consequences of this would have been even more widening of the gap between richer and poorer regions, with the former having gross underemployment and low, if not zero, marginal productivity of labour.

6.3. Constraints on the Impact of Industrial Movement

The fact that regional policy up to 1971 could still be described as only a holding operation, despite the movement of over half a million jobs in the development areas, requires an explanation. After all, it might reasonably have been expected that new demand for labour of this magnitude and the extra income generated by the incoming establishments ought to have closed the gap between these regions and the rest of the country more effectively. However, there have clearly been processes operating which have perpetuated regional differences in most of the key indicators. Broadly, these fall into three categories which, singly or together, account for the relative failure of policy. The first is the nature of regional problems. These have not been static but, rather, have continued to unroll at much the same rate as new opportunities have been created. New industries have replaced, rather than augmented, old ones. As a result, employment has not changed at the same rate as population of working age and migration has remained necessary. Secondly, differentials have been perpetuated because non-assisted areas have continued to perform at least as well as the assisted areas. This is particularly true of the non-manufacturing sectors and applies especially to London and the South East, and other major cities which benefited from disproportionate shares of office development in the 1960s. But it applies also in the manufacturing sector where, despite a fall in total employment, there has continued to be a relatively tight labour market.

Thirdly, it appears likely that the impact of industrial movement in the development areas has been less than expected and, possibly, less than the impact which equivalent investment might have had in non-development areas. Unfortunately, on the subject of the impact of industrial movement we have to acknowledge a major deficiency of empirical research despite its importance to the formulation of policies and objectives. But impact studies have to surmount difficulties which are greater than those found in research on movement *per se* (Moseley, 1973). There is a need to distinguish between different kinds of impact falling on different populations or organizations. The first such distinction which must be made is between effects on incomes and effects on employment. The two are related, but not so closely that they can be used interchangeably. This is particularly true when one discusses regional growth. Here, for example, the replacement of a declining industry by new high value-added firms may do little to increase employment or reduce unemployment, but it may have an effect on levels of earnings. Secondly, it is important to make at least a general distinction between short- and long-term effects. The arrival of large new employers in a region is likely to upset whatever equilibrium existed in the labour market, and a period of time will need to elapse before a new equilibrium is established. Also, the external relations of a newly arrived firm or branch plant are likely to be similar to those existing at its previous location, and it will take time to forge new links in the region. Thirdly, within the category of long-term effects, it is possible to identify those related to growth and those influencing stability or the ability to withstand cyclical or seasonal fluctuations. Fourthly, we need to face the problem of discriminating between the impact of a particular change, such as a new firm, and the effects of the other sources of change. To a large measure the difficulty of making such an identification is related to the size of the region and the speed with which it is undergoing change. In a small, stagnant area the problem might be minimal; in a large, dynamic region the opposite is true. Hence it is valuable to test the impact of similar kinds of development against typologies of regions. At its most basic, this might take the form of similar-sized firms, with similar technologies, one group relocating in a development area and one in, say, southern England. This might be profitably extended to a regional typology such as that proposed by Friedmann (1966), consisting of core regions, upward and downward transitional areas, resource frontier regions, and special problem regions. The dynamism implied in this typology would lend greater precision to forecasts of the impact of industrial development than would a simple twofold classification, since the categories in the latter can be quite heterogeneous.

Nevertheless, although faced with a hiatus in empirical findings, there are several aspects of the impact of industrial movement which have been studied in some depth and which are important in the present context. These include the effects of movement on regional levels of productivity, on mobile firms and on labour markets, and on regional development via input–output linkages. The evidence on each is eclectic, but the overall picture drawn from them helps to explain why development areas have not achieved a marked narrowing of the differentials between themselves and the rest of the country.

6.3.1. *Industrial Productivity*

It is a prerequisite for the long-term narrowing of differentials that the level of productivity in new establishments should not only exceed those in declining industries (of which the development areas have a disproportionate share), but should also at least be equal to that found at the parent plant or original location. High productivity is simultaneously a measure of success (though not the only one) and provides a basis for high earnings. However, some care is needed in interpreting apparent differences in productivity, since they depend to some extent on the measure adopted. Also, some industries have higher average net output per unit of labour or capital employed than others, but at the same time grow more slowly or even contract due to lower marginal net output. This is reflected in the position and trend of Wales and Northern England (Table 6.5) in relation to the rest of the country in the level of net output per employee in manufacturing. Between 1958 and 1968 they were above the national average but falling rapidly. This was due mainly to industrial composition; the growth industries moving in were displacing "heavy" industries with higher average net output per employee and often with higher-than-average wage levels. However, in other development areas the trend was opposite and, as a whole, these regions maintained an average net output equal to the national level.

Industrial composition is a major determinant of net output, but it is not necessarily the only one, and it is important to inquire whether

TABLE 6.5. NET OUTPUT PER EMPLOYEE, 1958–68, CENSUS OF
PRODUCTION INDUSTRIES (UK = 100)

	1958	1963	1968
All development areas	100	100	100
North	109	105	100
Wales	117	115	105
Scotland	95	100	96
South East	107	112	110

Source: census of production.

development areas inherently are less productive than other regions;
that is, whether a given establishment would be likely to meet with
less success (assuming the absence of subsidies) here than in non-
development areas. On this issue the evidence is very thin and has to
be interpreted with caution. The general picture afforded by an interregional comparison of average net output per industry (Table 6.6) is

TABLE 6.6. INDUSTRIAL PRODUCTIVITY BY REGION, 1963
(MANUFACTURING INDUSTRIES)

	%Minimum List Headings with net output *per capita*		Net output *per capita* (UK = 100) All manufacturing
	Above UK average	Below UK average	
North	20	71	104
Wales	25	53	114
East Anglia	29	62	100
Yorkshire and Humberside	30	68	91
Scotland	31	64	98
North West	32	65	96
South West	32	59	100
West Midlands	33	66	96
East Midlands	47	48	91
South East	76	23	110

that for most industrial subcategories (of which the census lists 112) there was little difference between most regions. This conclusion is based on a calculation of net output of each industry for which there was data in every region. These are then classed as above, equal to, or below the national average. Thus, in Northern England only 20% of industries had average net output above the mean against 71% below it, compared with the South East with 76% above and only 23% below, and the East Midlands with 47% and 48% respectively. Such polarity between regions could be partly the result of different capital/labour ratios, but this is unlikely to account for much of the difference in the present case. In fact, in 1963, capital invested per head in the South East was lower than the national average in almost every industry group, but net output per unit invested was above average (Table 6.7). Although data for one year can give a misleading impression, these observations do suggest that the South East has some inbuilt advantage, possibly related to stronger external economies than other regions. Apart from the outstanding position of the South East and, to a lesser degree, the East Midlands, net output per employee varied very little between regions. Wales and Northern England were the weakest, but Scotland, industry by industry, was not much different from the West Midlands.

These figures relate to average net output for all establishments; a more important regional comparison would be the productivity of mobile firms. As a rule, these tend to be the more productive, faster-growing members of their industries, and it may be that their extra efficiency permits them to override the conditions reflected in the regional variations of Table 6.6. Studies by Luttrell (1962) and the North East Development Council (1973) were directly concerned with this question, seeking to establish what the initial handicaps of relocation were and what continuing cost differences there might be after the initial difficulties were overcome. The great variety of firms' responses to relocation problems and the lack of a regional analysis make it difficult to draw sound conclusions, but Luttrell found that initial costs at branch plants tended towards parity by, or shortly after, the fourth year. Continuing cost differentials tended to be negligible, on average, though a significant proportion had costs 10% or more above that of the parent factory in the fifth year, but

TABLE 6.7. PRODUCTIVITY IN THE UNITED KINGDOM AND THE SOUTH EAST, 1963 BY SIC GROUP

SIC Group	Capital expenditure (£) per employee: South East	United Kingdom	Net output (£) per £ capital expenditure: South East	United Kingdom
III Food, Drink and Tobacco	172	182	98	93
IV Chemicals	232	312	108	76
V Metal manufacture	176	248	83	58
VI/VII/IX Engineering, Shipbuilding and metal goods	94	89	146	143
VII Vehicles	177	120	97	112
X/XI/XII Textiles, Fur and Leather, and Clothing	37	65	250	145
XV Paper and printing	119	133	138	109
XIII/XIV/XVI Bricks, pottery, etc., Timber and furniture, Miscellaneous manufacturing	120	122	114	104

Source: Census of Production, 1968.

Luttrell found no consistent factor governing this. Transport costs incurred by branches tended to be higher, but only by about 3–5% of total operating costs and were not, therefore, the major determinant of the differential. Few of the firms in the survey considered their chosen location to be bad and locational difficulties were normally outweighed by differences of operating efficiency. The lack of an analysis by region of destination means that Luttrell's findings must be interpreted with care, but his study presented no evidence to show that branches or firms moving to development areas performed differently from those moving to other locations or than firms expanding *in situ*. However, the Cameron and Clark study (1966) of firms moving to development areas provided further useful information on this issue. About 10% of the firms in their sample still regarded their development area locations, chosen under government pressure, as second-best some time after the move, because of the duplication of plant and staff, extra transport costs, and lower labour productivity (at least in the short run), and higher costs of planning, building, and operating the new plants compared with expansion at their original site or parent plant. Many of these were among the largest firms to move, so the effect was out of proportion to their numbers.

Finally, the impact on firms which move can be gauged by their rates of subsequent closure. Keeble (1968) found that, among both branches and relocated firms, the proportion subsequently closing was considerably greater in development areas than elsewhere. However, the more detailed analysis of closures by region (reported in Chapter 3) based on the Board of Trade's 1945–65 and 1966–72 surveys, shows the differences adjusted by cohorts to have narrowed and, later, to have favoured the development areas chiefly as a result of financial assistance.

6.3.2. *Labour Markets*

The next constraint on the rate of progress of assisted areas has been that the direct impact of industrial movement on labour markets has been relatively small. In particular, the effect on unemployment rates, and their difference from the national average, has been negligible. This stands in contradiction to some of the optimistic statements about the likely job-creation resulting from industrial movement. Thus, Lloyd (1970) quotes a Board of Trade prediction in 1961 that "new developments in the vehicle industry would bring some 30,000 additional jobs to Merseyside" (pp. 396–7). Certainly, this number of jobs was created in that particular industry on Merseyside, but the effect was not an increase in total employment of 30,000 in the region. Much of the confusion in statements like this arises from an oversimplified polarization of labour market conditions in different regions. For example, the National Economic Development Council argued (1963) that "new factories in the more prosperous regions . . . recruit a large part of their manpower from other firms there. To this extent the gain in output is only that resulting from the transfer of labour from less to more productive work. By contrast, new factories in the less prosperous regions will, to a much greater extent, employ labour that otherwise would have produced nothing" (pp. 18–19).

There are no fundamental errors in this statement; its shortcomings lie in its lack of corroborative evidence and the element of exaggeration. The first sentence is substantially correct; studies have pointed to labour markets in areas in the South East which have attracted firms becoming very tight, and for new employers to recruit from existing firms with a consequent bidding-up in wages (Sant, 1970). The latter, it must be emphasized, is not necessarily inflationary: it is likely to be associated with higher marginal productivity of labour in the new firms and increases in productivity in the existing firms. However, it is the third sentence of the National Economic Development Council statement which is most relevant to the development areas, since it implies that industrial movement significantly reduces unemployment or, in the case of female labour, induces it into the labour market. The latter has been shown to be true; female activity rates have risen faster in the development areas than elsewhere. Grime and Starkie (1968), in a case study of a factory moving to Furness, showed that over 10% of the female labour force had been housewives (i.e. inactive). A further 43% had been at school and thus technically inactive. But the effect on unemployment has fallen below this. In the same study, only 3% of the firm's labour force had been registered as unemployed. This was a medium-sized firm, employing 600, and it might be expected that larger firms would need to rely more heavily on the register of unemployed. However, this was barely true in two cases where the motor industry has been involved. Jones (1968) found that in a branch of a motor firm located near Swansea only 8% out of a workforce of about 1000 had been unemployed immediately before recruitment. Likewise, Salt (1967) estimated that less than 10% in a workforce of over 20,000 in the two motor firms locating on Merseyside were unemployed at the time of their engagement.

Clearly, therefore, if new firms have a relatively small impact on unemployment, they must have recruited from existing firms. In the two case studies from the motor industry the proportion in this category lay near to 90%; even establishments locating in the South East could not have taken a much higher proportion. The Furness study, with a higher female component, had a lower proportion, but, even so, this exceeded 50%. With this level of interfirm labour mobility, it is important to ask what the effect was on firms losing labour and the degree to which the level of wages was altered.

Two common features of the effect on existing firms are that they face the largest loss among skilled workers and that at this end of the labour market wage levels are bid up by the newcomer. Jones (1968) calculated that rates of pay in the new motor firms were between 8 and 16% above the local average. The same trend occurred on Merseyside (Salt, 1967), but here, unlike the Swansea case, it was contended that one effect was to accelerate the closure of some of the less-profitable firms losing skilled labour. Salt summarized that the skilled labour market, "for so long a buyers' market . . . has been seen well on the way to becoming a sellers' market". On the other hand, the effect on unskilled labour tends to be diluted because of an initial oversupply.

The effectiveness of industrial movement is also constrained by the occupational structure of the employment which it creates. Initially we can expect movement to development areas, composed mainly of branch plants, to contain a relatively low proportion of management, administrative, and professional jobs, and a greater-than-average proportion of operative functions. Further, in several areas the latter group contains a large unskilled female workforce. The implications of this, apart from continuing the concentration of control functions in the metropolitan regions, is that average incomes tend to be lower in branches than at parent establishments and, hence, the level of consumer expenditure in assisted areas is also likely to be lower. Assuming that this expenditure is localized, it would follow that the impact derived from consumer spending is also likely to be smaller in the case of long-distance branch moves than for the shorter single-plant transfers which are more typical of moves within the South East and Midlands. Evidence on the occupational structure of industrial mobility is inadequate, but Westaway (1973) has calculated, on the basis of a "shift and share" analysis, the gain or loss of professional, managerial, and administrative jobs in each standard region relative to the national trend during 1961–6. The disparities are marked; the South East and Midlands had an upward shift of 35,000 jobs (i.e. above what they would have had if they followed the national trend), while Scotland Wales, Northern England, and the North West had a downward shift of the same magnitude. While one cannot attribute this to industrial movement, it does appear that the creation of new establishments has done little to combat the trend.

6.3.3. *Leakages Through Interregional Trade*

The movement of industry creates jobs in the reception areas, although, as we have seen, the net addition to employment need not be equal to the labour force in the new firms. The employment so created, which has been called the "direct" impact (Yeates and Lloyd, 1969; Moseley, 1973) is not, however, all that ensues from the new investment. In a closed regional economy with a surplus labour supply, additional employment would be brought about through the demand for intermediate goods, and services consequent upon the net gain to household incomes. The former have been labelled "indirect" effects and the latter "induced" effects. The regional economy can be conceived as a matrix of intersectoral flows comprising industries, households, the government, savings, and so on, in which a change in one sector will be transmitted to others through their inputs and out-puts. The ratio between the ultimate impact on the system and the initial investment (the multiplier), depends upon the strength of the input–output coefficients. By making assumptions about their stability, it is possible, if present coefficients are known, to use the matrix as a predictive device. However, even when not being used for forecasting, the concepts employed in input–output analysis and the multiplier still provide a useful framework for estimating the impact of industrial movement. Thus, having identified the direct effect, it is possible to identify and estimate the subsequent indirect and induced effects, at least in the early rounds of the transmission process. In addition, with open regional economies, it is possible to assess a fourth impact which partly offsets the indirect and induced effects, namely leakages through the import sector. For the multiplier effect on a region to be maximized, the whole impact must be kept within the region. In practice, however, this does not occur because no region is actually or potentially self-sufficient. Thus indirect and induced effects are at least partially transmitted to other regions.

The question is, how much of the effect leaks out of regions, and is the leakage greater from development areas than from others? The practical problems associated with accurately measuring leakages and, subsequently, multipliers for each region are virtually insurmountable with existing data (Archibald, 1967), but it is possible to provide estimates. On *a priori* ground alone it can be convincingly argued that regional variations are normal because the marginal propensity to add value in production differs. Given assumptions about this propensity, Archibald estimates the income multipliers of standard regions in the United Kingdom to lie between 1·20 and 1·70. No attempt is made to place individual regions in this range, but since a major determinant of these values is the proportion of regional output consumed internally, and since regional consumption functions are not greatly different, it can be inferred that the multiplier is closely related (inversely) to the level of specialization. This would put the South East, the Midlands, and the North West towards the upper end of the range, and Wales and Northern England towards the lower end (Brown, 1972). Allen (1970) estimated the Scottish multiplier to be about 1·4. However, it might be deduced that since regions have become more alike in their industrial composition, their multipliers should also have tended towards parity.

The way in which leakages occur in practice has been the subject of several studies concerned with the impact of industrial movement.

Moseley (1973), conducting surveys of the direct, indirect, and induced effects of industrial development in two East Anglian expanding towns, found the indirect effects to be small initially. Only about 8% of materials used by new firms was produced within the region. But about a third of the new firms were increasing their dependence on local sources, although these were mainly smaller producers (i.e. with a turnover below £1m per annum). The induced effect, estimated from a survey of household expenditure, showed less leakage from the region, but because the towns studied are relatively small (below 15 000 population), the higher-order consumer goods had to be purchased in larger regional centres. The tendency for incoming firms gradually to increase their linkages with suppliers in the region to which they move is a process which might be expected: proximity should add convenience and save costs. However, James (1964) argued that long-standing relationships with suppliers are likely to continue after a firm has moved to a development area to a large degree because local suppliers lack the competitiveness to make use of their proximity to the new potential market. The reason may be shortage of new capital to improve their own productivity, but it might also be a lack of experience in subcontracting. A conclusion from this was that financial assistance should be directed towards indigenous firms to avoid an undesirable dualism within development areas; legislation in the latter half of the 1960s did, in fact, recognize this need.

Considerable variety occurs among new firms in their degree of linkage with existing suppliers. This is partly an interindustrial variation, but there are also differences among firms in the same industry. Lever (in press), in a small sample of twenty-four firms from six industries in West Central Scotland, showed that purchases from Scottish suppliers ranged from 54% down to 8%. Small firms tended to purchase more within Scotland (28%) than did large ones (18%), and large firms bought more from South East England and the West Midlands (38%) than did small ones (7%). Supporting James (1965), it was also found that immigrant branches bought substantially more from outside the region; generally, their linkages with their region of origin (i.e. usually the South East) remained strong.

CHAPTER 7

The Future of Regional Policy in Britain

WHEN Parliament passed the 1972 Industry Act (Cmnd 4942), the latest in a long series of measures related to regional policy, the government undertook to preserve the new framework until at least 1978. In large measure that was to facilitate the first phase of membership of the EEC, but it was also believed that greater stability was needed to enable planners and industrial decision-makers to operate on a more secure basis, not fearing that their actions might be thwarted by a change in the instruments of policy. However, in this final chapter, we put forward the assertion that the 1972 provisions are still unlikely to be sufficient to "solve" the regional problem, although they are likely to be more effective than their predecessors. This implies two, not necessarily conflicting, courses of action. The first is an acceptance of some continuing disparities; the second involves an investigation of additional measures to give the inhabitants of less prosperous regions a greater range of opportunities to achieve higher incomes.

7.1. Institutional Dimensions

It is unrealistic to speak of "policy" as if it were a unique, homogeneous, and self-contained function. Instead, we should be aware that policy-making (not only in regard to regions) is one of several stages in the process of intervention by government. The full set of stages, following the definition of problems, comprises:

(i) identification of objectives;
(ii) formulation of policies;
(iii) designation of policy instruments.

To these can be added (iv) implementation, and (v) monitoring. The last is an important process, since it allows the success of the policy and its instruments to be calculated and permits further debate to proceed on methods of improving the system. We should add, also, that although it is simple to identify these stages, in practice they are often obscure, and the impression is given (not least by politicians) that success is not always related to the speed with which objectives are met. In addition, at least in regard to regional policy, there is not one single objective, as we shall see in the following subsection. Thus what we have is a system in which policy exists to meet a number of objectives and in which policy is itself served by a number of instruments. This distinction, despite being a simplification, is valuable in discussions of the relative success of the system and subsequently of ways in which it might be improved.

7.1.1. *Objectives*

Diamond (1974) has listed six broad objectives which remain in current usage:

(1) relief of localized high unemployment;
(2) restraint of expansion of employment in the congested conurbations;
(3) fuller utilization of national resources, notably labour:
(4) reduction of interregional differences to assist with macroeconomic management of the economy and control of inflationary pressure;
(5) maintaining and strengthening of provincial cultures and identity;
(6) assisting in achievement of a balance between population and environmental resources.

From time to time the emphasis placed on each of these has altered perceptibly and, with it, the regional patterns of resource allocation. However, at no time have there been stated easily quantifiable, operational objectives. Nor has there been an explicit statement of the permanence of regional policy. The statements which have been made, like that referring to Central Scotland (Cmnd 2188, 1963), have undertaken commitments which tend to be open-ended; in that case it was to stimulate viable growth. At its most strict, "viability" could be interpreted as self-sustaining growth in *per capita* incomes without any form of regional protection, at a level at which full employment could be maintained, with a balanced distribution of factor endowments. However, "viability" ultimately depends upon "acceptability", so that as long as disparities remained between Central Scotland and, say, the South East or Midlands, there would still be a cause for concern. In another instance it was found to be impossible, due to political pressures, to relegate Merseyside from development area to intermediate area status, as the Hunt Committee (Cmnd 3998, 1969, p. 147) recommended.

7.1.2. *Policies and Policy Instruments*

The evolution of policy has been reviewed in detail elsewhere (McCrone, 1969; Brown, 1972), and there is no need for more than a general statement of recent trends. One should note, firstly, that the regions designated for assistance have, over the years, accounted for an increasing proportion of Britain's area and population. At the same time, there has evolved a hierarchy of designations, ranging from special development areas where assistance is greatest, to Greater London where controls on development are most stringent, with perhaps half a dozen categories in between. It should be emphasized, however, that although the government has expressed an interest in the "growth centre" concept, this has never been incorporated in the designation of areas for assistance, unlike the practice in a number of European countries.

Secondly, controls, in the form of industrial development certificates (IDCs) and office development permits (ODPs), have become less severe. Under the 1972 Act, the limit for which an IDC is required for industrial building is now 10,000 square feet in the South East and 15,000 square feet elsewhere outside the assisted areas. There has also been an easing of the ODP system, with the West Midland conurbation no longer controlled. Applications in London (scrutinized against the criterion of whether it would enhance the city's prospects as an international financial and commercial centre) now recognize the capital's aspirations to be the leading centre in the EEC.

Thirdly, while controls have been eased, there has been a parallel rise in the level of government assistance to private investment and spatially discriminant public expenditure. At current values, aid to industry in the assisted areas rose from £39m in 1965 to £329m in 1971, and will probably reach £450–500m in 1974–5. One should note, however, the arguments of Moore and Rhodes (1973) that this is an Exchequer cost rather than a real resource cost, and that the expenditure has, in fact, generated a higher GNP than would have occurred in its absence. The element of subsidy to firms in assisted areas varies from case to case, but Wilson (1973) has calculated that the development grant (for new plant and machinery and a depreciation allowance on buildings) will give producers in development areas a cost advantage of about $1-2\frac{1}{2}\%$ of total manufacturing costs. In addition, producers are eligible for a regional employment premium (or labour subsidy), selective assistance in the form of low interest loans, interest relief grants, removal grants and training grants, which together can give a further substantial subsidy.

7.2. Success or Failure?

In making a distinction between objectives, policies, and instruments, the purpose was to provide a framework to discuss the relative success of public intervention. Subsequently, the same framework can be used to consider which, if any, of its elements might require modification. Thus, for simplicity, we can ask whether or not the instruments have served the needs of the policy and then whether or not the policy has fulfilled the objective.

Although varying estimates have been put forward of the volume of job creation and industrial movement in response to policy, there is no doubt that the total is a large one. Howard (1968) estimated that 438,000 jobs in manufacturing had been created in the "peripheral areas" (approximately the present development areas) between 1945 and 1965 by firms moving from other regions; of these 122,000 occurred during 1960–5. On the same definitions over 60,000 jobs were created through interregional movement during 1966–71. Brown (1972) compared the progress of the four major development areas (Scotland, Wales, North East, and North West England) in 1953–9, when the available instruments and implementation were weak, and 1960–6, when they had been markedly strengthened. His conclusion was that relative performance was improved by about 50,000 jobs per annum. Of these, 30,000 were in new jobs associated with IDC approvals, including 15,000 which were the direct result of interregional movement, and the rest were induced by the multiplier effects of these two categories. Another estimate, by Moore and Rhodes (1973), using a "shift and share" analysis, is that manufacturing employment in the development areas at the end of the period 1963–70 was 12% higher than it would have been if policy had been as passively implemented as it had been in the 1950s. In absolute terms, this amounted to about 200,000 jobs. Lastly, the results of a survey by the Department of Trade and Industry (House of Commons, 1973) indicated that firms moving to assisted areas were significantly influenced by the various policy instruments. One can conclude, therefore, that the instruments of policy have been strikingly successful.

But what of the policy itself? Can that, too, be described in such unequivocal terms? To answer this, one needs to return to the objectives listed above and estimate the contribution of regional policy to each. Also, to make matters more complicated, we should ideally assign a weight to each objective since, *a priori*, we should expect them to differ in importance from each other. However, such an exercise is impracticable, and all that can be achieved is a discursive account.

For practical reasons, the last two objectives in the list ought to be discounted. The idea that the loss of interregional cultural diversity represents a social cost (Stilwell, 1972) has been bitterly attacked by West (1973): "Welfare economics does not countenance the idea that people should be regarded as collector's pieces, cherished for their ability to speak old dialects or perform in Morris dancing. Many people *want* to shrug off their dialects" (p. 119). Another, perhaps more realistic, view is that cultural heterogeneity, or its disappearance, is most affected by mass media and travel (both symbols of development), and that regional policy is unlikely to play more than a neutral role. The problem of defining a balance between population and environmental resources is no less difficult. The "environment", in its broadest sense, has no legal meaning in Britain. Regional strategic planning teams have been charged in their terms of reference with taking account of environmental qualities and constraints, and there are policy instruments dealing with the clearance of derelict land. But this is a long way removed from a general policy towards the use of environmental resources. Before this could happen effectively, it would be necessary to have a national "environmental survey". Moreover, there is a fundamental reason why this objective is not a proper one for a developmental regional policy, and this is that, in practice, the aim of achieving a balance between population and environmental resources is inherently conservative.

The third and fourth objectives are closely related, being based on the belief that regional policy can dampen the cyclical swings in the national economy (exacerbated by inflationary pressures in the south and midlands) and increase the rate of growth in GDP by diverting demand, especially for labour, to areas of underemployment. In these, it is argued by Moore and Rhodes (1974), policy has proved to have been successful. On the assumption that the productivity of the additional employment was similar to that of the national average, the 200,000 jobs created in the development areas between 1963 and 1970 led to additional output in the United Kingdom of about £400–500m per annum. This is approximately 1% of GDP as at 1970. If these figures are correct (and, it should be stated, the Moore and Rhodes thesis has not been fully accepted yet), then these two objectives would appear to be in the process of being achieved.

The same is also true of the second objective, restraint of expansion in congested conurbations, although this is being done as much—if not more—by intraregional planning as by interregional policy. Decentralization has occurred both to the fringes of all the British conurbations (Cameron and Evans, 1973) and to new and expanded towns. All the conurbation centres have lost employment, and total conurbation populations have grown slowly or even decreased. However, research undertaken for the Greater London Development Plan indicated not only how far decentralization has gone, but also that it has been unbalanced, and it concluded that if trends continued, the labour shortage of the 1960s could be turned into a labour surplus in the 1970s notwithstanding national employment cycles (Foster and Richardson, 1973).

This leaves the first objective, the reduction of regional disparities, especially in unemployment. Here the achievement is less clear-cut. Disparities have proved to be obdurate. The rank order of regions on a number of indicators (unemployment, activity rates, incomes, etc.) has changed little over at least the last decade, and the differentials have tended to remain stable (North East Development Council, 1971). Largely as a result, interregional migration has continued with the assisted areas all showing substantial net losses. However, as has been pointed out on numerous occasions, these facts do not necessarily amount to an absolute failure. Without the effects of regional policy, the differentials might have grown and migration might have reached more serious dimensions. In this respect, the achievement has been that of a "holding operation", despite the massive movement of industry since 1945. The reasons for this can be found in a number of factors such as the continued run-down of older industries, the leakage of induced and indirect (i.e. multiplier) effects to the Midlands and South, and the propensity of new firms in the assisted areas to recruit labour from existing workforces rather than from among the unemployed.

7.3. Existing Requirements and Resources

From the above section we can conclude that there is an ongoing need to use regional policy for macro-economic demand management. Also, in certain cases at least, it continues to have a role in combating congestion in major conurbations, although it has been argued that higher social costs may not be inherent in large cities but may be due to transient factors, such as too fast a rate of immigration relative to the increase in urban capacity (Richardson, 1972). However, the key to the future of regional policy lies in the requirements for reducing labour market disparities, since it is their magnitude and distribution which is most likely to influence the vigour and character of government action. Here it is important to refer to the operational targets listed by Ridley and outlined above, which identify a requirement of about a million jobs in the main assisted areas. Compared with the estimates for job creation in the past, this would represent an enormous goal if it were undertaken. Clearly, therefore, there is a need to examine the present and possible future sources of additional employment and, in the event of their being insufficient, alternative ways of approaching the problems.

The list of possible sources of employment growth has been examined in some detail by Cameron (1974), but it is useful to make a few comments under each of the headings.

7.3.1. *Industrial Movement*

As the main arm of policy it might be expected that government will continue to create and divert the movement of manufacturing industry to assisted areas. However, it is not clear whether this process can continue indefinitely or whether the supply of mobile industry might begin to diminish. Our analysis suggests that the supply is unlikely to grow much larger, although the modern sector of industry does appear to be more footloose. Also, it is clear that industrial movement to the assisted areas is directly affected by the rate of economic growth and investment in manufacturing and by the demands of new towns, several of which are programmed for development in the 1970s. Nor can it be expected that a significantly larger volume of jobs arising from foreign investment will take place than the 3000–5000 per annum currently occurring, although membership of the EEC might have a slight effect. Lastly, we should repeat the fears of the two main sources of industry in the past, London and the West Midlands, that they are in danger of becoming unbalanced employment-deficient economies if the process continues much further. Whether wholly true or not, such arguments are likely to carry weight.

7.3.2. *Office Relocation*

Most studies of the private office sector have concluded that while there is great scope for the movement of "lower order" offices out of conurbation centres, it is unlikely that they would move much further than the peripheral suburbs or nearby towns. Part of the reason is that the rent–distance relationship is a hyperbolic curve; that is, it is steep between the city centre and its periphery, but very shallow thereafter. Rhodes and Kan (1971) estimated that only 1% of the office jobs decentralized from Central London during 1963–70 went to the development areas. It is unlikely that ODPs, unless accompanied by large inducements, would alter this sufficiently to make great inroads into the existing requirements of the assisted areas.

The same is true, at least in the immediate future, of the dispersal of government offices from London. The Hardman report (Cmnd 5322, 1973) recommended the movement of about 31,000 jobs, but that only about 17,000 should be destined for assisted area locations. (This was significantly increased by a government decision in 1974.) Moreover, all the towns, with one exception, chosen as possible locations had, or are planned to have, populations greater than 200,000. These are places which already have substantial office sectors and, compared with other parts of the assisted areas, fairly high female activity rates. Thus, although they are the most rational places to put new office employment, the dispersal process still leaves areas with the more serious problems relatively untouched.

7.3.3. *Indigenous Growth*

Recognition that industrial movement cannot be sufficient to meet the needs of the assisted areas has been followed, perhaps logically, by a shift of attention to the possibility of fostering indigenous growth in the assisted areas. There is, of course, an initial paradox to be overcome, namely that the past records of the ability of these areas to generate new companies and to expand their existing companies has been weak, largely because of their industrial composition. Thus one needs, on the one hand, a new composition to generate indigenous growth and, on the other, the prospect of indigenous growth to create a new industrial composition and a better climate for new companies and further expansion.

Nevertheless, employment in indigenous industry has been *evidence ?* fostered. The first major policy instrument to do this was the regional employment premium, paid as a standard, per capital labour subsidy. More recently, the 1972 Act introduced a new instrument—"selective financial assistance"—which makes available loans and interest relief grants to new projects and expansions which create additional employment and to projects (e.g. modernization or rationalization) which safeguard existing employment. Selective assistance has also been made available outside these categories to cases where there is an imminent risk of significant redundancies unless help is provided (e.g. in shipbuilding). The effectiveness of selectivity will not become fully apparent for some years, but it is interesting to note that at least one of the regions applying it (Yorkshire and Humberside) has done so in a strongly entrepreneurial manner, attempting, in the words of the regional director of the Department of Industry, to establish "profits centres"—industrial units with a complete spectrum of management and professional services, giving them autonomy in decision-making.

Although it is too early to judge the effectiveness of selective assistance, it is not unreasonable to suggest that this, together with the other policy instruments, is unlikely to meet the requirements identified by Ridley. Even if policy in the present decade resulted in job creation at the rate claimed by Brown to have occurred in the 1960s, this would still leave a major discrepancy. Clearly, therefore, to meet the regional disparities objective, it is necessary to look to new approaches to augment the existing ones.

7.4. Future Policies

The argument so far has led in one direction, namely that policy, as hitherto formulated, has been well served by its instruments, but that while it has met some of the major aims, the leading socio-economic objective (removing regional disparities) has not been achieved. Nor, given the magnitude of existing requirements, is it likely to be achieved in the foreseeable future.

One escape from such a dilemma would be to restate the objectives, substituting a less-ambitious goal than that calculated by Ridley. But while it might be economic realism to do so, taking into account the inevitability of some disparities arising from differences in industrial composition, it appears to be politically impracticable to suggest an explicit operational objective based on anything less than interregional equality. Nevertheless, as discussed below, there is a case for an inquiry into the objectives of regional policy.

The opposite approach would be to strengthen the instruments of existing policy. Moore and Rhodes (1973) have argued that this would not impose real resource costs on the economy but would, on the contrary, produce extra growth in GDP and, incidentally, lead to lower taxes in the more prosperous regions. However, this approach is constrained by bottlenecks of various kinds (e.g. the availability of mobile industry, the supply of skilled labour, etc.), which impose a limit on the possible rate of development in the assisted areas.

But before adopting this, it is valuable to investigate the scope for new approaches to augment the existing ones of industrial movement and, more recently applied, indigenous industrial development. We would emphasize that our argument is for an exploration of possibilities, not the adoption of untested ideas.

A number of proposals concerning regional policy and its objectives have been put forward over recent years. Most of them share one feature in common: that is an interest for the long-term evolution of the regional economic system. In its present form regional policy deals essentially with the short term by aiming to correct inequalities in the distribution of unemployment and the immediate problems of labour market adjustment. Largely, this is because there are no firm long-run objectives dealing with the possible directions in which the national space-economy might evolve. In this it contrasts strongly with regional strategic plans, which project developments within individual regions to the year 1991 and beyond, albeit often with unsatisfactory techniques, whereas the most that regional policy has undertaken is a six-year period of stability.

The need for a division of objectives into long-term perspectives and short-term aims has been justified by Diamond (1974) as a means of achieving a more coherent approach to regional development. There are, of course, major problems associated with such a division. Not least is the classification of relevant sets of objectives and ensuring that both sets are understood and accepted. Diamond notes a major paradox in this: "While the logic of analysis and evaluation requires a long-term view, the practical needs of political decision-making require clear shorter-run policy guidance. Thus it only becomes feasible to adopt a longer-term perspective if a workable short-run aim can be devised."

However, a satisfactory short-run mechanism already exists in the present use of regional policy by the government as a way of influencing the rate of change in regions by stimulating development or moderating decline. The next step, therefore, ought to be an investigation of the content and implications of long-term objectives. Of course, it might be the case that such an exercise would give rise to one or more of three negative results: namely, that a long-term perspective is (a) not identifiable, (b) not desirable, or (c) not practicable. However, until we know that these are the case, there remains a need for inquiry, if only to dispel the confusion which persists about long- and short-term requirements.

If, ultimately, it is considered that a division of long- and short-term objectives is feasible and desirable, then there are a number of implications which follow from this. Not least of these is a need to integrate regional policy with strategic planning in a more effective manner. Hitherto, strategic plans and subregional studies have been prepared individually. They have paid little regard to each other and their relationship with regional policy has been tenuous. Yet, in discussing the long-term distributions of population, services and economic activities within large areas, they clearly ought to play a greater role in the wider process of policy formulation. Among the more important functions which might be fulfilled is a more constructive attitude towards the designation of areas for assistance. Our own analysis has given support to this, showing that in the short-term a relatively systematic response can be predicted from a change in policy instruments.

In addition, the long-term view requires a more explicit acceptance of the role of migration in relation to regional policy. Hitherto, the "workers to the work" argument, conducted so heatedly in the 1950s and early 1960s, has been concerned with the short-term effects of migration. But now that a well-established short-term policy exists, in the form of industrial movement, it ought to be possible to carry out a more constructive appraisal of the long-term functions of migration and the ways in which it might be used as a resource for development.

A further implication is the need to augment the concern for industrial movement with an analysis of the role of occupational distributions and modern corporate structures. British regional policy has been firmly grounded in industrial development and the movement of manufacturing establishments. In consequence, the majority of studies have neglected the nature of jobs that people do, the skills and training which they require, and the distribution of occupations. Yet it is now considered that important disparities exist among the occupation structures of regions, that these are widening, and that neither distributions nor trends are related in any simple way to the industrial composition of regions. Also, there are grounds for believing that the implementation of regional policy has done little to narrow the gap. Most of the movement to assisted areas has consisted of branch plants. In the context of the corporate structures of multiplant and multinational companies, such establishments probably have a disproportionately large share of production workers, while the source regions retain the majority of professional, scientific, technical, and specialist managerial functions in head offices and parent factories. But, notwithstanding work on office linkages and their effect on location decisions (Goddard, 1973), there is still a lack of conclusive evidence on a number of important issues.

Forty years of regional policy have left their beneficial mark in Britain. Even so, some old problems remain and new ones are emerging, and it would be easy to confine the present requirement to "more of the same". There is no doubt that this course will be followed. But, equally, there is no doubt that the discussion of regional policy should be broadened to give it an enriched long-term perspective.

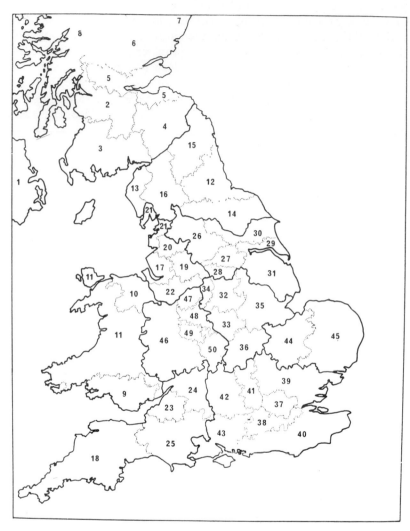

FIG. A.1. Areas used in recording the movement of firms, 1945–65.

APPENDIX A

Areas Used in Recording the Movement of Firms

1. 1945–65 (see Fig. A.1)

1. Northern Ireland

SCOTLAND
2. Central Scottish DA*
3. South-west Scotland
4. Eastern Borders
5. East Central Scotland
6. Eastern Scotland
7. North-east Scotland
8. Highlands and Islands

WALES
9. South Wales DA*
10. North-east Wales
11. Rural Wales

NORTHERN ENGLAND
12. North-eastern DA*
13. West Cumberland DA*
14. North Yorkshire
15. Northumbria
16. Rural Cumberland and Westmorland

NORTH WEST
17. Merseyside and South-west Lancashire
19. East Lancashire and North-east Cheshire
20. North-east Lancashire
21. North-west Lancashire
22. South Cheshire and High Peak

SOUTH WEST
18. Devon and Cornwall
23. Bristol and Bath
24. Gloucester and North Wiltshire
25. Somerset, South Wiltshire, and Dorset

YORKSHIRE AND HUMBERSIDE
26. West Riding—Textile
27. West Riding—Coal
28. West Riding—Steel
29. North Humberside

* Development Area as constituted in 1953.

Note: areas 1–17 constitute the "peripheral areas".

30. Mid Yorkshire
31. Lindsey

32. Nottingham, Derby, and Notts./Derby Coalfield
33. Leicester and South Derbyshire and Leicestershire Coalfield
34. West Derbyshire
35. Holland, Kesteven, Melton Mowbray, and Newark
36. Northamptonshire

SOUTH EAST
37. Greater London
38. Surrey and West Kent
39. Essex, Hertfordshire, and Bedfordshire

40. Sussex and East and Central Kent
41. Buckinghamshire and East Berkshire
42. Oxfordshire, West, and Central Berkshire
43. Wessex

EAST ANGLIA
44. Western East Anglia
45. Eastern East Anglia

WEST MIDLANDS
46. Shropshire, Herefordshire, Worcestershire
47. North Staffordshire
48. Central Staffordshire and Warwickshire Coalfield
49. West Midlands Conurbation
50. Central and South Warwickshire

2. 1966–71 (see Fig. A2)

1. Northern Ireland

SCOTLAND
2. Glasgow
3. Falkirk/Stirling
4. Edinburgh
5. Tayside
6. Borders
7. South-west
8. North-east
9. Highlands

WALES
10. Industrial South Wales: Central and Eastern Valleys

11. Industrial South Wales: West
12. Industrial South Wales: Coastal
13. North-east Wales
14. North-west Wales: North Coast
15. North-west Wales: remainder
16. Central Wales
17. South-west Wales

NORTHERN ENGLAND
18. Industrial North-east: North

19. Industrial North-east: South
20. Rural North-east: North
21. Rural North-east: South
22. Cumberland and Westmorland

NORTH WEST
23. Furness
24. Fylde
25. Lancaster
26. Mid Lancashire
27. North-east Lancashire
28. Merseyside Conurbation
29. South Lancashire
30. Manchester
31. South Cheshire and High Peak

SOUTH WEST
32. Northern
33. Central
34. Southern
35. Western

YORKSHIRE AND HUMBERSIDE
36. North Humberside
37. South Humberside
38. Mid Yorkshire
39. South Lindsey
40. South Yorkshire
41. Yorkshire Coalfield
42. West Yorkshire

EAST MIDLANDS
43. Nottingham/Derbyshire
44. Leicester
45. Eastern Lowlands
46. Northampton

SOUTH EAST
47. Greater London
48. Outer Metropolitan Area
49. Outer South-east: Essex
50. Outer South-east: Kent
51. Outer South-east: Sussex Coast
52. Outer South-east: Bedfordshire and Buckinghamshire
53. Outer South-east: Berkshire and Oxfordshire

EAST ANGLIA
54. South-east
55. North-east
56. North-west
57. South-west

WEST MIDLANDS
58. Central
59. Conurbation
60. Coventry Belt
61. Rural West
62. North Staffordshire

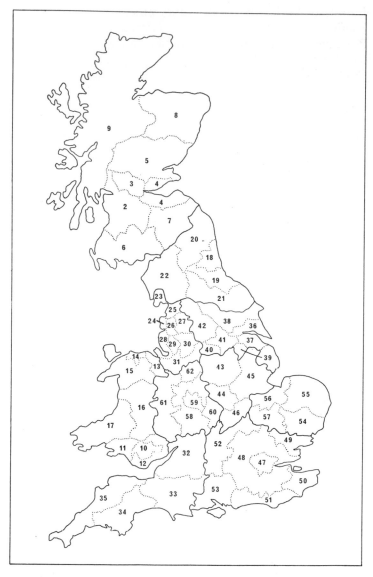

Fɪɢ. A.2. Areas used in recording the movement of firms, 1966–71.

APPENDIX B

Explanations and Definitions

(Extract from *The Movement of Manufacturing Industry in the United Kingdom* 1945–65)

THE following paragraphs describe the definitions used in identifying and allocating moves which occurred during 1945–65.

For the purpose of compiling the Record of Movement of Firms the United Kingdom was divided into fifty areas. These areas are listed in Appendix A.

The Record relates to the opening of new manufacturing establishments when the development in question could be considered to have originated outside the area in which the new establishment was opened. The term establishment is used in a sense very close to that given it in the census of production. In most cases it comprises the whole of the premises under the same ownership or management at a particular address.

For the opening of an establishment to qualify as a move, the firm or enterprise concerned must not have been operating in that area in the industry (Minimum List Heading of the Standard Industrial Classification) in question at the time the new establishment was opened. The terms firm and enterprise are used in the sense in which they are employed in the census of production. A firm means one or more productive establishments operated under the same trading name. An enterprise means one or more firms under common ownership or control. When subsidiary firms were, as far as was known, subject to the control of their parent enterprise with respect to location policy, the organization unit considered in the context of this paragraph was the enterprise. However, in cases where this was known not to be so, the firm was the unit considered, or in the case of

229

some very large firms where individual manufacturing divisions appeared to be in control of their own locational policies, such divisions were considered as units for this purpose.

Moves include both:

(i) "transfers" or complete moves in the sense that the observed opening of an establishment in one area was associated with the closure of another establishment in another area; and

(ii) "branches", in the sense that the firm or enterprise concerned opened an additional establishment in an area where it was not manufacturing previously.

The data recorded in connection with any move included the destination, i.e. the area where the new establishment was opened, and the origin. The origin of a transfer was the area in which the associated closure of an establishment took place. The origin of a branch move was primarily the area in which was situated the manufacturing establishment publicly recognized or declared to be the manufacturing headquarters of the firm. Where there was no recognized manufacturing headquarters, the origin was taken to be that area where the largest manufacturing unit or group of units, in terms of numbers employed, was located. If the firm in question had not previously manufactured, e.g. if it had been concerned solely with wholesaling, similar tests were applied to ascertain the firm's operating headquarters. Note that the address of the firm's registered offices were not necessarily a guide. In a limited number of cases it was not possible to determine a single area of origin, and these cases were unallocated in analyses of origins.

The tests of origin referred to in the previous paragraph (and the other criteria of a move) were applied equally to new establishments opened by overseas firms. Thus new overseas-owned establishments which were transfers from other areas (of the United Kingdom) were recorded as having originated in those other areas. Where a new establishment was a branch of an overseas enterprise, the origin was taken as the country where the manufacturing headquarters of the enterprise was situated. However, in a few cases where a British subsidiary of an overseas enterprise appeared to be in complete control of its location policy, that firm was treated separately for the purpose of determining the origin of a move. In the case of new establishments owned jointly by British and overseas firms, or of new establishments owned by firms themselves owned jointly by British and overseas enterprise, overseas ownership was considered to be predominant for the purpose of tracing the origin if the overseas interest equalled or exceeded 50% of the whole.

Where an establishment transferring to another area had itself been recorded as a move from elsewhere at an earlier date, the origin of the later move was taken as the area in which the originating establishment was located immediately prior to the later move.

If an establishment was opened in an area where the firm or enterprise in question already had another establishment manufacturing in the same industry and if the latter establishment had already qualified as a move, the new establishment did not qualify as a move in the sense of adding to the number of moves but its employment was added to that of the first establishment for the purpose of assessing the amount of employment attributable to movement.

To qualify as a move an establishment must have employed more than ten persons at one date at least for which employment data were available. The acquisition by a firm of another firm or of an existing establishment did not constitute a move, even though the new owners were thereby manufacturing in an area for the first time, unless a radical change in the product manufactured at the establishment was introduced at the same time.

The Record did not include the opening of an establishment by an entirely new firm.

An establishment which qualified as a move according to the above criteria did so irrespective of whether it was opened in premises newly built to house it or in a previously existing premises.

The definitions used for movement during 1966–71 were generally the same, with the following exceptions:

The establishments recorded include:

(i) first occupiers of new premises of 5000 ft^2 or more on a new site for which an industrial development certificate was issued;

    (ii) occupiers of premises of 5000 ft^2 or more for which an industrial development certificate was issued for a change of use; and

   (iii) occupiers of other sorts of premises provided that:

      (a) employment had at some time reached 100,* and

      (b) the establishment had not transferred from other premises in the same "travel-to-work" group of employment exchanges.

This definition includes establishments opened by firms or individuals not previously engaged in manufacturing. No account is taken of these in the analysis of movement.

---

* The figure of 100 refers to the national and certain regional totals. In other regions the minimum employment required for enumeration was less than 100.

APPENDIX C

Employment in Industrial Movement

Numbers of Moves versus Employment in Moves, 1945–65

For the most part this study is concerned with mobile establishments rather than the volume of employment involved in factory movement. There are two reasons for making this distinction. Firstly, the data collected by the DTI is much more detailed when dealing with numbers of firms; secondly, employment is calculated at the end of the period (1966), regardless of when the establishment moved, thus giving a bias to earlier moves which had had longer to develop and expand. In choosing to concentrate on moves rather than employment, however, there is a danger that valuable information will be lost if the areal correlation between them is weak. That is, some areas may prove to have been massive recipients of employment but to have gained disproportionately few firms, and vice versa. Fortunately, this does not appear to have been a serious factor in either the generation or attraction of industry. Graphing total employment against number of firms entering or leaving each area does show that some areas deviate widely from the mean ratios, but the overall relationships between movement and employment are close. Leaving aside the areas with zero entries and carrying out linear regression analyses provides the results contained in Table C1, the correlations between establishments and employment generated are almost perfect and those between establishments and employment attracted are high enough to permit analysis on the basis of numbers of firms.

Multivariate Analysis of Employment in Moves

Earlier (Table C.1) it was shown that this measure and another possible one, employment in surviving moves, were high correlated;

TABLE C1. NUMBERS OF FIRMS AND EMPLOYMENT IN MOVEMENT:
REGRESSION ANALYSIS, 1945–65

(a) *Movement generation*

Variables	Correlation	α	β	Sy
Total moves versus:				
(1) Total employment ('000)	0·995	1·348	0·260	0·0045
(2) Male employment ('000)	0·988	0·814	0·160	0·0044
(3) Female employment ('000)	0·995	0·808	0·092	0·0017
$n = 33$				

(b) *Movement attraction*[a]

Variables	Correlation	α	β	Sy
Total moves versus:				
(1) Total employment ('000)	0·897	−1·389	0·313	0·0223
(2) Male employment ('000)	0·887	−0·878	0·194	0·0146
(3) Female employment ('000)	0·887	−0·608	0·122	0·0092
$n = 49$				

[a] Includes moves from abroad and from unallocated origins.

in the case of movement generation the correlation was almost perfect ($r = 0·99$), although the alternative measures of attraction were less well related ($r = 0·90$). Because of this high degree of similarity, and because the basic data (the unpublished matrices) gave much greater detail of numbers of moves, it was believed to be desirable to concentrate upon these through the main body of the analysis. However, it is accepted that a less than perfect correlation between alternative dependent variables might lead to differences in the relationships with the independent variables. For this reason, a part of the analysis is repeated in this appendix. Using the same independent variables as before, the numbers employed (1966 values) in moves occurring during each of the first three periods (generated and attracted by, and between, each area) has been subjected to correlation and regression analyses in exactly the same way as before. The results are contained in Tables C.2 and C.3.

As might be expected with such similarity between the alternative measures of movement generated by areas, their correlations with the independent variables are closely alike. On the other hand, the results from analysis of patterns of attraction show some marked changes which might have been foreseen. These are of two types. Firstly, the labour variables tend to be more important than before; larger establishments (given an equal number of moves) tended to locate in areas where the numbers and rates of unemployment were greater. Secondly, the two policy variables (assisted area employment and new town targets) were affected in opposite ways. The former were significantly improved, the latter had their importance diminished. The remaining variables retained their correlations with very little change. In view of the circumstantial evidence noted previously (the relationship between size of establishment and distance moved, and between size and labour availability), these changes in levels of correlation conform to expectations.

TABLE C.2. CORRELATION COEFFICIENTS BETWEEN EMPLOYMENT IN MOVES GENERATED AND ATTRACTED BY AREAS AND INDEPENDENT VARIABLES, 1945–65

(a) *Generation*

Variable	1945–51	1952–9	1960–5
1. Manufacturing employment	0·90***	0·85***	0·86***
2. Urban employment density	0·62***	0·62***	0·62***
3. Area with urban status	0·72***	0·66***	0·65***
4. Size of area	−0·19	0·16	−0·17
5. Female activity rates	0·43**	0·34*	0·39**
6. Male earnings	0·36*	0·32*	0·38**
7. Female earnings	0·24	0·22	0·43**
8. Male unemployed (%)	−0·12	−0·08	−0·11
9. Female unemployed (%)	−0·23	−0·17	−0·20
10. Total unemployed (%)	−0·16	−0·10	−0·15
11. Assisted area weight	−0·12	−0·09	−0·15
12. New town target weight	0·04	−0·01	−0·01
13. Industrial composition	0·34*	0·33*	0·37**
14. Employment change, 1951–61	—	—	−0·01

(b) *Attraction*

Variable	1945–51	1952–9	1960–5
1a. Total numbers unemployed	0·65***	0·34*	0·61***
2. Urban employment density	0·02	−0·06	0·14
3. Area with urban status	0·18	0·11	0·18
4. Size of area	0·01	0·07	0·02
5. Female activity rates	−0·13	−0·03	0·01
6. Male earnings	0·20	0·29*	0·30*
7. Female earnings	0·02	0·10	0·06
8. Male unemployed (%)	0·42	0·11	0·40**
9. Female unemployed (%)	0·40**	0·10	0·24
10. Total unemployed (%)	0·43**	0·12	0·3*
11. Assisted area weight	0·78***	0·14	0·36*
12. New town target weight	0·16	0·70**	0·45**
13. Industrial composition	Not applicable		
14. Employment change, 1951–61	Not applicable		
15. Assisted area employment	0·89***	0·26	0·73***
16. New town target population	0·30*	0·81***	0·63***
17. Modified gravity measure	0·04	0·44	0·11

Significance levels: 95% *; 99% **; 99·9% ***.

The differences are also carried over into the multiple regression models (Table C.3), although it should also be noted that overall levels of explanation are, in general, no higher in the employment analysis than they were in the analysis of surviving moves. The differences occur in two categories, of which the more important is the promotion or relegation of variables to significantly different ranks in the models. The second change is found in the weights of the standardized regression coefficients of variables common to both the employment and the "number of moves" models. In the first category the ranks of variables comprising the generation models are very little different from those derived from the number of moves; this is expected, for the two measures were very highly correlated. In addition, there were only very minor changes in the weights assigned to regression coefficients.

By contrast, the variables constituting the attraction models are markedly different in both categories. Whereas in the number of

TABLE C.3. ATTRACTION AND GENERATION MODELS BASED ON EMPLOYMENT
IN MOVES

(a) *Generation*

1945–51	1952–9	1960–5
$+1\cdot45\,X_1$ $10\cdot2$***	$+1\cdot38\,X_1$ $10\cdot1$***	$+1\cdot36\,X_1$ $10\cdot1$***
$-0\cdot21\,X_{11}$ $4\cdot1$***	$-0\cdot54\,X_3$ $3\cdot6$***	$-0\cdot54\,X_3$ $4\cdot0$***
$-0\cdot46\,X_3$ $4\cdot1$***	$-0\cdot32\,X_5$ $2\cdot8$***	$-0\cdot15\,X_8$ $2\cdot1$**
$-0\cdot17\,X_2$ $2\cdot2$**	$-0\cdot15\,X_{11}$ $2\cdot2$**	$+0\cdot15\,X_{13}$ $2\cdot0$*
	$+0\cdot17\,X_{14}$ $1\cdot9$*	$-0\cdot13\,X_{12}$ $1\cdot9$*
	$-0\cdot05\,X_{12}$ $1\cdot7$*	$-0\cdot13\,X_5$ $1\cdot8$*
$r^2 = 0\cdot89$	$r^2 = 0\cdot84$	$r^2 = 0\cdot85$

(b) *Attraction*

1945–51	1952–9	1960–5
$+0\cdot56\,X_{11}$ $6\cdot1$***	$+1\cdot14\,X_{12}$ $7\cdot3$***	$+0\cdot66\,X_{1a}$ $5\cdot1$***
$+0\cdot54\,X_{1a}$ $5\cdot1$***	$+0\cdot44\,X_{1a}$ $4\cdot8$***	$+0\cdot34\,X_8$ $2\cdot8$***
$-0\cdot29\,X_2$ $3\cdot2$***	$+0\cdot28\,X_{17}$ $3\cdot0$***	$+0\cdot30\,X_{12}$ $2\cdot8$***
$+0\cdot19\,X_{17}$ $2\cdot5$**	$-0\cdot24\,X_2$ $2\cdot8$***	$+0\cdot30\,X_{17}$ $2\cdot3$**
		$-0\cdot26\,X_2$ $2\cdot3$**
$r^2 = 0\cdot78$	$r^2 = 0\cdot78$	$r^2 = 0\cdot67$

Significance levels: 95% *; 99% **; 99·9% ***.

moves models the most significant variable was the volume of unemployment (X_{1a}), which dominated in two of the periods, in the
employment models the dominant variables in two periods relate to
regional policy attractions (X_{11} in the period 1945–51, and X_{12} in the
period 1952–9). The volume of unemployment is the second most
significant in these periods and urban employment density (X_2)
appears in each period as a significant negative influence on attraction.

On balance, one may conclude that the explanation of movement
patterns differs when the dependent variable is employment in

movement, but not so markedly as to alter significantly the generalizations based on number of moves. Moreover, the models themselves are no better, having similar coefficients of multiple correlation and patterns of residuals which are not much removed from those discussed above. It is possible that a different set of results would emerge if the dependent variable were employment in moves at the time of movement instead of at the end of 1966 (due to possible regional differentials in growth rates), but there is no data on which to test this.

References

ALEXANDERSSON, G. and NOSTROM, G. (1963) *World Shipping: An Economic Geography of Ports and Seaborne Trade*, Wiley, New York.

ALLEN, K. (1970) The regional multiplier: some problems in estimation, in *Regional and Urban Studies* (edited by J. B. Cullingworth and S. C. Orr), Allen and Unwin, London.

ARCHIBALD, G. C. (1967) Regional multiplier effects in the U.K., *Oxford Economic Papers* **19**, 22–45.

AYRES, R. U. (1969) *Technological Forecasting and Long Range Planning*, McGraw-Hill, New York.

BATER, J. M. and WALKER, D. F. (1970) Further comments on industrial location and linkage, *Area* **4**, 59–63.

BEACHAM, A. and OSBORNE, W. T. (1970) The movement of manufacturing industry, *Regional Studies* **4**, 41–47.

BEESLEY, M. (1955) The birth and death of industrial establishments: experience in the West Midlands conurbation, *Journal of Industrial Economics* **4**, 45–61.

BOUDEVILLE, J. R. (1974) European integration, urban regions and medium-sized towns, in *Regional Policy and Planning for Europe* (edited by M. E. C. Sant, Saxon House, London.

BOWERS, J. (1970) *The Anatomy of Regional Activity Rates*, NIESR, Regional Papers I, London.

BRONFENBRENNER, M. (editor) (1969) *Is the Business Cycle Obsolete?*, Interscience, New York.

BROWN, A. J. (1969) Surveys in applied economics (1) regional economics with special reference to the United Kingdom, *Economic Journal* **79**, 759–96.

BROWN, A. J. (1972) *The Framework of Regional Economics in the United Kingdom*, Cambridge U.P., Cambridge.

BROWN, C. M. (1966) Industry in the new towns of the London region, in *Greater London: An Industrial Geography*, by J. E. Martin, Bell, London.

BURNS, A. F. and MITCHELL, W. C. (1946) *Measuring Business Cycles*, NBER, New York.

CAMERON, G. C. (1970) Growth areas, growth centres and regional conversion, *Scottish Journal of Political Economy* **17**, 19–38.

CAMERON, G. C. (1974) Regional economic policy in the United Kingdom, in *Regional Policy and Planning for Europe* (edited by M. E. C. Sant), Saxon House, London.

CAMERON, G. C. and CLARK, B. D. (1966) *Industrial Movement and the Regional Problem*, Oliver and Boyd, Edinburgh.

CAMERON, G. C. and EVANS, A. W. (1973) The British conurbation centres, *Regional Studies* **7**, 47–55.

CAMERON, G. C. and JOHNSON, K. M. (1969) Comprehensive urban renewal and industrial location—the Glasgow case, in *Regional and Urban Studies* (edited by J. B. Cullingworth and S. C. Orr), Allen and Unwin, London.

CAMINA, M. M. (1974) Local authorities and the attraction of industry, *Progress in Planning*, Pergamon, Oxford.

CHANNON, D. F. (1973) *The Strategy and Structure of British Enterprise*, Harvard U.P., Boston, Mass.

CHISHOLM, M. (1964) Must we all live in South East England?, *Geography* **48**, 1–14.

CHISHOLM, M. (1966) *Geography and Economics*, Bell, London.

CHISHOLM, M. (1970) On the making of a myth? How capital intensive is industry investing in the development areas?, *Urban Studies* **7**, 289–93.

CHISHOLM, M. and MANNERS, G. (editors) (1971) *Spatial Policy Problems in the British Economy*, Cambridge U.P., Cambridge.

CLARK, C., WILSON, F., and BRADLEY, J. (1969) Industrial location and economic potential in Western Europe, *Regional Studies* **3**, 197–212.

COATES, B. E. and RAWSTRON, E. W. (1971) *Regional Variations in Britain*, Batsford, London.

COMMISSION OF THE EUROPEAN COMMUNITIES (1969) *A Regional Policy for the Community*, Brussels.

COMMISSION OF THE EUROPEAN COMMUNITIES (1973) *Report on the Regional Problems of the Enlarged Community*, Brussels.

CMND 2188 (1963) *Central Scotland: a Programme for Development and Growth*, HMSO, London.

CMND 3998 (1969) *The Intermediate Areas*, HMSO, London.

CMND 4942 (1972) *Industrial and Regional Development*, HMSO, London.

CMND 5322 (1973) *Dispersal of the Civil Service*, HMSO, London.

CMND 6153 (1940) *Royal Commission on the Distribution of the Industrial Population: Report*, HMSO, London.

COMMITTEE OF INQUIRY ON SMALL FIRMS (1971) *Dynamics of Small Firms*, Research Report 12, HMSO, London.

CULLINGWORTH, J. B. and ORR, S. C. (editors) (1969) *Regional and Urban Studies*, Allen and Unwin, London.

CYERT, R. M. and MARCH, J. G. (1963) *A Behavioural Theory of the Firm*, Prentice Hall, Englewood Cliffs.

DANIELS, P. W. (1969) Office decentralization from London—policy and practices, *Regional Studies* **3**, 171–8.

DARWENT, D. F. (1969) Growth poles and growth centres in regional planning—a review, *Environment and Planning* **1**, 5–31.

DAVIES, G. (1967) Regional unemployment, labour availability and redeployment, *Oxford Economic Papers* **19**, 59–74.

DEPARTMENT OF THE ENVIRONMENT (1971) *Long Term Population Distribution in Great Britain*, HMSO, London.

DIAMOND, D. R. (1974) The long term view of regional policy, in *Regional Policy and Planning for Europe* (edited by M. E. C. Sant), Saxon House, London.

DICKEN, P. (1971) Some aspects of the decision making behaviour of business organizations, *Economic Geography* **47**, 426–37.

DONNISON, D. and EVERSLEY, D. E. C. (editors) (1973) *London: Urban Patterns, Problems and Policies*, Heinemann, London.

DOWNS, A. (1957) *An Economic Theory of Democracy*, Harper and Row, London.

DZIEWONSKI, K. (1966) A new approach to the theory and empirical analysis of location, *Regional Science Association Papers* **16**, 17–25.

ESTALL R. C. and BUCHANAN, R. O. (1961) *Industrial Activity and Economic Geography*, Hutchinson, London.

EUROPEAN FREE TRADE ASSOCIATION (1971) *Regional Policy in EFTA: Industrial Mobility*, Geneva.

EVERSLEY, D. E. C. (1965) Social and psychological factors in the determination of industrial location, in *Papers on Regional Development* (edited by T. Wilson), Blackwell, Oxford.

EVERSLEY, D. E. C. (1973) Problems of social planning in inner London, in *London: Urban Patterns, Problems and Policies* (edited by D. V. Donnison and D. E. C. Eversley), Heinemann, London.

FLORENCE, P. S. (1948) *Investment, Location and Size of Plant*, Cambridge U.P., Cambridge.

FLORENCE, P. S. (1962) *Postwar Investment, Location and Size of Plant*, Cambridge U.P., Cambridge.

FLORENCE, P. S. (1970) *Atlas of Economic Structure and Policies*, Oxford.

FORSYTH, D. J. C. (1972) *U.S. Investment in Scotland*, Praeger, London.

FOSTER, C. D. and RICHARDSON, R. (1973) Employment trends in London in the 1960s and their relevance for the future in London: *Urban Patterns, Problems and Policies* (edited by D. V. Donnison and D. E. C. Eversley), Heinemann, London.

FRIEDMANN, J. (1966) *Regional Development Policy*, M.I.T. Press, Cambridge, Mass.

GARNER, B. J. (1967) Models in urban geography, in *Models in Geography* (edited by R. Chorley and P. Haggett), Methuen, London.

GODDARD, J. B. (1973) Office linkages and location, *Progress in Planning* **1**, 109–232.

GOLDBERG, M. A. (1969) An economic model of intrametropolitan industrial location, *Journal of Regional Studies* **10**, 75–79.

GORDON, I. R. (1970) Activity rates: regional and sub-regional differentials, *Regional Studies* **4**, 411–24.

GREATER LONDON COUNCIL (1970) *Greater London Development Plan; Statement*, London.

GRIME, E. K. and STARKIE, D. N. M. (1968) New jobs for old: an impact study of a new factory in Furness, *Regional Studies* **2**, 57–67.

HAGUE, D. C. and DUNNING, J. H. (1954) Costs in alternative locations: the radio industry, *Review of Economics and Statistics* **22**, 203–13.

HAGUE, D. C. and NEWMAN, P. K. (1952) *Costs in Alternative Locations: the Clothing Industry*, NIESR, Cambridge.

HAINES, V. G. (1970) *Business Relocation: A Guide to Moving a Business*, Business Books, London.

HALL, M. (editor) (1959) *Made in New York*, Harvard U.P., Cambridge, Mass.

HALL, P. G. (1962) *The Industries of London Since 1861*, Hutchinson, London.

HALL, P. G. (1968) Land use—the spread of towns into the country, in *Forecasting and the Social Sciences* (edited by M. Young), Heinemann, London.

HALL, P. G. (1973) *The Containment of Urban England*, 2 vols., Allen and Unwin, London.

HAMILTON, F. E. I. (1967) Models of industrial location, in *Models in Geography* (edited by R. J. Chorley and P. Haggett), Methuen, London.

HART, P. E. and MACBEAN, A. I. (1961) Regional differences in productivity, profitability and growth, *Scottish Journal of Political Economy* **8**, 1–11.

HOLMANS, A. E. (1964) Industrial development certificates and the control of growth of employment in South East England, *Urban Studies* **1**, 138–52.

HOOVER, E. M. (1948) *The Location of Economic Activity*, McGraw-Hill, New York.

HOOVER, E. M. (1954) Some institutional factors in business investment decisions, *American Economic Review* **44** (Suppl.), 201–13.

HOROWITZ, I. (1970) *Decision Making and the Theory of the Firm*, Holt, Rinehart, New York.

HOUSE OF COMMONS (1973) *Inquiry into Location Attitudes and Experience*, Minutes of Evidence, Expenditure Committee (Trade and Industry Sub-Committee), 42, xvii, HMSO, London.

HOWARD, R. S. (1968) *Movement of Manufacturing Industry in the United Kingdom*, 1945–65, HMSO, London.

ISARD, W. (1956) *Location and Space Economy*, MIT Press, Cambridge, Mass.

ISARD, W. (1969) *General Theory: Social, Political, Economic and Regional*, MIT Press, Cambridge, Mass.

JAMES, B. G. S. (1964) The incompatibility of industrial and trading cultures, A critical appraisal of the growth point concept, *Journal of Industrial Economics* **13**, 90–94.

JONES, R. M. (1968) The direction of industrial movement and its impact on recipient regions, *Manchester School* **36**, 149–72.

KAST, F. E. and ROSENZWEIG, J. E. (1970) *Organization and Management. A Systems Approach*, McGraw-Hill, New York.

KEEBLE, D. E. (1967) Models of economic development, in *Models in Geography* (edited by R. J. Chorley and P. Haggett), Methuen, London.

KEEBLE, D. E. (1968) Industrial decentralization and the metropolis: the North West London case, *Institute of British Geographers, Transactions* **44**, 1–54.

KEEBLE, D. E. (1969) Local industrial linkage and manufacturing growth in outer London, *Town Planning Review* **40**, 163–88.

KEEBLE, D. E. (1970) The movement of manufacturing industry—comments, *Regional Studies* **4**, 399–408.

KEEBLE, D. E. (1971) Industrial mobility in Britain, in *Spatial Policy Problems of the British Economy* (edited by M. Chisholm and G. Manners), Cambridge U.P., Cambridge.

KEEBLE, D. E. and HAUSER, D. P. (1971) Spatial analysis of manufacturing growth in outer South East England, 1960–1967: I, Hypotheses and variables, *Regional Studies*, **5**, 229–62.

KEEBLE, D. E. and HAUSER, D. P. (1972) Spatial analysis of manufacturing growth in outer South East England, 1960–1967: II, Methods and results, *Regional Studies* **5**, 11–36.

KING, L. J. (1969) *Statistical Analysis in Geography*, Prentice Hall, Englewood Cliffs.

KLAASSEN, L. J. (1965) *Area Economic and Social Redevelopment*, OECD, Paris.

KRUMME, G. (1969a) Towards a geography of enterprise, *Economic Geography* **45**, 30–40.

KRUMME, G. (1969b) Notes on locational adjustment patterns in industrial geography. *Geografiska Annaler* **51B**, 15–19.

KUKLINSKI, A. R. (1967) *Criteria for Location of Industrial Plants*, United Nations, New York.

LEFEBER, L. (1958) *Allocation in Space: Production, Transport and Industrial Location*, North Holland, Amsterdam.

LEVER, W. (1972) Industrial movement, spatial association and functional linkages, *Regional Studies* **6**, 371–84.

LEVER, W. (1973) Cyclical changes in factors affecting industrial location, *Land Economics* **49**, 218–21.

LEVER, W. (1975) Selectivity in British regional policy, *Proceedings of the First British–Hungarian Geographical Seminar*, National Academy of Sciences, Budapest.

LINGE, G. J. R. (1967) Governments and the location of secondary industry in Australia, *Economic Geography* **43**, 43–63.

LLOYD, P. E. (1970) The impact of development area policies on Merseyside, 1949–67, in *Merseyside: Social and Economic Studies* (edited by R. Lawton and C. M. Cunningham), Longman, London.

LOGAN, M. T. (1966) Locational behaviour of manufacturing firms in urban areas, *Annals of the Association of American Geographers* **56**, 451–66.

LOMAS, G. M. (1963) Labour and life in London, in *London: Urban Patterns, Problems and Policies* (edited by D. Donnison and D. E. C. Eversley), Heinemann, London.

LOMAS, G. M. and WOOD, P. A. (1969) *Employment Location in Regional Economic Planning*, Cass, London.

LOSCH, A. (1954) *The Economics of Location*, Yale, New Haven.

LOWRY, I. S. (1966) *Migration and Metropolitan Growth*, University of California Press, Los Angeles.

LUTTRELL, W. F. (1962) *Factory Location and Industrial Movement*, NIESR, London.

McCRONE, G. (1969) *Regional Policy in Britain*, Allen and Unwin, London.

McGOVERN, P. D. (1965) Industrial dispersal, *Planning*, vol. 31.

MARTIN, J. E. (1966) *Greater London: An Industrial Geography*, Bell, London.

MARTIN, J. E. (1969) The size of plant location of industry in Greater London, *Tijdschrift voor Economische en Sociale Geografie* **60**, 369–74.

MEADE, J. E. (1955) *The Theory of Customs Unions*, North Holland, Amsterdam.

MINISTRY OF LABOUR (1962) Characteristics of the unemployed, *Ministry of Labour Gazette* **70**, 131–2 and 347.

MINISTRY OF LABOUR (1966) Characteristics of the unemployed, *Ministry of Labour Gazette* **74**, 156 and 385.

MOORE, B. and RHODES, J. (1973) *The Economic and Exchequer Implications of Regional Policy*, Minutes of Evidence taken before the Expenditure Committee (Trade and Industry Sub-Committee), House of Commons, 42, xvi, HMSO, London.

MOORE, B. and RHODES, J. (1974) The effects of regional economic policy in the United Kingdom, in *Regional Policy and Planning for Europe* (edited by M. E. C. Sant), Saxon House, London.

MOSELEY, M. J. (1973) The impact of growth centres in rural regions: I, An analysis of spatial patterns in Brittany: II, An analysis of spatial flows in East Anglia, *Regional Studies* **7**, 57–94.

MYRDAL, G. (1957) *Economic Theory and Underdeveloped Regions*, Duckworth, London.

NATIONAL ECONOMIC DEVELOPMENT COUNCIL (1963) *Conditions Favourable to Faster Growth*, HMSO, London.

NEEDLEMAN, L. (1965) What are we to do about the regional problem ?, *Lloyds Bank Review* **75**, 45–58.

NEEDLEMAN, L. (editor) (1968) *Regional Analysis*, Penguin, London.

NEEDLEMAN, L. and SCOTT, B. (1964) Regional problems and the location of industry policy in Britain, *Urban Studies* **1**, 153–73.

NORDLING, C. O. (1967) Origin of a depression, *Land Economics* **43**, 64–70.

NORTH-EAST DEVELOPMENT COUNCIL (1971) *The North in the Sixties*, Newcastle-upon-Tyne, mimeo.

NORTH-EAST DEVELOPMENT COUNCIL (1973) *The Move to the North: A Survey of the Experience of Industrial Plants*, mimeo.

OLSSON, G. (1965) *Distance and Human Interaction*, Regional Science Research Institute, Philadelphia.

PARSONS, G. F. (1972) The giant manufacturing corporations and balanced regional growth in Britain, *Area* **4**, 99–103.

POCOCK, D. C. D. (1970) Economic renewal: the example of Fife, *Scottish Geographical Magazine* **86**, 123–33.

PRED, A. (1967) *Behaviour and Location: Foundations for a Geographic and Dynamic Location Theory*, Gleerup, Lund.

RAY, D. M. (1965) *Market Potential and Economic Shadow: A Quantitative Analysis of Industrial Location in Southern Ontario*, University of Chicago Press, Chicago.

RENNER, G. T. (1947) Geography of industrial localization, *Economic Geography* **23**, 168–89.

RHODES, J. and KAN, A. (1971) *Office Dispersal and Regional Policy*, Cambridge U.P., Cambridge.

RICHARDSON, H. W. (1969) *Regional Economics*, Weidenfeld and Nicholson, London.

RICHARDSON, H. W. (1972) Optimality in city size, systems of cities and urban policy: a sceptic's view, *Urban Studies* **9**, 29–48.

RICHARDSON, H. W. and WEST, E. G. (1964) Must we always take work to the workers ?, *Lloyds Bank Review* **7**, 35–48.

RIDLEY, A. (1972) Regional policy—theory and practice, *Urban Studies Conference on Regional Policy*, Oxford, mimeo.

ROBERTSON, D. J. (1965) A nation of regions ?, *Urban Studies* **2**, 121–36.

ROSS, E. A. (1896) The location of industries, *Quarterly Journal of Economics* **10**, 247–68.

SALT, J. (1967) The impact of the Ford and Vauxhall plants on the employment situation of Merseyside, *Tijdschrift voor Economische en Sociale Geografie* **58**, 255–64.

SANT, M. E. C. (1970) Age and area in industrial location, *Regional Studies* **4**, 349–58.

SANT, M. E. C. (1973) *The Geography of Business Cycles*, London School of Economics, London.

SANT, M. E. C. (1974a) *Regional Disparities*, Macmillan, London.

SANT, M. E. C. (editor) (1974b) *Regional Policy and Planning for Europe*, Saxon House, London.

SANT, M. E. C. (1975) Interregional industrial movement: the case of the non-survivors, in *Essays in Honour of S. H. Beaver* (edited by B. J. Turton and A. D. M. Phillips), Longman, London.

SKENE-SMITH, N. (1966) *Economics, Commerce and Administration*, Pergamon, Oxford.

SMIDT, M. DE (1966) Foreign industrial establishments located in the Netherlands, *Tijdschrift voor Economische en Sociale Geografie* **57**, 1–19.

SMITH, B. M. D. (1970) Industrial overspill in theory and practice: the case of the West Midlands, *Urban Studies* **7**, 189–204.

SMITH, D. M. (1971) *Industrial Location: An Economic Geographical Analysis*, Wiley, New York.

SOUTH-EAST JOINT PLANNING TEAM (1971) *Strategic Plan for the South East*, HMSO, London.

SPOONER, D. J. (1972) Industrial movement and the rural periphery: the case of Devon and Cornwall, *Regional Studies* **6**, 197–215.

STEED, G. P. F. (1971) Locational implications of corporate organization of industry, *Canadian Geographer* **15**, 54–56.

STEVENS, B. H. and BRACKETT, C. A. (1967) *Industrial Location: A Review and Annotated Bibliography of Theoretical Empirical and Case Studies*, Regional Science Research Institute, Philadelphia.

STEWART, J. A. (1974) Objectives for regional policy: the view from industry, in *Regional Policy and Planning for Europe* (edited by M. E. C. Sant), Saxon House, London.

STILWELL, F. J. B. (1972) *Regional Economic Policy*, Macmillan, London.

STONE, P. A. (1962) *The Economics of Factory Buildings*, HMSO, London.

TAYLOR, J. (1968) Hidden female labour reserves, *Regional Studies* **2**, 221–31.

TAYLOR, M. J. (1970) Location decisions of small firms, *Area* **2**, 51–54.

THOMAS, R. (1969) The financial benefits of expanding in the development areas, *Bulletin of the Oxford University Institute of Economic and Social Studies* **31**, 77–87.

TOWNROE, P. M. (1969) Locational choice and the individual firm, *Regional Studies* **3**, 15–24.

TOWNROE, P. M. (1970) Industrial linkage, agglomeration and external economies, *Journal of the Town Planning Institute* **56**, 18–20.

TOWNROE, P. M. (1971) *Industrial Location Decisions: A Study in Management Behaviour*, Centre for Urban and Regional Studies, Birmingham.

TOWNROE, P. M. (1973) The supply of mobile industry: a cross sectional analysis, *Regional and Urban Economics* **2**, 371–86.

TULPULE, A. H. (1969) Dispersion of industrial employment in the Greater London area, *Regional Studies* **3**, 25–40.

WEBER, A. (1929) *Theory of Location of Industries*, University of Chicago Press, Chicago.

WELCH, R. V. (1970) Immigrant manufacturing industry established in Scotland between 1945 and 1968: some structural and locational characteristics, *Scottish Geographical Magazine* **86**, 134–48.

WEST, E. G. (1966) Regional planning: fact and fallacy, *Lloyds Bank Review* **80**, 33–49.

WEST, E. G. (1973) "Pure" versus "operational" economics in regional policy, in *Regional Policy for Ever?*, by G. Hallett, P. Randall, and E. G. West, Institute of Economic Affairs, London.

WESTAWAY, J. (1973) *Contact Potential and the Occupational Structure of the British Urban System, 1961–1966: An Empirical Study*, London School of Economics, Graduate School of Geography Discussion Paper 45, mimeo.

WILSON, T. (1973) British regional policy in the European context, *The Banker* **123**, 164–9.

WOOD, P. A. (1969) Industrial location and linkage, *Area* **1**, 32–39.

YEATES, M. H. and LLOYD, P. E. (1970) *Impact of Industrial Incentives: South Georgia Bay Region, Ontario*, Department of Energy, Mines and Resources, Ottawa.

YOUNG, M. (1968) *Forecasting and the Social Sciences*, Heinemann, London.

Index

Activity rates   9, 19, 127–9, 142–3
   148, 150, 191–2
Alexandersson, G.   183
Allen, K.   209
Archibald, G. C.   209
Assisted areas
   designation   30–4, 87–8, 213
   in movement models   87–8, 91,
      100, 134–5, 143, 149–51, 157
Australia   23
Ayres, R. U.   160

Backwash effect   4
Barlow report   13
Beacham, A.   186
Behavioural theories   6, 154, 157
Belgium   34
Boudeville, J. R.   24
Bowers, J.   191
Branch plants   41, 108–9
Bronfenbrenner, M.   161
Brown, A. J.   19, 30, 66, 105, 186,
   188, 209, 214, 220
Brown, C. M.   46
Buchanan, R. O,   21, 44
Burns, A. F.   161

Cameron, G. C.   13, 22, 44–5, 52,
   186, 205, 216, 218
Camina, M. M.   24, 180
Central Scotland report   17, 212

Channon, D. F.   82
Chisholm, M.   21, 170
City size   13
Clark, B. D.   52, 186, 205
Clark, C.   23, 183
Closures   19, 72, 101–9
Coates, B. E.   178, 190
Colonization effect   48
Committee of inquiry on small firms
   103
Comparative advantage   2
Corporate structure   82, 177
Cost differentials   34, 106–7, 214
Cumulative causation   1, 4

Data sources   xi, 67, 110
DATAC areas   77
Decentralization   178–9, 216
Decision making   12, 48, 81–2
Definitions   xi–xii, 224–32
Derelict land clearance areas   31
Development areas   31–3
Development districts   33
Development grants   214
Diamond, D. R.   212, 221
Disparities   15–16, 165, 190–9, 216
Distribution of Industry Act 1945
   86
Distribution of Industry Act 1958
   31
Donnison, D.   180
Downs, A.   10, 17

Dual population hypothesis 62
Dunning, J. H. 106
Dziewonski, K. 20

Earnings 190
Economic dualism 4
Economic bases 7, 197
Economies of scale 44
Employment
  changes 132–4, 194–5
  in movement 233–8
  projection 173
Environment 14
Equilibrium 1–7
Estall, R. C. 21, 44
European Economic Community
  23, 182–3
Evans, A. W. 216
Eversley, D. E. C. 5, 12, 157,
  179–80
Exchequer costs 9–10
Exogenous variables 37
Expenditure on regional policy
  28–30, 72–4, 86–7, 166, 214
External economies 44–6

Factor price equalization 3–4
Federalism 23
Florence, P. S. 44
Forecasting
  experimental 167–71
  general, 160–2
  long-term 171–84
  requirements 162–3
Foreign companies 52, 121–2
Forsyth, D. J. C. 52, 121, 183
Foster, C. D. 217
Free depreciation 30, 107
Friedmann, J. 200

Garner, B. J. 178
Goddard, J. B. 223

Goldberg, M. A. 44
Gordon, I. R. 128
Gravity model 115, 118, 139–40,
  148, 151, 183
Greater London Council 14
Grime, E. K. 206
Growth centres 24

Hague, D. C. 106
Hall, M. 46
Hall, P. G. 44, 178–9
Hardman Report 219
Hauser, D. P. 65
Holmans, A. E. 81
Hoover, E. M. xii, 5
Horowitz, I. 81
Howard, R. S. xi, 41, 125, 214
Hunt Committee Report 12, 33,
  189, 213
Hypotheses 68–71, 81–3, 122–4

Impact of movement
  constraints 199–210
  employment 61–6, 214–5
Indigenous growth 219
Industrial composition 19, 125,
  145, 195–7, 201
Industrial Development Act 1966
  33
Industrial development certificates
  52, 54, 213
Industrial estates 28, 86, 100
Industrial Location Attitudes Group
  53–8
Industrial mobility
  creation 23, 71
  diversion 23, 71
  prospects 171–84
Industry Act 1972 7, 30, 185, 211
Inertia 20–7
Inflation 9, 11–12

Infrastructure 13, 30, 33
Intermediate areas 31–3
Interregional industrial movement
  characteristics 50–9
  description of patterns 111–21
  destinations 113
  explanatory variables 124–40
  impact on employment 61–6,
    214–5
  models 122–4
  motives 52–3, 81–3
  origins 60–1, 112, 114–8
  residual distributions 151, 154–9
  statistical analysis 140–53
  supply areas 118–20
Intervening opportunities 123
Intraregional movement 37–50
Investment grants 30
Isard, W. xii, 1, 124
Italy 34

James, B. G. S. 210
Johnson, K. M. 22, 44–5
Jones, R. M. 207

Kan, A. 173, 178, 219
Kast, F. E. 164
Keeble, D. E. 44, 46, 52, 62, 65,
  68, 82, 96, 107–8, 186, 205
King, L. J. 95
Klaassen, L. J. 13
Krumme, G. 2, 81

Labour
  costs 58, 125–8, 142, 148, 150,
    174, 176, 178
  markets 205–8
  mobility 5, 11–12

supply 41, 46–8, 58, 127, 137,
  150
Lag effects 69, 133
Land values 178
Leakages 6–7, 208–10
Lefebre, L. 4
Lever, W. 52, 68, 210
Linkages 44–8, 210
Lloyd, P. E. 7, 189, 206, 208
Local authorities 24, 180
Local Employment Act 1960 32–3
Local Employment Act 1963 52,
  86
Location factors 53–8
Location theory 1–3
Logan, M. T. 48
Lomas, G. M. 44
London 13–14, 41–3, 157, 213
Lösch, A. xii, 141
Lowry, I. S. 163
Luttrell, W. F. 58, 82, 103, 203

McCrone, G. 14, 27, 33, 72, 86, 94,
  167, 213
McGovern, P. D. 52
Manufacturing
  employment 124–6, 142–3, 166
  output 73, 84, 166
Martin, J. E. 41, 44
Mass factor 124
Meade, J. G. 183
Metropolitan economic labour areas
  178
Metropolitan influence 78
Migration 4, 11–12, 192–4
Mitchell, W. C. 161
Moore, B. 9–12, 86, 165, 186, 196,
  213–4, 216, 221
Moseley, M. J. 7, 130, 200, 208,
  210
Multipliers 19, 208–10
Myrdal, G. 1, 4

National Economic Development
  Council 206
Needleman, L. 5, 9, 11–12
Netherlands 23
New Towns 73, 76, 88, 100, 134,
  136, 149–50, 179
New York 46
Nordling, G. 183
North East Development Council
  58–9, 198, 203, 217
Nostrom, G. 183

Occupation structure 207–8
Office development permits 213
Office relocation 218–9
Olsson, G. 115, 124
Osborne, W. T. 186

Policy
  goals and objectives 8, 16–18,
    34–5, 212–3
  impact on GDP 10, 165, 216
  impact on industrial movement
    166, 185–9
  instruments 213–4
  long-term and short-term 7,
    221–3
  marginal costs 181–2
  selectivity 157
Post-move experience 58–9, 204–5
Pred, A. xii, 1, 81
Productivity 201–4
Profitability 58–9
Profits centres 220
Public investment 30

Radial movement 46–7
Raw materials 182
Rawstron, E. W. 178, 190

Regional employment premium 30,
  107
Regional indicators 189–99
Regional typology 200–1
Regionalism 14
Renner, G. T. 3
Rents 21, 45, 58
Rhodes, J. 9, 10, 11, 12, 86, 165,
  173, 178, 186, 196, 213–4, 216,
  219, 221
Richardson, H. W. 3, 5, 8, 13, 217
Richardson, R. 217
Ridley, A. 18, 180, 220
Rosenzweig, J. E. 164
Ross, E. A. 21

Salt, J. 207
Sant, M. E. C. 16, 46, 48, 78, 102,
  166, 206
Scott, B. 5, 11
Selective assistance 30, 219
Shift and share analysis 187–8
Size of factory 41–4, 46, 121, 176–7
Skene-Smith, N. 82
Smidt, M. de 23, 70, 183
Smith, B. M. D. 45, 158
Smith, D. M, xii, 12, 70, 140
South East Joint Planning Team
  40, 48, 180
Spatial margins model 70
Special areas 86
Special development areas 31–3
Spooner, D. J. 48–9, 78
Spread effect 4
Stabilization 10–11
Starkie, D. N. M. 206
Steed, G. P. F. 177
Stewart, J. A. 48
Stilwell, F. J. B. 5, 8, 14, 215
Stone, P. A. 177
Systems theory 164

Tariffs 23
Taylor, J. 128
Tertiary sector 173
Thomas, R. 34
Time Series
    composition 69–71, 84–5, 93–4
    independent variables 84–8
    multivariate analysis 88–102
    national 71–5, 95–7
    problems of analysis 83–4, 92
    regional 75–81, 96–101
Town Development Act 1952 76
Town expansion schemes 76, 78, 88, 100, 134, 136
Townroe, P. M. xii, 2, 5, 22, 48, 69, 87, 125, 154, 172, 174
Transferred establishments 41
Transport costs 34, 174
Tulpule, A. H. 46

Unemployment 9, 19, 74, 85, 129–31, 137, 139, 142–3, 145, 148, 150, 190–1, 206–7, 217
United States 10, 13, 44
Urban employment density 131–2, 142, 145, 150
Urbanization 178
Urban areas 131, 133, 142–3, 145

Weber, A. xii, 1, 140
West, E. G. 9, 14, 19, 215
West Midland conurbation 44–5
Westaway, J. 208
Wilson, T. 24, 107, 213
Wood, P. A. 44

Yeates, M. H. 7, 208
Young, M. 160

THE URBAN AND REGIONAL PLANNING SERIES
Other Titles in the Series

CHADWICK, G. F.: A Systems View of Planning: Towards a Theory of the Urban and Regional Planning Process (Volume 1)

BLUNDEN, W. R.: The Land Use/Transport System: Analysis and Synthesis (Volume 2)

GOODALL, B.: The Economics of Urban Areas (Volume 3)

LEE, C.: Models in Planning: An Introduction to the Use of Quantitative Models in Planning (Volume 4)

FALUDI, A.: A Reader in Planning Theory (Volume 5)

COWLING, T. M. & STEELEY, G. C.: Sub-Regional Planning Studies: An Evaluation (Volume 6)

FALUDI, A.: Planning Theory (Volume 7)

SOLESBURY, W.: Policy in Urban Planning: Structure plans, programmes and local plans (Volume 8)

MOSELEY, M. J.: Growth Centres in Spatial Planning (Volume 9)

LICHFIELD, N., KETTLE, P. and WHITBREAD, M.: Evaluation in the Planning Process (Volume 10)

Other Titles of Interest

CLOUT, H.D.
Rural Geography

JOHNSON, J. H.
Urban Geography, 2nd edition

The terms of our inspection copy service apply to all the above books. A complete catalogue of all books in the Pergamon International Library is available on request. The Publisher will be pleased to consider suggestions for revised editions and new titles.